CAMBRIDGE STUDIES IN ENGLISH LEGAL HISTORY

Edited by
H. A. HOLLOND
*Fellow of Trinity College, Cambridge
and sometime Rouse Ball Professor of English Law*

THE ATTORNEY
IN
EIGHTEENTH-CENTURY ENGLAND

BY

ROBERT ROBSON

Fellow of Trinity College
Cambridge

CAMBRIDGE
AT THE UNIVERSITY PRESS
1959

PUBLISHED BY

THE SYNDICS OF THE CAMBRIDGE UNIVERSITY PRESS

Bentley House, 200 Euston Road, London, N.W. 1
American Branch: 32 East 57th Street, New York 22, N.Y.

©

CAMBRIDGE UNIVERSITY PRESS

1959

Printed in Great Britain at the University Press, Cambridge
(Brooke Crutchley, University Printer)

TO
THE MEMORY OF
MY FATHER

CONTENTS

GENERAL EDITOR'S PREFACE

IN the preceding volume in this series Professor Plucknett, in a masterly first chapter entitled 'Maitland's View of Law and History', shows that the notion, if it were entertained, that legal history must be annexed to the study of law would be entirely misconceived, and that to make legal history the preserve of professional lawyers would indeed be to condemn it to extinction. A glance at the list of authors in this series of studies shows that, if the general editor had been compelled to limit his choice to qualified lawyers, the series would long ago have come to an end.

Once more the general editor has prayed in aid the sister faculty, with he believes great profit to the student of legal and social history. The pages of the popular press show how large a part law and lawyers play in the social life of the present day. It has always been so, and yet in any book on social history the proportion of it which is devoted to the functioning of the law is far smaller than that topic merits. The reason for this defect is, no doubt, the fact that the writer of a general survey must base himself on the detailed research of others, and that research upon the relation of law to life has been meagre. But gaps are being filled. The most notable modern contribution in this field has been that of Professor Bertha Putnam to our knowledge of the work of justices of the peace in the Middle Ages. It is fortunate that one of the leaders in eighteenth-century studies set to Dr Robson the task of bringing similarly to life the attorney of the latter period. It was an exacting task for it required the scrutiny of archives ranging from Essex to Cumberland.

The title of his book will puzzle the many who do not know that attorneys and solicitors were separate classes of the legal profession until the middle of the eighteenth century. The amalgamation of those two branches, and the supersession of the more ancient and dignified title by the more modern and lowly one, are part of Dr Robson's story.

In the seventeenth century solicitors were men who performed in cases before the Council and in Chancery functions similar to those of attorneys in the common law courts. Attorneys had an ancestry reaching back to the thirteenth century, solicitors were newcomers.

In a valuable monograph on the Star Chamber, written before 1635 by William Hudson, of Gray's Inn, but not published until 1792, there occurs the passage, 'In our age there are stepped up a new sort of people called solicitors, unknown to the records of the law, who, like the grasshoppers in Egypt, devour the whole land'.

But by the end of the eighteenth century the wheel had turned full circle. Dr Robson tells us, on page 152, that one of the characters in Maria Edgeworth's novel, *Patronage*, published in 1814, remarked, 'There are no such things as attorneys now in England, they are all turned into solicitors and agents, just as every *shop* is become a *warehouse*, and every *service* a *situation*'.

Dr Robson explains this change of fashion by the fact that the adjective 'pettifogging' had come to be linked all too frequently with the noun attorney, while solicitor suffered from no such pejorative association.

At any rate it is as 'solicitors' that the 'gentlemen practisers in law and equity' preferred to be known, and the title was given statutory recognition in the Judicature Acts, 1873–5. And so the sonorous title 'attorney' survives in England only as that of the Leader of the Bar, though in the United States it flourishes in high esteem side by side with the excellent word 'counsellor'.

I hope that some of the thousands of solicitors practising in this country may catch sight of an advertisement of Dr Robson's book, and may be inspired to purchase it for their firms and thus encourage further research into the antiquities of their profession.

H. A. H.

December 1958

PREFACE

THERE has been no previous attempt at a social history of the profession of attorneys and solicitors in eighteenth-century England. In recent years there have been studies of the parish clergy and of the medical professions during this period. These are as yet unpublished, and I am grateful to their authors, Mr P. A. Bezodis and Dr B. M. Hamilton, for allowing me to see their work. My own research has in some ways proved complementary, and has suggested that this was a period of crucial importance for the history of the professions in England. It has also tried to show how important the attorneys were in the working of English society in the eighteenth century.

The main MS. sources which have been used are indicated at the end of the work. In general, the working papers of attorneys have proved of limited use for a study of this kind, and are difficult to quote briefly and intelligibly. They have, however, been extremely useful in creating an impression of the nature and of the importance of the attorney's work, even when, as is often the case, the attorney's personal papers have been destroyed and only those belonging to his clients have been preserved. I am most grateful to the various county archivists and librarians whose papers I have used, and particularly to Mr F. G. Emmison of the Essex County Record Office, and Mr W. P. Lamb, formerly the City Librarian of Sheffield, for their kindness in depositing bulky collections of documents for lengthy periods in my college library. Mr T. Gray of the Cumberland County Record Office allowed me to arrange the unsorted Hodgson papers so that I might use them more conveniently.

For permission to use the Wentworth Woodhouse papers at Sheffield I am indebted to Earl Fitzwilliam and his trustees of the Wentworth Woodhouse Settled Estates. The Librarian of the Royal Institution of Cornwall enabled me to see the Journal of Christopher Wallis deposited with him by Mr J. Percival Rogers. I quote from W. E. Beasley, *The Early History of a Leicester Firm of Attorneys*, by permission of Mr Beasley's Executors, and from *The Memoirs of William Hickey*, vol. 1 (1913) by permission of Messrs Hurst and Blackett, Ltd. I have also received help from many persons and societies who possessed records of eighteenth-century attorneys. These include Mr A. N. L. Munby, Mr R. C. Reginald Nevill, Mr Henry Potts, and the secretaries of the Liverpool Underwriters' Association and of the provincial law societies mentioned in chapter IV.

The many pamphlets which have proved valuable are listed at the end. Some of these are only available in the Library of the Law Society in Chancery Lane, and I am indebted to the Council of the Law Society for permission to consult them there.

The attorneys touched society at many points, and there are traces of their activities in many of the contributions which have been made to the social, political, and economic history of the period. Where I have made use of these, I have indicated the work in footnotes, and for that reason I have not compiled a separate bibliography of secondary works. The only ones which are directly relevant are three short volumes by E. B. V. Christian, *A Short History of Attorneys and Solicitors* (London, 1896); *Leaves of the Lower Branch: the Attorney in Life and Letters* (London, 1909); and *Solicitors: an Outline of their History* (London, 1925).

This subject was suggested to me by Dr J. H. Plumb, and my work on it was supervised by Dr Plumb and by Dr G. S. R. Kitson Clark. I am deeply indebted to both of them for much encouragement and advice over a lengthy period. I have also benefited greatly at a later stage from the comments of Professor H. J. Habakkuk, Professor Edward Hughes, and of the Editor of this series, Professor H. A. Hollond. It is my fault that this work is not more worthy of the attention which has been bestowed upon it by these scholars, and of the generosity with which the Master and Fellows of Trinity College surrounded its writing and rewarded its completion.

R. R.

TRINITY COLLEGE
CAMBRIDGE

26 June 1958

CHAPTER I

ATTORNEYS AND SOLICITORS
BEFORE 1700

THE present division of the legal profession into barristers and solicitors existed in the eighteenth century, and the division of labour in its present form had in many respects already been established. Indeed, as far as the essential difference between the two branches of the profession was concerned, the distinction between those who were permitted to plead a client's cause before the judges, and those who could only conduct it up to this stage, it may be said to have existed in the sixteenth century. This distinction was marked by a difference in the organisation and regulation of the two branches, and was itself the product of the theory and practice of the law in medieval England.[1]

The idea that a man could stand in place of another in legal disputes, that he could be his attorney, was alien to early conceptions of the law, and was perhaps inappropriate to the simpler structure of society. To appear in court by attorney was at first a privilege restricted to the king, for whom such a representation was an obvious necessity. Gradually the privilege was extended to others, but it survived surprisingly long as a privilege, and was not readily conceded as a right to be demanded by all litigants. Eventually, however, the concession which the king at first allowed to favoured subjects was made to all who sought it. The growing complexity of society and of its laws involved more and more people in litigation, and in litigation so abstruse as to demand the technical assistance of those skilled in the law. It was in response to this need that the legal profession arose, and naturally enough, attorneys came to be chosen from those who, by habitual attendance on the courts, had acquired a special knowledge of their practices.

But if the appointment of an attorney was at first rare because it

---

[1] This historical introduction is based entirely on secondary sources, namely, F. Pollock and F. W. Maitland, *The History of English Law* (2nd ed., Cambridge, 1923); W. S. Holdsworth, *A History of English Law*, II (3rd ed., London, 1923), VI (1924), and XII (1938); and E. B. V. Christian, *A Short History of Solicitors* (London, 1896).

conflicted with early notions of the law, the assistance of a pleader was commonly allowed and was entirely in harmony with these ideas. The pleader or barrister did not stand in his client's place, but only used his skilled voice on his behalf, and this was not a function which had to be conceded as a privilege by the king or his judges. Consequently there was in the case of the barristers no basis for the kind of control to which the attorneys, in their highly privileged and slightly unusual position, were submitted. They lived in the Inns of Court in circumstances chosen for their own convenience, and admitted newcomers to membership on conditions which they themselves laid down.

The attorneys in contrast were early subjected to close regulation by the judges and by parliament. And, whereas the barristers organised themselves in the Inns of Court, the attorneys were compelled to belong to the Inns of Chancery by the judges, and the Inns of Chancery were themselves dependent on, and subordinate to, the control of the Inns of Court. 'The attorney was never allowed to forget that he was an officer of the court and subject to its discipline. The barrister, on the other hand, was in no sense an officer of the court, and was much less directly under its control.'[1]

As early as 1292, 'The king directed his justices to provide for every county a sufficient number of attorneys and apprentices from among the best, the most lawful, and the most teachable, so that the king and people might be well served'.[2] On this occasion it was suggested that 140 such men might be enough, but the matter was left to the discretion of the judges.

This matter of the number of attorneys was a chronic complaint, and in 1402, as a result of such grumbling, it was enacted that all attorneys should be examined by the judges before being put on the Roll.[3] They were to be 'good and virtuous and of good fame', and 'received and sworn well and truly in their offices'. And it was further laid down that 'if any such attorney be hereafter notoriously found in default of record or other wise, he shall forswear the court and never be received to make any suit in any court of the king'. In London, and later elsewhere also, special rules governed the behaviour of attorneys who were admitted to practise in the local courts.

---

[1] Holdsworth, *op. cit.* VI, 434.
[2] Pollock and Maitland, *op. cit.* I, 216.
[3] 4 Henry IV, c. 18: Christian, *Short History*, p. 19.

But the complaints about attorneys continued, and the act of 1455[1] to limit the number of attorneys in Norfolk and Suffolk was in answer to a petition which said that there were many people 'not being of sufficient cunning to be any attorney, which go to every fair, market, and other places where congregation of people is, and stir, procure, move and excite the people to make untrue suits, foreign suits, for light offences and small sums of debt', and asked that the number of attorneys allowed to practise in the two counties should be limited to fourteen—six for each county and two for Norwich.

By the sixteenth century the present distinction between barristers and attorneys existed and was insisted on. It was given institutional representation in the deliberate attempt to exclude attorneys from the Inns of Court in order to prevent them being called to the bar. The character of the attorneys' work can be defined negatively as comprising all that barristers did not insist on keeping to themselves. Beyond this, it was decided by the demands of society, demands which ultimately had the result that attorneys did much work which had habitually though not legally been confined to the bar. In the sixteenth century it is possible to say that attorneys existed as a professional class in the sense that men now generally turned for legal aid to a man of some professional training and experience, and that many such men existed. But it would be too much to say that they were a professional class if by that is implied the existence of professional institutions and fixed standards of professional education and conduct. Indeed, it may be that a professional class in this sense existed less and less during the sixteenth and seventeenth centuries as the almost exclusive concentration of lawyers in London was broken down, and men were increasingly able to find enough problems of a legal sort to occupy them in a country practice, problems which might only rarely bring them up to attend on the courts in London.

This being so, whatever degree of institutional representation had formerly been given to the attorneys by membership of the Inns of Court or Chancery was diminished, though the attempt of the judges to insist on it, in order to have some control over the profession, went on long after it ceased to be desirable, or even feasible. These attempts may, indeed, be indirect recognitions on the part of the judges that the profession was growing larger and

---

[1] 33 Henry VI, c. 7.

more scattered and hence less controllable, compelling them to insist on outmoded means of regulation because no others existed.

In the main act of parliament which sought to control the attorneys before the eighteenth century, they were linked with the solicitors.[1] Just as the attorneys had come to perform whatever were not the exclusive functions of barristers, and to fill a need which the barristers could not completely satisfy, so the solicitors arose to answer needs catered for neither by barristers nor attorneys. The solicitors were a group known in the fifteenth century.[2] They assisted the attorneys, and managed business which fell outside their scope. They were not officers of the common law courts, and it was to the development of 'the new work and new needs introduced by the growth of the jurisdiction of such courts as the Star Chamber, the court of Chancery, and the court of Requests, that the solicitor owes his elevation from the position of the servant or agent of the litigant or attorney, to the position of a professional man on a level with the attorney'.[3] By the middle of the sixteenth century they were a group sufficiently definite to be excluded along with the attorneys from the Inns of Court.[4] During the seventeenth century attempts were made to define the solicitors' work, claiming that 'It is not enough for the Solicitor to be, as it were, the Loader to the Attorney, or the Intelligencer to the Client'.[5] These had been the earlier functions of the solicitors, but by the middle of the century certainly they had come to have a more closely defined sphere of practice in which they were alone. A certain amount of prejudice against solicitors was still felt by attorneys, but as attorneys came to practise as solicitors, and solicitors of five years' standing could practise as attorneys, the division between them became blurred.

At any rate they were lumped together in 1605, and contrasted with the 'just and honest serjeant and counsellor at law', who considered themselves 'greatly slandered' by the disrepute into which the conduct of their inferior brethren brought the profession of

---

[1] 3 Jac. I, c. 7; an act 'to reform the multitudes and misdemeanours of attornies and solicitors at law'.

[2] By c. 1450 the term 'solicitor', used earlier simply of one who 'urges, instigates, or conducts business on behalf of another person', had come to mean one who concerned himself with legal business but who was neither an attorney nor a barrister (Holdsworth, *op. cit.* VI, 449).

[3] *Ibid.* pp. 454–5.   [4] *Ibid.* p. 449.

[5] *Compleat Solicitor*, 1668; quoted *ibid.* p. 452.

the law. Some differences between attorneys and solicitors were recognised. Attorneys were required to have been brought up in the King's Courts, or be 'otherwise well practised in soliciting of causes', and also 'have been found by his dealings to be skilful and of honest disposition'. All that was required of a solicitor was that he should 'be a man of sufficient and honest disposition'.[1] The act further provided that an attorney was to produce receipts for any fees he claimed to have paid on behalf of his 'client or master', together with an elaborate statement of all the work he claimed to have done. Heavy penalties were imposed for delaying suits, and attorneys were not to allow unqualified persons to bring suits in their names.[2]

Although there was no more legislation to discipline the profession between this act and that of 1729, there were frequent complaints about the excessive numbers of attorneys. There was a parliamentary committee on the subject in 1672, and a bill in parliament in 1700. In the absence of legislation, however, there was a good deal of activity on the part of the judges to control the profession. They tried to keep down numbers by insisting on a fixed period of apprenticeship before admission. A rule of the court of Common Pleas of 1633 prescribed six years' service as a clerk to an attorney. It was followed in 1654 by a rule of the Judges of the Upper Bench prescribing a period of five years' apprenticeship, and an examination to prove the candidate 'of good ability and honesty for such employment'. At least twelve examiners were to be appointed every year to conduct this examination. It was claimed that these examinations were not rigorously insisted on for many reasons, among them the conduct of the judges themselves. 'A judge considers every attorney he admits as a new client who may bring him business, and therefore his lordship is not severe respecting the attorney's knowledge, the want of which tends to increase the business of the judge's chambers.'[3]

Nevertheless, both in London and on circuit the judges did

---

[1] Quoted Holdsworth, *op. cit.* p. 456.

[2] By the regulating act of 1729 sworn attorneys were entitled to practise as solicitors without paying additional fees, but it was not until 1750 that sworn solicitors were granted the reciprocal advantage of practising as attorneys. All trace of the division disappeared when the Judicature Acts of 1873 classed them all as solicitors of the Supreme Court.

[3] Cunningham, *The History and Antiquities of the Four Inns of Court...*, extracted from Dugdale (1780); quoted Christian, *Short History*, p. 82.

something to control the professional conduct of attorneys. In Cambridge, for example, in 1665, 'John Patteson an Attorney at Law stood in the pillory on the Pease Hill...from about a quarter after eleven in the forenoon, to about half an hour after twelve of the clock having fastened to the fore part of his hat being on his head a paper written in capital letters (a common barrator) being sentenced by Judge Keeling at the...Assizes'.[1]

In theory the control of the profession was complete at the beginning of the eighteenth century. The practice and the numbers of the attorneys were controlled by parliament, and this was supplemented in detail by the orders of the judges which affected all who wished to practise in their courts. In theory there was a fixed period of apprenticeship, and an examination before admission to the Roll. In theory they were all 'brought up in the courts or otherwise well practised in soliciting causes and proved by their dealings to be skilful and honest'. No one in the early eighteenth century could have believed that this was the case with the profession: there were, perhaps, not many who believed that any laws could ensure that attorneys would be 'skilful and honest', 'good and virtuous and of good fame'. Fewer still can have expected that attorneys themselves would ever be concerned to see that theory and practice should in this matter more nearly coincide.

[1] Cambridge Antiquarian Society, Octavo Publications, XXIII (1890), *The Diary of Samuel Newton, 1662–1717*, p. 10.

CHAPTER II

REGULATION OF THE PROFESSION

ON 4 February 1700 Evelyn noted in his diary that the House of Commons had 'voted that the exorbitant number of attorneys be lessened, (now indeed swarming and...eating out the estates of people, provoking them to go to law)'. In March 1701 leave was given to bring in a bill for the reduction of the number of attorneys and solicitors, and for regulating their practice.[1] It received its second reading on 16 April, and was committed to the legal members of the house, but is not mentioned again.

The judges continued their work in the absence of this act, and controlled the profession with the means at their disposal. In 1704 they laid it down that all attorneys should belong to some Inn of Court or Chancery. This, however, proved impossible to enforce. The Inns of Court existed for quite other purposes than the judges were seeking to use them for, and could not be compelled to admit attorneys. The barristers, perhaps resenting the encroachments of the attorneys, and determined to preserve some distance and distinction between them, were successful in their attempt to exclude the attorneys from the Inns of Court.[2]

What in part the judges had wanted was that each attorney should have a London address where writs and the like could be served on him, as well as putting them under the control of some body which could supervise them more closely than had been possible in the past. It may be that the judges knew that the Inns of Court would not admit the attorneys, and that they would in consequence be forced into the Inns of Chancery, which had been more properly their province, and which in the early stages of the

[1] *Commons Journals*, XIII, 31 March 1701. It seems to have aroused at least one pamphlet: *Observations on the Dilatory and Expensive Proceedings in the Court of Chancery*, etc. (1701) (see bibliography for full title).

[2] On this, see Holdsworth, *op. cit.* VI, 441; and H. Hale Bellot, 'The Exclusion of the Attorneys from the Inns of Court', *Law Quarterly Review*, XXVI, 137–45. In 1706 a bill was introduced by Lord Somers into the House of Lords to regulate proceedings at law. The bill was passed by the Lords, but defeated in the Commons, where 'the interest of under-officers, clerks, and attornies, whose gains were to be lessened by this bill, was more considered, than the interest of the nation itself' (Cobbett, *Parliamentary History*, VI, 517–18).

profession had played some part in their education. But by the eighteenth century, these were decaying bodies. And, moreover, as the country attorney became more important, and, as provincial life grew richer, more stationary in his own locality, membership of an Inn in London became increasingly pointless. The system of moots and readings in the Inns of Chancery had greatly declined, and in any case was no substitute for the apprenticeship system as a training for an attorney. Nor was the profession yet sufficiently coherently organised for the Inns of Chancery to play the sort of role that the Metropolitan Law Society was to adopt as a controlling, and, above all, as an examining body.

But there were signs fairly soon in the century that such ideas and needs as would eventually produce the Law Society were being discussed. The Society of Gentlemen Practisers was in being at least as early as 1739. The attorneys had, after all, the example of the barristers as a highly organised and articulate body always before them, and more particularly, before the more affluent members of their profession in London and the provincial centres, from whom the stimulus to reform was likely to come in the first instance. But the solution of the problem which was provided by internal regulation is a separate story, and will be treated later. In the meantime, further suggestions were being made for the external regulation of the profession, and the first moves towards the act of 1729 become discernible.

Proposals for reform were many, some idealistic and too general in character, others extremely detailed and realistic in their suggestions, and clearly springing from a close acquaintance with the conditions of the attorneys' employment, and the needs of their clients. A pamphlet published in 1724 abandoned generalities, and included lengthy proposals for regulating the profession in the form of a draft bill to be put before parliament.[1] In some ways the measures suggested closely resembled those incorporated in the act of 1729, but in others, especially in the matter of controlling entry into the profession, they went far beyond them.

It was proposed to permit no one to practise as an attorney or

---

[1] *An Essay on the Amendment and Reduction of the Laws of England, for the ease of the subject, the advancement of justice, and regulating the profession of the law.* Quotations are from the second, corrected, edition of 1726. An earlier pamphlet touching on these matters, *Proposals Humbly offered to the Parliament for remedying the great charge and delay of suits at Law and in Equity,* was published in 1707, and ran into at least seven editions.

solicitor who had not served a clerkship of five years with a qualified practitioner, under a penalty of £500. After this apprenticeship, it was suggested that the clerk should apply for membership of one of the Inns of Court, who would examine him, and administer to him an oath 'To do no falsehood or deceit in his practice, not to delay causes for lucre, nor increase any fees, or undertake any false or malicious suits, etc.'. Those admitted were to be given a certificate of the examination and the oath, which would permit them to practise as attorneys in any of the king's courts. For the convenience of country attorneys the judges were to appoint examiners 'from among the oldest and most experienced practisers of the law', who would vouch to the Inns of Court for the character and qualifications of such as they approved. Country attorneys were also to be exempt the expenses of the Inn, save a small fee as 'out-members'.

No attorney was to have more than two clerks at any one time. Beyond this, and most significantly, it was to be laid down that attorneys should not 'take or admit into their offices, any persons to be their clerks, whose parents or themselves have not freehold estates in lands, tenements, or hereditaments, of the value of £40 per annum, or are not worth £1000 in money'. Attorneys were not to permit unqualified persons to practise in their names, under pain of disqualification, and heavy fines were prescribed for those attorneys convicted of making malicious arrests, delaying suits needlessly, making false bills and the like. It was further suggested that once a year the judges should hold a court for hearing complaints against attorneys. 'A jury of honest clerks and attorneys shall...inquire into and try the abuse and the extortions of the attorneys and solicitors complained of, and if the said jury of attorneys shall shew any favour or partiality...they shall be liable to attaint, and to forfeit each juror £100.'

Whether or not these suggestions had any direct effect on the act of 1729 does not appear. But at least they are among the signs that thought was being given to the problem of regulating the profession, and they are clearly the work of an informed and responsible critic. The petition of the justices of the West Riding, which was presented to the House of Commons in February, 1728/9, and which was directly responsible for the act, complained principally of the activities of unqualified persons who were practising as attorneys.[1] This

---

[1] *Commons Journals*, XXI, 236, 25 February 1728–9. It is not clear why so much of the stimulus to legal reform should have come from Yorkshire. Professor

petition, together with others in identical terms from the justices of the East Riding, and from the Liberty of St Peter at York, were referred to a committee presided over by Sir William Strickland, M.P. for Scarborough, and a Lord of the Treasury. This committee conducted a close investigation into the problems raised, in the obvious way available to them, which was to examine the officers of the various courts who were responsible for the admission of attorneys. Their findings, which were communicated to the House on 14 March, give a detailed picture of the state of the profession from this special point of view, a picture perhaps less violent in its colourings than that painted by many contemporary pamphleteers and commentators, but which nevertheless suggests that there was some justice in their complaining.

Sir George Coke, Prothonotary of the Court of Common Pleas for twenty years, gave evidence about the attorneys of that Court. He claimed that he 'never entered any clerks in his office, but such as had served their time, or were well recommended by practisers, that he knew, or the Master with whom they served their clerkship'. More than a thousand clerks were entered on his books: he did not claim to know them all by name, but knew some of them 'by person'. Many had been entered on the recommendations of the agents of country attorneys without his having seen them personally. He said that many people were accustomed to sue out writs from his court who were not on its Roll. All who were sworn as attorneys paid a stamp duty of £6. Attorneys' bills were in Court hand and in Law Latin, but Sir George saw no reason why they should not be in English, and in ordinary hand. He agreed that a great many trifling actions were brought in the prothonotaries' offices, but thought that there was more business at the present time than there had been formerly.

The corresponding officer of the court of King's Bench said that none were admitted attorneys of that court unless they produced a certificate to show that they had served at least five years with some clerk or attorney of the court. The clerks of judges and serjeants at law had the privilege of being sworn in order to practise without

Hughes suspects that the clerks of the peace, jealous of encroachments on their preserves, were behind these petitions (Edward Hughes, 'The Professions in the Eighteenth Century', *Durham University Journal*, New Series, XIII, ii, 50). Petitions against law proceedings in Latin came from the East and North Ridings in 1731, and the bill to rectify this was introduced by Sir George Savile (Cobbett, *Parliamentary History*, VIII, 843–4, 858–9).

these requirements. He too admitted that a great many practised as attorneys who had never been sworn, but maintained that there was no power to prevent them. It was also the case that sheriffs' officers often took out writs in the name of an attorney without first obtaining his permission. John Croft, of the Middlesex Office, also told the committee that writs were frequently taken out in the names of attorneys without their cognisance. He said that he had known 1100 writs to be issued in a vacation, and about 3000 in a year. Similar evidence was produced by an officer of the Exchequer Office.

Another witness claimed that many people who called themselves prothonotaries' clerks practised as attorneys, and that he had heard that 'several broken tradesmen and bailiffs, do practise as attorneys and often set the people at variance, and have got £10 or £20 of each party, by being concerned, and, before the matter comes to trial, make the affair up between their clients for a bottle of wine and a treat'. Robert Appleton said that he knew 'one who is a farmer, and another a sailor, and about 20 or 30 more who practise and never were sworn: that he knew one that made out a bill for £24 and took £5 for the whole'. He claimed that there were only six sworn attorneys in the whole of the East Riding.[1]

Finally, the committee questioned the Commissioners of Stamp Duties. They too claimed that a great many practised who had not been duly sworn, 'by reason of which (the revenue) is greatly injured and lessened'. Counsel had been consulted in this matter, but they had advised that as the law stood, such people could not be prosecuted.[2]

This evidence was held to be sufficient to prove the allegations of the petitioners, and leave was given to introduce a bill for the better regulation of the profession. This bill received the royal assent on 14 May.[3] Most of its stipulations were to be effective from

---

[1] One witness, from the Warrant of Attorneys Office, estimated that there were about 420 sworn attorneys in all; another that there were not more than 200 sworn attorneys and clerks in the court of King's Bench.

[2] This was not the first time attorneys were suspected of avoiding the stamp duties. In 1706 a reward of £150 was given to the Solicitor to the Stamps Commissioners for his diligence in 'discovering many great abuses committed in the Stamp Revenue by attorneys' (C[alendar of] T[reasury] B[ooks], xx, iii, 771–2). Attorneys were prosecuted on this account in 1707, and put forward the excuse that their clerks and others who practised in their names were responsible (C.T.B., xxi, ii, 440, 474).

[3] 2 Geo. II, c. 23. The stipulations of the act were extended to solicitors in 1750; 23 Geo. II, c. 26, which entitled sworn solicitors to become attorneys.

1 December 1730. After that date, no person was to be admitted as an attorney unless he had taken the prescribed oath,[1] and had been duly admitted and enrolled in one of the courts. Before they admitted any clerk, the judges were to 'examine and inquire, by such ways and means as they shall think proper, touching his fitness and capacity to act as an attorney'. Clerks were to serve an apprenticeship of five years to an attorney 'duly sworn and admitted',[2] and no attorney was to have more than two clerks at any one time. Attorneys of one court were permitted to sue out writs in another if they had the permission of an attorney of the court to so do, but those attorneys who allowed persons to practise in their names who had not been admitted were to be debarred from practice, and those suing out the writs fined £50. Sworn attorneys were able to practise as solicitors, without paying an additional fee.[3] They were obliged to put their names on all writs before delivering them, and were not to begin any action for the recovery of fees until one month after the delivery of their bills. After June 1729, the names of all who were admitted were to be enrolled on lists kept in the respective courts. Nothing in the act was to be held as either requiring or authorising the judges to admit a greater number of attorneys 'than by the ancient custom and usage of such court hath heretofore been allowed'. The act, which was not to extend to the Six Clerks in Chancery, their sworn clerks, cursitors, or to various officers of the courts, was to remain in force for nine years after 1 June 1729.

This act, like it predecessors, and most social legislation of the period, laid down the penalties of misbehaviour, rather than tried to prevent it. It was not part of any wider programme of legal reform, and left all the old temptations and opportunities largely as they had been before. Like all prohibitive legislation, it depended for its success on the willingness of those whom it affected to enforce it. The examination it suggested was too general in character, and depended on the individual judges conducting it, without fees and in addition to their normal work on the bench.[4] It left much to

---

[1] 'I, A. B., do swear, That I will truly and honestly demean myself in the practice of an attorney, according to the best of my knowledge and ability.'

[2] A suggestion that the period of apprenticeship should be seven, instead of five years, was defeated by 65 votes to 62.

[3] This act was amended in 1750 so as to allow sworn solicitors to practise as attorneys without paying additional fees, provided they were otherwise deemed well-qualified (23 Geo. II, c. 26, sect. xv).

[4] Cf. Joseph Day, *An Address*, etc. pp. 91–2, on the ineffectiveness of judges for this purpose.

human initiative, and in retrospect, may seem to have been too optimistic for its time. But it was by no means without effect: some influential groups were willing to enforce it, and it provided the basis on which the Society of Gentlemen Practisers did its work from 1739 onwards.[1]

But the malpractices of attorneys did not cease overnight, nor were the critics of the profession silenced. Some, indeed, considered the act as worse than useless, in so far as it allowed too many to enter the profession or to remain in it who were in no way qualified to do so. One of these critics maintained that 'not one out of above six thousand, who before practised as attorneys, but was again admitted to practise, upon the payment of the six pound stamp duty'.[2] Another, writing much sooner after the passing of the act, said: 'I am sensible a tiny effort was made in the late act to qualify such Gentlemen for practice, intending perhaps to distinguish between good and bad; but it only discovered, to the grievance and shame of the Nation, that the Numbers were large enough to ruin the four Quarters of the World, however unhappily confin'd to the miserable Portion of Land that makes not a millioneth part of the Whole.'[3] Both these writers were concerned for the dignity of the profession, and both insisted on making a distinction between the upright and honourable attorney, and the pettifogger. Unfortunately, the act under discussion, and another of the same period,[4] had merely detracted from the dignity of the profession, and made it easier than ever before for illiterate and unprincipled men to become attorneys, so that a profession which before 1729 'was held in such estimation that it was no disgrace to a gentleman, or to a younger son of one higher born, to be bred to it',[5] was now despised.

Although there were no further general acts specifically designed to regulate the profession until the nineteenth century, the imposition of an annual licence in 1785, and of a stamp duty on articles of clerkship in 1794, which are perhaps more properly regarded as aspects of Pitt's financial policy, did impose additional and important

[1] For this Society, see pp. 20–34 below. The act of 1729 was renewed in 1739, and modified on several occasions.

[2] *Reflections or Hints...touching the Law, Lawyers, officers, attorneys,* etc. (1759).

[3] Dim Sasson, *Law Visions; or, Pills for Posterity* (1736).

[4] 4 Geo. II, c. 26, 1731, laid down the rule that law proceedings should be in English. For another view, see *Gentleman's Magazine,* February 1733.

[5] *Reflections or Hints,* etc; a similar point was made in the *Present State of the Practice and the Practisers of the Law,* etc. n.d.

rules on the attorney. And it is significant of an increased concern among attorneys themselves, apparent also from other sources, that many men were ready to interpret them in this way, and to welcome them.

Complaints were made as early as 1689 that attorneys were not specially mentioned in the poll tax acts.[1] They were included in 1694 for the first time,[2] but complaints were now made that attorneys were too leniently treated by the local commissioners. On 28 September, for example, the Treasury Lords rebuked the Commissioners in Cornwall for their neglect in 'wholly omitting, or taxing at only 4s. gentlemen of very good quality and great estates and rich attorneys in great practice...'.[3] It was difficult to assess the income of men whose wealth was drawn from so many sources, but it is some indication of the definitive place the attorneys had come to occupy in society that the attempt should have been made. But when the poll tax languished, the attorneys ceased to be directly taxed for their professional incomes.

There had been a kind of indirect tax on the profession since the introduction of the stamp duty on apprenticeship premiums in 1709. But this was at the low rate of 6d. in the £ on sums below £50, and 1s. on those above, and, moreover, was not a recurring duty. An annual licence to practice was imposed by an act of 1785.[4] Attorneys were to take out an annual certificate of their admission and enrolment in the court in which they practised. In London, Westminster, within the Bills of Mortality, and in Edinburgh, a stamp duty of £5 was to be paid; elsewhere, the tax was £3. Attorneys were to deliver to the court every year a statement of their names, and their usual residences, and the officers of the courts were to maintain a list of all admitted to practice. The penalty for practising without a certificate was £500, and prohibition from practice. This act, unlike that of 1729, was to apply to the Six Clerks and other officers of the courts.[5]

This act had a mixed reception from the profession. In 1786

---

[1] C[alendar of] T[reasury] B[ooks], IX, i, 298. The solicitor-general thought that the current poll tax did not warrant 'the assessing of attorneys for their practice'.

[2] 5 and 6 William III and Mary, c. 14, sect. iii.

[3] C.T.B. XIV, 135, 125.   [4] 25 Geo. III, c. 80.

[5] In 1792 the tax produced £18,943 (S. Dowell, *History of Taxation and Taxes in England*, 2nd ed. (London, 1888), III, 14). An annual licence, and a tax on articles were suggested in *Proposals Humbly Offered to the Parliament*, etc., as early as 1707.

and 1787 petitions were presented to parliament asking for certain modifications, and it was quickly followed by a demand for increased fees.[1] Several of the petitions complained of the unfairness in leaving the conveyancers untaxed, and took the occasion to point out further that very many ill-qualified persons did conveyancing, and suggested that legislation ought to be introduced to prevent this. The Bristol attorneys asked that conveyancers should be made subject to the same laws as attorneys, and also proposed that their own profession should be further controlled by imposing a large duty on articles of clerkship.[2]

These suggestions were referred to a committee, and in 1794, whether as a result of the petition from Bristol or not, a duty on articles of clerkship was imposed.[3] In February of that year the House was informed of the number of the attorneys in the various courts, and these figures were referred to the committee considering ways of raising the supply.[4] This committee recommended a stamp duty of £100 on articles of clerkship, except in the case of attorneys in certain inferior courts, who were to pay only £50. These rates were increased in 1804[5] (when conveyancers too were obliged to take out an annual certificate), and again in 1815.[6]

The discussion which these new measures aroused seems to indicate a new attitude on the part of many members of the profession towards their calling, and towards their responsibilities to society. Many of the points that were made in pamphlets were anticipated by the speech of William Adam in the House of Commons criticising the measure of 1794.[7] He followed Fox in

---

[1] For these petitions, see *Commons Journals*, XLI, 13 March, 11 June 1786, and 22 March 1787.

[2] The minutes of the Bristol Law Society are missing for these years, so it is impossible to say whether this petition was inspired by it or not. The Yorkshire Society concerned itself with the 1794 act.   [3] 34 Geo. III, c. 14.

[4]

	King's Bench	Common Pleas
1791	336	88
1792	190	71
1793	266	71 (*Commons Journals*, XLIX, 5 Feb. 1794.)

[5] 44 Geo. III, c. 98.   [6] 55 Geo. III, c. 184.

[7] William Adam, 1751–1839, was a nephew of Robert Adam. He was M.P. for Ross-shire, and a member of the English and Scottish bars. He had once fought a duel with Fox, but they had subsequently become intimate friends. He held various offices in North's administration, but by 1794 he was speaking as a member specialising on legal topics, and opposing Pitt on the trials of Muir and Palmer, etc. See *D.N.B.*

attacking the proposal, and said that he 'considered this tax as exposing the profession to unjust reflections. No persons', he continued, 'were professionally employed in more confidential transactions than the attorneys: they were necessarily entrusted with the secrets of individuals, and of whole families: the character of the profession ought therefore to command respect. Doubtless there were persons exercising it little to their credit, but this was no reproach to the profession itself, which contained as excellent individuals as any class of society. This additional tax', he maintained 'was a heavy incumbrance; as after paying it, together with the foregoing duty for a licence, a man was still liable to be struck off the list of attorneys, were a court of law to judge him unfit for the profession, in which case he lost not only his situation in life, but received no indemnification for the money he had expended in qualifying himself for it. The heads of the law', he concluded, 'and among them were those, the chief justice especially,[1] whose endeavours to raise the credit of the profession were well known, would become more averse than ever to degrade attorneys, from the consideration of the ruinous loss with which such a degradation must of course be attended.'[2]

It was maintained by some who did not welcome the tax that if its object were to raise the revenue, this would not be achieved, since the number of attorneys and of suits at law would thereby be decreased. It was also claimed that the profession was not sufficiently affluent as a whole to be the specific object of taxation.[3] More soberly, perhaps, it was objected by another writer that the tax was inequitable, in that it bore equally heavily on the man with only a small practice, as on 'the great opulent attorney, with 500 suits in his roll, and a dozen clerks at his back'.[4] It was unfair, too, in that the poor man, forced to live in the City where he worked, had to pay the higher rate of the tax, which the wealthier attorney, able to afford a house in the country, might be able to avoid. But

---

[1] Kenyon.   [2] *Annual Register* (1794), pp. 211–12.

[3] 'Every honest man in the profession knows, and will publicly declare, that very few attornies or solicitors get fortunes in this age. I declare, upon my honour, I do not believe there are thirty in London who get one thousand a year; and the greater part can scarce keep their heads above water' (*A Word to the Wise; or, a Hint to the Minister, about taxing Attornies, Solicitors, Proctors, etc., by an untaxed Attorney*, 1785). Cf. also Charles Ilsley, *A Brief Inquiry concerning the origin, progress, and impolicy of taxing attorneys* (1804).

[4] *Considerations on the Attorney Tax, and proposals for altering and equalising the same, so as to render it easy in operation and just in principle* (1786).

he insisted that the tax was not wrong in principle: 'It will not readily be controverted that the profound mazes and intricacies of litigation are the proper objects of taxation; and it is believed, the liberal and considerate part of the practitioners of the law are as much of that opinion as any ministers or set of men whatever.' The tax was only wrong in that it was undiscriminating, and he suggested instead a stamp duty to be paid on each suit carried on, to vary in proportion to the amount of money which was being sued for. This, he said, would be 'something more agreeable, and probably convenient for many, whose external appearance is not irrespectable, to pay it by degrees, than all in one sum. They can, by this means, pay it in a gentlemanly manner, and wipe away the ridiculous aspersion, thrown on the profession, "that LAW, like BEER, is now sold by RETAIL by HIS MAJESTY'S ROYAL ANNUAL LICENCE".'

There were those who defended the tax as being likely to keep undesirable men out of the profession, and maintained that it would probably serve as a most effective supplement to the regulations concerning the profession which already existed, but which were clearly inadequate. It was 'calculated to render the profession more respectable and eventually to cause the members of it to rank higher in the estimation of society, inasmuch as it will have a tendency to drive out of the profession the vile and needy petti-foggers, to whom alone is attributable all the obloquy which the public, for want of a due discrimination, attaches to the whole body'.[1] This commentator believed that attorneys could well afford to pay the tax,[2] and suggested that the 'loyal attorney' should not embarrass the government by refusing to pay, but should do so cheerfully, and 'by setting...so good an example to his country-men...convince them that the obloquy which has long been cast upon himself and brethren, has been unmerited'. It was on the basis of such principles as these that other men were endeavouring at the end of the eighteenth century to regulate the profession from the inside, at a time when state intervention in matters of social concern was still viewed with suspicion.

[1] *A Defence of Attornies* (*reasons why they should pay the tax*), *by a Friend to the Profession* (1804).

[2] 'Look at our country towns, and see if the best houses are not occupied by attornies—Look at the Habitations of the London solicitors. When entertained at the table of either, do, gentle reader, take the trouble of asking yourself, no matter before or after the cloth is removed, if the means of attornies in general, are not more than adequate to an abstemious mode of living?'

But in addition to these new regulations by parliament, and these more private endeavours, the profession continued to be under the control of the judges in a more minute way. Most of the cases cited in the law reports refer to small points of practice, but there are one or two which have a more general interest. Perhaps the most famous of these was Frazer's Case of 1757, in which the Society of Gentlemen Practisers was concerned. Frazer was an attorney of the court of King's Bench, and had taken as his clerk a turnkey of the King's Bench prison, so that he could be concerned professionally for all the prisoners who needed legal assistance. Since 1755 he had been concerned in sixty-three cases of this kind. Complaint was made to the court, and it was decided that the articles were merely collusive, and they were ordered to be cancelled. The judge gave it as his opinion that 'the exercise of the office of a turnkey in a prison was, both in itself, and also according to the intent and spirit of the act for regulating attornies, a very improper education for an attorney'.[1]

Blackstone considered that attorneys were 'peculiarly subject to the censure and animadversion of the judges',[2] and it is certainly true that many of them were not always able to resist the temptation to play to the gallery, and score off the attorneys. Jeffreys had set the tone, and it was taken up during the eighteenth century by others, Thurlow, Willes,[3] and Kenyon, for example.[4] Kenyon,

[1] Sir James Burrow, *Reports of Cases adjudged in the Court of the King's Bench*, 30 Geo. II to 12 Geo. III, 1 (1766), 291; 5 May 1757. For a case in which Mansfield was concerned, see *ibid*. IV, 2061 (1767). Mansfield was perhaps kinder to the profession than many of his colleagues on the Bench. It was he who was responsible for establishing the doctrine of lien, whereby attorneys could retain their clients' papers as a surety for the payment of their bills (Christian, *Short History*, pp. 165–6), and who was prepared to acknowledge that the 'part of the profession which is carried on by Attorneys is liberal and reputable, as well as useful to the public, when they conduct themselves with honour and integrity: And they ought to be protected when they act to the best of their skill and knowledge'.

[2] *Commentaries*, III (1768), 26.

[3] It was of Willes that Horace Walpole wrote: 'He had a great quickness of wit, and a merit that would atone for many foibles—his severity to, and discouragement of, that pest of society, attorneys. Hence his court was deserted by them, and all the business they could transport carried into Chancery, where Yorke's filial piety would not refuse asylum to his father's profession' (*Memoirs of the Reign of George III*; quoted Campbell, *Lives of the Chief Justices*, II (London, 1849), 276). Yorke was the son of a Dover attorney.

[4] For the case of an attorney who retaliated by laying an information against Camden and three other judges for wearing cambric bands in court, contrary to act of parliament, see W. E. H. Lecky, *A History of England in the Eighteenth*

indeed, according to Lord Campbell, was too often undiscriminating in this matter. 'He encouraged that universal prejudice against attorneys by which I have frequently seen the administration of justice perverted. Although bred in an attorney's office and long aspiring no higher than to be an attorney, he seemed to think the whole order pettifoggers and their occupation almost necessarily disreputable. Instead of restricting his animadversions to peccant individuals', Lord Campbell continued, 'he extended an angry suspicion to a whole class, containing many men as honourable as himself, and much his superiors in education and manners.'[1] But some attorneys welcomed Kenyon's concern for the professional behaviour of their colleagues. On one occasion at least he appears to have made just such a distinction as Campbell wanted,[2] and on another he gave judgment in favour of an attorney who complained that he had been libelled by a peer of the realm.[3] The effectiveness of the regulation of the profession by the judges, however, depended to a great extent on the willingness of other people to bring cases of misbehaviour by attorneys into the courts. The activities of the Society of Gentlemen Practisers in this matter will be considered in detail in the chapter which follows.

Century (ed. 1920), VII, 302 and n. 4. There are several cases of the regulation of the attorneys on points of practice in the various law reports of the period. For these, see Holdsworth, *op. cit.* XII, 118–26.

[1] Campbell, *op. cit.* III, 83; see also Christian, *Short History*, pp. 161–5.

[2] Cf. *Gentleman's Magazine*, LXIII, February 1793, 182: 'His Lordship said he believed that the majority of Attornies were honourable men, and of service to the community; but there were many others who were the greatest pests to society. He desired Attornies to take notice that they were bound to give their clients the best advice in their power, and to conduct the causes entrusted to them as if they were their own....' *The Pettifogger Dramatized* (1797), which was dedicated to Kenyon, insisted on such a distinction, and was prefaced by a quotation from a sermon by the Rev. Jethro Inwood making the same point.

[3] In a speech in the House of Lords on 17 June 1794, the Earl of Abingdon called attention to the immoral practices of attorneys, 'those locusts of the law, the pettifogging Attornies of this country; who, like the locusts in Africa, fall like a cloud upon the earth, and eat up everything they meet with'. He instanced the conduct of one of them, Thomas Sermon of Coney Court, Gray's Inn, who had been employed by himself, and sent his speech to the newspapers for publication. Sermon brought an information against Abingdon for libel in the court of King's Bench. The case was heard by Kenyon, and Abingdon was found guilty, and was sentenced to three months' imprisonment, and fined £100. (Cobbett, *Parliamentary History*, XXXI, 932–5; Isaac Espinasse, *Cases at Nisi Prius in King's Bench and Common Pleas*, I (2nd ed. 1801), 225–8; *D.N.B.*)

CHAPTER III

THE SOCIETY OF GENTLEMEN PRACTISERS

'At a meeting of the Society of Gentlemen Practisers in the Courts of Law and Equity, held on the 13th February, 1739, the Meeting unanimously declared its utmost abhorrence of all male [sic] and unfair practice, and that it would do its utmost to detect and discountenance the same.'[1] This is the first entry in the minute book of the society, and it seems to indicate that the society had not long been established. There is no information about the events leading up to its foundation. Like most professional bodies in England, it was voluntary in origin, and during the eighteenth century at least, it remained independent of external authority. The scope of existing regulations permitted it to put its first resolution into practice, without being specifically authorised to do so either by the judges or by parliament. For the rest, it was, like many others at this time, largely a convivial society, meeting twice a year to have a dinner, and to hear what the committee had been doing.

In retrospect, of course, the drawbacks of its independence are apparent, and even during the eighteenth century there were those who believed that such a society could not adequately control the profession.[2] But its minutes show a record of activity perhaps surprising to those who believed the attorneys to be wholly devoid of public spirit, or to those who, like Bentham, thought it unrealistic to suppose that they would ever concern themselves with professional morality. So the history of the society is another important sign of the growing concern which some attorneys were feeling about the public status of their profession. And it does not necessarily detract from its achievement that it owed much of its impetus to the realisation of its members—the more affluent part of the profession practising in London—that 'true self love and social'

---

[1] *Records* [*of the Society of Gentlemen Practisers*], ed. Edwin Freshfield (London, 1897), p. 1. Holdsworth dealt with the activities of this body in the *History of English Law*, xii, 63–75, but it seems desirable to deal with it at some length in the present context.

[2] See the criticisms of Joseph Day, pp. 31–4 below.

might coincide. Completely disinterested reformers are rare, and are inclined to an idealism which too readily ignores the general temper of the age in which they live. The effectiveness of the work of this society and of others like it was due to the fact that they were swimming with an increasingly powerful tide.

In addition to the two general meetings, held on the day after the beginning of the Hilary and Trinity Terms, it was agreed that a committee should meet once a month to consider how the aims of the society might best be achieved.[1] The officers of the society were a prolocutor, a secretary, and a deputy-secretary who acted as treasurer. At the beginning there were twenty-one committee members, five of whom constituted a quorum.[2] The main burden of the society's work fell on a small number of enthusiasts—so small indeed that the committee meetings had often to be postponed for want of a quorum. From time to time, *ad hoc* committees were appointed to study special problems, to draw up petitions and memorials, or to convey the thanks of the society to some benefactor. At critical times, the secretary's work could be very heavy, but he received no regular payment, and the office was commonly held by the same man for lengthy periods. On occasion, the society rewarded the devotion of its officers by voting them specific sums. In 1781, for example, 50 guineas were given to Edward Bowman in consideration of his 'long service...and the very small gratuities he had received for his trouble therein'.[3]

The subscription was fixed at half a guinea a year. In November 1758 it was raised to meet the costs of the society's dispute with the Scriveners' Company. When it had recovered from this heavy drain on its resources, the society began to invest in consols, and thus created a fund from which future needs of this kind, and all unexpected expenses, could be met. Occasionally, however, members were asked for special contributions for particular needs. By February 1810 the society held £1000 3% Consols, yet in July of that year the committee suggested that the subscription should

---

[1] See V. I. Chamberlain, 'The Early History of the Incorporated Law Society', *Law Quarterly Review*, VIII (1892), 41: 'The usual meeting place was the Old Devil Tavern...a place of resort...frequented by lawyers, who wrote up on their chamber doors "Gone to the Devil".'

[2] In order to ensure the attendance of a quorum, the numbers of the committee were increased from time to time, a rota was drawn up, and fines for absence were imposed. See *Records*, pp. 30, 145, 170, and 173.

[3] *Records*, p. 152.

be increased to two guineas a year[1] 'in order to support the credit and respectability of the society, and to defray the contingent expenses lately incurred in protecting and supporting the general interests of the profession, and to make provision for similar expenses in the future'.[2]

At a general meeting held on 23 February 1742 'it was ordered that all proper and necessary enquiries be made by the Committee to discover any attorneys or solicitors who had been or should be surreptitiously admitted: That every member of the society should use their utmost endeavours to discover and discountenance any such practice, and that the committee should use such ways and means as they should find most necessary to prevent such practices in the future'.[3] In 1752 this resolution was supplemented by the further one which instructed the committee to 'take notice of, and prosecute, at the society's expense, any attorneys found guilty of illegal practices, and every member was desired to give notice to the Deputy-secretary of all such illegal practices as should come to their knowledge'.[4] What the society did on the basis of these resolutions is shown in detail in the minutes.

It was clearly work which could be done more easily for attorneys and solicitors practising in London and the Home Counties. Until communications had improved, and the provincial law societies had come into existence, it was difficult to obtain accurate and up-to-date information about the activities of provincial attorneys and their clerks. But by 1802 at any rate, the activities of the society were sufficiently widely known for it to be asked to act against attorneys suspected of unprofessional conduct in Birmingham and in Jersey.[5]

In London, however, the society found much to occupy its attention, and from the start it acted with some vigour and success in controlling admissions to the Rolls, and in bringing instances of malpractice and the violation of the acts governing the profession to the notice of the courts. In 1753, it secured the removal from the Roll of the Court of King's Bench of an attorney who had continued to practice while detained in the Fleet prison,[6] and it was announced in the court that 'the society would at all times be

[1] It had previously been raised from half a guinea a year to three guineas payable over two years.
[2] *Records*, p. 228.   [3] *Ibid.* p. 11.
[4] *Ibid.* p. 51.   [5] *Ibid.* pp. 180, 184.
[6] Contrary to the stipulation of 12 Geo. II, c. 13, sect. ix.

ready, at their own expense, to prosecute attorneys for any unfair practices, and would use their utmost endeavours to detect all illegal practices, and to prosecute attorneys or solicitors who should be surreptitiously admitted'.[1]

One of the most curious cases which the society had to consider was that of William Wreathock, an attorney who had been found guilty of highway robbery, had been transported, and had resumed his profession on his return to England.[2] At the instance of the society, aided by the gratuitous services of three barristers, serjeants at law, Wreathock was struck off the Roll. In 1757 the secretary assisted a member of the society, Samuel John of Lyon's Inn in his appeal to have John Greenwood and John Sliper struck off the Roll, on the grounds that during his period of articles Sliper had acted as 'footman or common servant' to Greenwood. This appeal was successful, and was financed by the society. Again a barrister gave his services free, and Mr John was thanked for 'his laudible zeal in making the said motion for the honour of the profession'.[3] In the same year the society was concerned in Frazer's Case, already mentioned.[4]

In 1775, as a result of the intervention of the society, Robert Simpson was struck off the Roll for having signed the articles of William Hurley, who had, during the period of his alleged clerkship, been employed by Gregory Geering, a member of the society, as his paid servant.[5] In the same year the admission of Laurence Times was prevented when it was shown that he had continued to act as a schoolmaster during his clerkship.[6] A similar charge was brought against John Edkins in 1781, but on this occasion the petition was not successful, and the judge ordered him to be admitted.[7] In 1802 a caveat was entered on behalf of the society against the admission of Richard Gardiner, because it was claimed that he had served an apprenticeship to a grocer, that he had for

---

[1] *Records*, p. 65.

[2] In 1725 a highwayman, John Everett, had brought a suit for breach of partnership against his professional colleague, Joseph Williams. Their solicitors, of whom Wreathock was one, were both imprisoned and fined £50 for contempt of court. On a later occasion, Wreathock had been convicted of highway robbery and sentenced to death. This was transmuted to transportation, and on his return Wreathock had secured re-admission as an attorney. Cf. Holdsworth, *op. cit.* XII, 59, and *Law Quarterly Review*, IX (1893), 197–9.

[3] *Records*, p. 82.   [4] See above p. 18.

[5] *Records*, pp. 129, 132, 134, 306–8.   [6] *Ibid.* pp. 129–31.

[7] *Ibid.* pp. 147–50.

some years held the office of serjeant at mace to the City of London, and that he continued to receive part of the profits of his successor. It was further alleged that he had been accustomed to discount bills and notes for 'necessitous persons', and then to bring actions against the parties to these bills, in which he acted as plaintiff and his master as attorney. The court ordered that his admission should be postponed to allow time for further investigation of these charges.[1]

The society exercised some measure of control over the professional education of attorneys in the ways that have been shown, but it occasionally considered the subject in a more general light. In 1748 the committee suggested that certain clauses should be added to a bill, shortly to be put before parliament, for the purpose of 'more effectually obliging the clerks of attorneys and solicitors to an actual and menial service of their masters, until such time as each of them were regularly assigned over to another attorney or solicitor'.[2] In 1751 it expressed its approval of a pamphlet written by John Felton[3] offering suggestions to those who were articled to attorneys, and thanked him for having distributed 'many thousand' copies of it throughout England and Wales. In the following year, as a reward for his help to the profession in this and other ways, the society made him a gift of fifteen guineas.[4] In 1807 the committee was considering a proposal to set up another society 'for the articled clerks of members of the society and for the purpose of discussing legal questions under the patronage and direction of the society'.[5]

From time to time, the society proposed adjustments in the legal system for 'the ease and benefit of suitors'. Among such matters were alterations in the system of giving bail, bills for regulating trials at *nisi prius*, the more effective summoning of juries, the misuse of writs of error by debtors seeking to delay payment, alterations in the laws relating to fines, improvements in the bankruptcy laws and in the management of the Writ of Error Office in King's Bench. In 1783 the society turned its attention to the Court of Chancery, and considered whether it should draw up 'such regulations as may appear necessary for lessening the delays and

---

[1] *Records*, pp. 180–1.   [2] *Ibid.* p. 29.
[3] *Friendly Hints to young Gentlemen who are, or intend to be, bound by Articles to Attorneys and Solicitors.*
[4] *Records*, pp. 48, 61–2.   [5] *Ibid.* p. 201.

expenses of the proceedings in that court'.[1] It was suggested that the Lord Chancellor might be approached to introduce legislation for this purpose, but these efforts, like those of so many others who sought to reform this court, came to nothing, and it survived almost unscathed until *Bleak House* and beyond.[2] The matter was dropped and the orders relating to it were expunged from the minutes.[3] Many lesser obstacles in the way of an efficient legal service were removed at the society's instigation. The hours of attendance at various law offices were made more convenient, registers of the addresses of attorneys were proposed, and the fees of certain officers in the courts were scrutinised.

The society was always ready to resist the encroachments of other groups on what they felt to be the preserves of attorneys, and, by the same token, to insist on their own right to perform certain functions which others were seeking to deny them. It successfully opposed the application of the Clerks in Court to be admitted solicitors and to take clerks, and protested against their behaviour in refusing to sign certificates and in creating other difficulties.[4] To admit Clerks, it was held, would conflict with the 'intention of the legislature to prevent the undue and unnecessary increase of attorneys and solicitors, and that none should practise as such but persons of character and integrity regularly brought up, and well qualified to act in the profession'.[5]

It was perhaps a sign of the growing self-assurance of the society and of enhanced notions of professional solidarity, that the encroachments of the barristers were equally successfully resisted. In 1761 the committee was ordered to investigate means whereby barristers could be prevented from transacting business properly belonging to attorneys, and decided that the most effective course

[1] *Records*, p. 156.

[2] *Bleak House* did not begin to appear until 1852, but the Lord Chancellor described is generally assumed to be Lord Lyndhurst, so that the action of the story must take place about 1827, the period following the report of the first Chancery Commission, described by Holdsworth as 'the very worst period of the Court of Chancery' (W. S. Holdsworth, *Charles Dickens as a Legal Historian* (Yale University Press, 1928), p. 79).

[3] The society also dropped an attempt to get Masters in Chancery to attend in the afternoon when it was shown that some attended longer in the morning, and that 'others were so infirm that they could not attend in the afternoon (especially in the winter season)' (*Records*, p. 134).

[4] *Ibid.* pp. 9, 13, 14, 16. For a summary of the orders in Court relating to the Six Clerks' Office, and a list of the objections made by the society on these occasions, see pp. 295–302.   [5] *Ibid.* p. 300.

would be to prosecute individual cases as they occurred.[1] In 1800 it was reported that certain barristers were receiving clients and transacting their business without the intervention of an attorney, and it was resolved that 'such practices were highly improper, and ought to be discountenanced by the Society and the profession at large'. Copies of this resolution were sent to every member of the society 'in order that the sense of the meeting may be fully known, as a means of preventing in future a practice highly prejudicial to the interests of attorneys and solicitors'.[2] The society was also concerned to prevent conveyancers practising as attorneys.[3] From the opposite point of view, it endeavoured to break into the monopoly of the business connected with the soliciting of private bills in the House of Commons which the clerks of the House were seeking to keep to themselves.[4]

The most prolonged dispute of this kind in which the society was involved on behalf of the profession was that with the Scriveners' Company of London. The Scriveners, wanting to secure a monopoly of conveyancing business for themselves, tried to insist that attorneys and solicitors doing conveyancing in the City of London should become free of their company. The society denied the right of the Company to insist on this, and the dispute, fought out in several test cases in the Lord Mayor's Court, went on during the whole of the period 1749–60. Individual members were prosecuted by the Scriveners, and their defence was organised and paid for by the society. The expenditure of money and energy which the society was prepared to make in this affair is a striking indication both of the strength of professional feeling, and of the fact that conveyancing had now become recognised as one of the most important parts of the attorney's practice. And the additional fact that distinguished barristers were willing to represent the society in these disputes without retainers or fees, suggests that they realised that their interests were being threatened also, and that there were many points at which the interests of the whole legal profession coincided.[5] Besides, the threat was only local—though in a most

---

[1] This at a time when the society was presenting plate to those barristers who had given their services free in the dispute with the Scriveners' Company.

[2] *Records*, pp. 173–4.   [3] *Ibid.* pp. 180–3.

[4] The minutes end before the successful outcome of this matter; business of this kind eventually fell to barristers (*Records*, pp. xci, 221–2). See also O. C. Williams, *The Clerical Organisation of the House of Commons* (Oxford, 1954).

[5] As Fletcher Norton said in his speech on behalf of the attorneys: 'This is the case of the whole profession of the law...it is not only the profession of attorneys that is involved, but all the Serjeants at Law' (*Records*, p. 263).

important locality—and no insuperable constitutional or financial barriers were erected by the Scriveners to keep attorneys out of the Company, and hence deprive them of the right to do conveyancing. The Scriveners' Company was anxious to gain members, and the admission fees required were small. It seems, therefore, that what impelled the attorneys to engage in this prolonged litigation was a highly developed sense of professional prestige and solidarity in face of an attack which may have appeared impudent rather than dangerous.

The actions which were fought were based on a by-law of the City 'That no person not being free of the City of London, or any other employed by him, is to exercise any art or mystery whatsoever in the said City'.[1] Because of this, they were heard in the Lord Mayor's Court, before the Recorder. The attorneys tried without success to challenge the authority of this court to judge the question, and to get the action removed to King's Bench. In spite of this rebuff, however, the attorneys went on, and in 1760 the issue was decided in their favour.[2]

From the Scriveners' point of view, the affair looks like a desperate attempt to retain a monopoly in a type of business from which they derived much of their profit, and it represents the efforts of an old-established and decaying corporation to resist the latest—and perhaps the most serious—attack on its position. As a witness at the trial remarked: 'It was said that the Company was thrown into very great straits, and therefore must make use of this means to recover itself.'[3] The Scriveners seem to have been more successful in their dealings with other groups, the Notaries, for example, but the future lay with professional groups of another kind.[4] Others besides the attorneys seem to have been reluctant to join the City Companies at this time. They were sufficiently prosperous to do without the privileges, and anxious to avoid the inconveniences and petty restrictions which membership might impose. It was bodies like the Society of Gentlemen Practisers itself that men were beginning to want and to create, bodies in which efficiency counted for more than antiquity of foundation. And, as Mrs George com-

---

[1] *Records*, p. 247.

[2] The report of the trial is in *Records*, pp. 246–86; a separate account was published in 1769.

[3] *Records*, p. 277; see also Holdsworth, *op. cit.* XII, 70–1.

[4] Cf. E. R. Samuel, 'Anglo-Jewish Notaries and Scriveners', *Transactions of the Jewish Historical Society*, XVII (1951–2).

ments, 'The City's ceremonial...had become antiquated, but not yet historically interesting'.[1]

One of the obvious ways in which such a society could demonstrate its usefulness to the profession was by securing improvements in the conditions of employment, and the society proved itself in this respect by initiating a successful appeal to have the fees of the profession increased. In 1798 the committee decided to submit a memorial on this subject to the Lord Chancellor and the Master of the Rolls, pointing out that their fees had been fixed 'upwards of a century ago when the value of money was such as rendered the then allowance adequate to its purpose, but that the personal and particular imposts laid on the practisers within the last few years and other causes, render an increase of their fees absolutely necessary'.[2] This was not accomplished overnight. Both the Lord Chancellor and the Judges thought that it lay beyond their power to grant such an increase, though they were all agreed that it was desirable, and it was not until 1807 that Erskine, during his brief period as Chancellor, granted an increase of fees in his courts.[3] Fees in the common law courts were not increased until three years later, and then not to the extent that the society thought desirable, and when the minutes end, a further petition to parliament was being considered.[4]

Whatever their earlier attitude may have been, at this period the judges seem to have heard these petitions with sympathy, the more so there can be little doubt, because they were presented by such a society. The barristers, too, who early in the century had often adopted a somewhat haughty attitude towards the attorneys, had, by its end, become more respectful. It was a respect based as much on a nice appreciation on both sides of their mutual interests, as well as on more high-sounding ideas of professional solidarity, and it was made easier for the barristers by the improvement in the status of the attorneys since 1700. The attorneys were becoming increasingly sensitive about their public reputation, and the society

---

[1] M. D. George, *London Life in the Eighteenth Century* (London, 1951), p. 3 and note 4 (p. 323). See also J. R. Kellett, 'The Breakdown of Gild and Corporation Control over the Handicraft and Retail Trade in London', *Economic History Review*, 2nd series, x, 3 (1958), pp. 381–94.

[2] *Records*, pp. 163–4.

[3] On 3 July 1807, the society resolved that 'Lord Erskine' should be a standing toast at its dinners, as a token of its gratitude to the Chancellor (*Records*, p. 205).   [4] *Ibid.* p. 228.

was ready to demand apologies on behalf of any members who thought themselves shabbily treated by a member of the bar. In 1748, for example, it took up the case of Thomas Nuthall,[1] one of its members who considered that his professional reputation had been wrongly impugned by a note placed in the Retainer Book of a barrister, Hume Campbell, to the effect that no more briefs were to be accepted from Nuthall. Campbell replied at some length to the representations made on Nuthall's behalf, and blamed the entry on the officiousness of his clerk. He concluded his explanation by expressing his 'hearty wishes for the prosperity of the Society, declaring whether in or out of parliament he would in all places and at all times be ready to serve the Society in the best manner he was able, not only as bound in point of gratitude, but that he considered the worthy part of the profession, whether attorneys, solicitors, or counsel, as one body'.[2]

He evidently kept his word, for six years later it was announced that on his retirement from the bar he had been replaced as counsel for the society in its dispute with the Scriveners by Fletcher Norton, another barrister of distinction. Fletcher Norton, too, served the society well, and, with the aid of the attorney- and solicitor-general, brought this action to a successful conclusion.[3]

In 1766 an eminent barrister who had spoken in disparaging terms of attorneys[4] was quickly brought to heel by a resolution of the society that 'any counsel...making use of suchlike reflections upon the attorneys in general ought not to be employed by any member of the society'.[5] He sent a very full apology, and made further amends in a similar statement made in open court, and later by giving his services free to the society in their attempt to have one Robert Simpson removed from the Roll.[6] Once the tradition had been established which forbade barristers from dealing directly with clients, they found they could no longer afford to indulge in the common sport of abusing attorneys. The society even objected to rulings of the Inns of Court which were thought to

---

[1] Chatham's attorney was called Thomas Nuthall; see pp. 80–1 below.
[2] *Records*, pp. 32–3.
[3] The society presented Norton and his juniors with plate to mark the victory.
[4] Serjeant Davy was alleged to have told a jury: 'You gentlemen who are on the outside of the curtain do not see the tricks and management within; we that are on the inside see the whole, and I will take it upon me to say, that out of the many mistakes that happen in the management of causes, 19 out of 20 happen by the ignorance of attorneys' (*Records*, p. 114).
[5] *Ibid.*   [6] *Ibid.* p. 132. Davy's apology is printed in full, pp. 114–15.

be harmful to attorneys. In 1763, for example, a lengthy statement was prepared objecting to an order of the Benchers which prohibited attorneys and solicitors from being called to the bar for two years after they had ceased to practice.[1] There was a case, too, in 1809, in which the society protested against the admission to Gray's Inn of one William Harwood, who in their opinion was 'not duly qualified to act as a solicitor.'[2] This is unusually late for a solicitor to be admitted as a member of an Inn of Court, but the abrupt end of the minutes leaves the details of the case unknown.

The society also served the profession by scrutinising proposals for legislation which would affect attorneys, and by providing a central agency through which petitions and memorials could be presented to parliament. In 1740, for example, a bill 'for regulating trials at *nisi prius* and for the more effective summoning of juries' was considered, and at the next meeting 'a deputation was appointed to attend the gentlemen in the House of Commons who had the bill under consideration, and to give them their assistance in settling the bill'.[3] In the following year, the committee considered the Land Tax bill which was before parliament, and attempted to have those clauses removed which prevented attorneys and solicitors from acting as commissioners. The Speaker, the Lord Mayor, and the members for the City of London were all approached on the society's behalf.[4] In 1742 the situation was reversed when a member of parliament asked the help of the society in preparing a bill for the easier recovery of small debts. The existing laws on this matter were a subject of constant complaint, and it was commonly thought that the attorneys had a vested interest in preserving

[1] *Records*, p. 111.

[2] *Ibid*. pp. 214–15. William Harwood (Horwood), aged 29, son of Thomas Gee Harwood, yeoman deceased; admitted 2 December 1808 (*Gray's Inn Admission Register*, p. 411).

[3] *Ibid*. pp. 2–3.

[4] *Ibid*. pp. 6–7. Cf. W. R. Ward, *The English Land Tax in the Eighteenth Century* (Oxford, 1953), p. 88. Dr Ward notices a decline in the social status of the commissioners by this time, and quotes Hardwick's taunt that they were 'Some of the lowest people of any kind of property in the kingdom'. He adds 'Attorneys, who might have helped, were often excluded from the boards "because if they were let into the management of other people's property, they would be sure to set them together by the ears"' (Hist. MSS. Comm. *Egmont Diary*, 1, 87). This remark was made apropos of a clause which was to be added to a bill for erecting a workhouse at Worcester to the effect that 'No attorney shall be capable of being elected, or of acting as, a Guardian of the Poor in the City of Worcester'. Sir Joseph Jekyl (whose wife's family included attorneys) protested against this as a 'reflection on an honourable profession'.

their complexities and absurdities. The society, however, even at this early stage in its history, resolved to give what help it could, and thanked the member for 'the mark of his regard for them'.[1] In 1747 it considered an application to parliament to revive several recent acts on the matter of vexatious arrests,[2] and in the following year applied to the standing committee on expiring laws to have the acts regulating the profession continued.[3]

Lastly, the society performed many acts of benevolence and charity to distressed members of the profession and their families. In 1778 Mrs Colston, widow of John Colston and mother of two children, applied to the committee for relief. Colston had been a member of the society and had 'rendered great service' during its dispute with the Scriveners' Company, for which he had not been recompensed. In recognition of this, his widow was given twenty guineas to alleviate her distress.[4] In 1806 Thomas Searle wrote saying that for the last twenty years he had been afflicted with a disease which had compelled him to give up his partnership with another solicitor, and had made it impossible for him to receive clients. He had, unwillingly, been forced to seek the aid of the society, having in the past been helped by several members individually. 'To whom', he wrote, 'can I so properly apply as to those of my profession who by the blessing of God having had their health and abilities continued to them, have with honour to themselves and benefit to their fellow-creatures been raised to states of independence and affluence.'[5] It was decided to leave members to contribute to Searle's relief if they thought fit; the secretary was to collect the donations, and employ them as he should judge best. In the following year it was suggested that a fund should be established 'for the relief of decayed members of the profession, their wives and children', but there is no record of what came of this proposal.[6]

In spite of this striking record of professional and charitable service to the attorneys, the society was not without its critics. The most energetic and voluble of these was Joseph Day, an attorney,

[1] *Records*, p. 8.   [2] *Ibid.* p. 25.
[3] *Ibid.* pp. 29–31. The society frequently applied to have indemnifying acts passed for the benefit of attorneys who had neglected to perform certain duties in the statutory time.
[4] *Ibid.* p. 139.
[5] *Ibid.* pp. 193, 196. For a similar petition, see *ibid.* pp. 321–3.
[6] *Ibid.* p. 205.

who devoted much time and trouble to attacking the society, and
making proposals for establishing another, more efficiently organised, and officially sanctioned.[1] The point at which he attacked it
most vigorously—that it was independent in origin and voluntary
in membership—was that at which it was probably most vulnerable.
But while it is true that the society represented only part of the
profession, it might be replied with equal truth that Day represented only himself.

He maintained that a society constituted as this one was must
be inadequate.

Scarcely a day passes during any term [he wrote] without complaint to
some of the courts against one or more attorneys; the censures passed,
and the punishments inflicted neither tend to prevent a continuance of
the numerous and serious evils with which the lower and unprincipled
members of the profession torment society, nor in the smallest degree
diminish the vast load of obloquy, that has long been attached by public
prejudice to the general body of practitioners.[2]

This may have been true, and it is a view expressed by others,[3]
but it was something at least that the complaints were made—many
of them by the society itself—and their number might also be
interpreted as evidence of an increased concern for the behaviour
of the profession. Both in its origin and in the methods by which
it proceeded, the Society of Gentlemen Practisers was more typical
of eighteenth-century society and government than that which Day
proposed to establish in its place, but it is to his credit that when
the Law Society was founded in the nineteenth century, its constitution bore striking resemblance to that which he had advocated
thirty years earlier. But in the meantime, it was hardly fair to
blame those making complaints about the behaviour of attorneys
if the disciplinary action taken in consequence was not sufficiently
severe.

---

[1] Details of his criticisms of the society and of his efforts to create a substitute
for it are contained in two pamphlets written by him, *An Address* [*to the Attorneys
at Law and Solicitors*, etc.] (1796); and *Thoughts* [*on the Necessity and Utility
of Examinations*, etc.] (1795).

[2] *An Address*, pp. 11–12.

[3] Cf. A. Grant, *The Progress and Practice of the Modern Attorney*, etc. (1796).
'It is a truth...that while the officers of the sheriff of Middlesex are more
respectable now than formerly, the pettifogging tribe of attornies have not only
increased in numbers but in infamy.'

Yet, although Day appears to have underestimated the effectiveness of the society, and to have been as ready to discern selfish motives behind their conduct as they were to see them in his own, there was probably some truth in his claims that only a society which was officially authorised to govern the profession, to which all attorneys would belong, and which would conduct a rigorous examination of their qualifications, would be sufficiently powerful to perform the Herculean task that confronted it. What he proposed was a Royal College of Attorneys and Solicitors, similar to that of the surgeons and physicians. It would be established by royal charter, and entrusted with the task of examining and governing the profession. Its governors would include the Lord Chancellor, the judges, and the Master of the Rolls, and they would be assisted by the attorney- and solicitor-general and other senior barristers. This board would appoint examiners who would award a certificate. Day further suggested that a library should be established, lectures given, and a register of practitioners maintained. Membership of such a society as this would clearly mark off the upright and honourable attorney from the pettifogger, and guarantee to his client a certain standard of professional competence and behaviour.

According to Day, many distinguished legal figures supported this plan. But attorneys, and the Society of Gentlemen Practisers, objected that it placed the profession under external control, and gave the impression that it was incapable of ruling itself. To Day, however, only a society constituted in the way he suggested would have the appearance of dignity and impartiality that was necessary if the public was to be brought to respect the profession. 'Incorporating the attorneys', he maintained, 'would create a marked distinction and oppose an insurmountable barrier against the host of evils which daily assail the really respectable practitioners from the misconduct of those of another description.'[1]

The society was not convinced. It paid scant attention to his advances, and even suggested that he wanted to create such a college mainly in order to become its first secretary. But Day was not easily discouraged. Thurlow, Kenyon, the king himself, were told of his plans. George Rose assured him that the government would support the necessary bill if it were backed by the judges. It was all in vain. The society would have none of it, and Day's plan fell through. It voted him substantial sums for his expenditure

---

[1] Day, *An Address*, p. 173.

of time and trouble,[1] but he was not to be mollified. 'But the die is cast', he wrote, 'I have promised acquiescence, and I will honestly keep my word. I *now see* that there are *interests* to combat, which, though formidable, would perhaps not be unconquerable; but I will submit, and not oppose them.'[2]

Day's professed aims, and those of the society, were closely akin. Both were concerned to distinguish the respectable attorneys from those of another complexion, but Day's proposals would have created an institution which in the scope of its work and in the social ideals it embodied went far beyond those of the type represented by the Society of Gentlemen Practisers. The present Law Society, which performs many of the functions which Day planned for his own, was founded in 1825. The minutes of its predecessor end in 1810, and those who founded the new society apparently conceived of themselves as founding a new society, not as reviving an earlier institution. This is surprising, for the older body had been influential and respected, and it is strange that it should have been forgotten. The new society was given a royal charter in 1831; in 1832 it possessed a library of more than a thousand volumes; in 1836 the first examination of articled clerks was held under its auspices.[3]

Attorneys and solicitors, however, never attained that degree of independence accorded to barristers. The new society, like the old, was in essence an instrument for putting into effect parliamentary regulations concerning the profession. In accordance with new social ideals and in answer to more pressing social needs, the powers given it were such as its increased jurisdiction demanded. But for its successful working, it depended on a spirit of professional pride and social responsibility such as that which had brought the Society of Gentlemen Practisers into being, and enabled it to perform its most useful work, in an age with which these qualities are not usually associated.

[1] He was given £98. 18s. 8d. for his expenses in this matter, and £100 for his trouble. Day is not mentioned in the published minutes of the society.

[2] Day, *An Address*, p. 182.

[3] See E. B. V. Christian, *A Short History of Solicitors*, pp. 176 *et seqq.*

CHAPTER IV

THE PROVINCIAL LAW SOCIETIES

MEMBERSHIP of the Society of Gentlemen Practisers was, as has been shown, practically restricted to attorneys in London and the Home Counties, if only for the reason that they alone would be able to attend its meetings. This, indeed, was an objection raised by Joseph Day in his attack on the society. But it is true that the cases of malpractice dealt with by the society were not restricted to those which occurred in London, and further, that it scrutinised the entire lists of those seeking admission to the Roll at the beginning of each Term—though here also, the difficulty of obtaining reliable information increased with the distance from London, even if it was mitigated by the development of the practice of every country attorney having a London agent.

Yet this was a private society, owing its existence to the initiative of a few men in London, and the development of the provincial law societies took place independently of it. So far as can be seen, there was no formal connection between them and the London society in the early stages of their existence. During the period up to about 1830, indeed, there were occasions when the provincial societies seemed to resent the increasing importance and presumptions of the London society. But it seems likely—and the records of the Yorkshire Law Society amply support the impression—that when the interests of the profession were at stake, provincialism would give way to professional solidarity. It is probable that the provincial societies, like the Society of Gentlemen Practisers itself, can in origin best be regarded as examples of a phenomenon that was common enough in the eighteenth century—groups of men with common interests meeting together for reasons that were primarily social and convivial, and finding that collectively they were able to do things for their common benefit which as individuals they were unable to accomplish. And, as the secretary of the Manchester society told the Select Committee on Legal Education in 1846: 'These Societies are altogether voluntary, and have originated from the zeal and exertions of a few respectable individuals.'[1]

[1] *Reports, Committees* (1846), x, xvi.

In addition to those bodies which are to be described, there were apparently others even more informal in character, such as that which met at King's Lynn in 1797 to draw up a list of conveyancing charges, and the meetings of the Northern Agents mentioned by William Hodgson at the end of the century.[1]

There are four provincial law societies which were founded in the eighteenth century: Bristol, founded in 1770, Yorkshire in 1786, Somerset in 1796, and Sunderland in 1800.[2] Between 1800 and 1835 fourteen were founded: Leeds in 1805, Devon and Exeter in 1808, Manchester in 1809, Plymouth in 1815, Gloucester in 1817, Birmingham, Hull, and Kent in 1818, Bolton and Newcastle upon Tyne in 1826, Liverpool in 1827, Carlisle in 1831, Preston in 1834, and Dorset in 1835. It is not surprising that Bristol should be the first city outside London to have its own law society, nor that Yorkshire should follow it, when it is remembered that it was from Yorkshire that the first moves came which culminated in the act of 1729.[3] And it was to be expected also that such centres of growing size and importance as Leeds, Manchester, Birmingham, Newcastle, Liverpool, and Hull, would early support their own law societies. It is interesting that there is no immediate connection between these early societies, nor are they the result of any pressure exerted by the judges or by the London society. This, and the similarity of their early histories and functions, lends some support to the view suggested elsewhere that it was during the latter years of the eighteenth century, and the early years of the nineteenth, that ideas about professional conduct and professional solidarity began to be common and important, calling for societies like these to express and implement them.

The Bristol Law Society was apparently founded in 1770, but the minutes which survive do not begin until 1774, and there is an unfortunate gap for the crucial period 1780–1819. It may even be the case that the society expired shortly after 1780; a letter of 1814 seems to suggest that there was no society in existence then, and

---

[1] Some sort of arrangement must also have been available to arrange for the presentation of a petition of 1169 attorneys protesting against a threatened prosecution for infringing the laws relating to Stamp Duties (*Calendar of Treasury Books*, xxx, ii (1706–7), 440; 16 September 1707).

[2] This date is not claimed by the existing Law Society in Sunderland, but it is given by other authorities.

[3] It was in Yorkshire that the first Land Registry was set up, at Wakefield.

another of 1805 advocates the setting up of a law library, apparently in the absence of any other comparable organisation.[1]

The minutes from 1774 to 1780 give the impression of a society interested almost exclusively in social activities. The rules were revised and printed in 1774, and begin: 'Whereas divers attorneys at law and solicitors in chancery, did in the month of October in the year 1770 upon consideration of the many advantages which might arise from a regular and well ordered association of the practisers of the laws of this realm, form themselves into a society, which has continued from that time to the present to be held at the Bush Tavern in Corn Street, Bristol....' The society was to include barristers as well as attorneys and solicitors. It was to meet for dinner every second Tuesday, and on the first and last days of each Term. There were fines for non-attendance, and for the infringement of the rules such as that which forbade dice, cards, and betting. Eight members attended the first meeting mentioned in the minutes, and the number continued to be fairly small.[2]

There are only a few indications that the society was anything other than a social one. In July 1775 new regulations were adopted 'as to the manner of stating and debating law questions in this society'. At the same meeting it was suggested that £5 be paid out of the society's funds towards the cost of the funeral of an attorney, William Edwards. This proposal was not agreed to, but it was agreed that 6s. 3d. should be paid to the landlord of the Bush who had supplied Edwards with certain provisions during his illness. From time to time law books were bought for the use of members, but these can never have been very numerous, for they were kept along with other records of the society in a single chest locked by three keys, and in July 1775 a proposal that Viner's *Abridgement of the Law* should be bought was dropped because the proposer did not turn up at the meeting at which the matter was to be discussed. In January 1776, 20 guineas were subscribed to the fund raised in Bristol for the relief of soldiers, widows, and children who had suffered 'in the prosecution of the measures lately adopted by Government against rebelling North Americans', and in January 1778, £50 was given to the fund for raising men in support of

---

[1] The present secretary of the Bristol Law Society kindly arranged for me to see these records.

[2] The *Law List* for 1777 gives the names of 35 attorneys in Bristol; that for 1790, 61. The *Bristol Directory* for 1794, 72.

the 'constitutional authority of Great Britain over her rebellious colonies in America'.[1]

The society's money was invested in turnpike tickets until March 1778, when they were sold and the money invested in the funds. Occasionally also shares in state lottery tickets were bought for the society. There does not seem to have been a great deal of enthusiasm for the society; on more than one occasion a quorum was not present, and on 14 May 1776 it was recorded that 'The president and most of the members being engaged at Gloucester in the Election not one member was present at this meeting'.

There seems to have been no organised body of attorneys in Bristol during the period 1780–1819. A printed circular of December 1805 mentions that a meeting had been held to discuss the setting up of a law library, and asks attorneys to join. Another circular of 21 November 1814, signed by Arthur Palmer of the Sheriff's Office in Bristol, asks attorneys to attend a meeting to discuss 'a communication from a committee of respectable solicitors [in London] on the subject of an application by the profession to the judges of the Courts of King's Bench, Common Pleas and Exchequer respecting the present practice in the taxation of costs', and commends the proposals as being 'calculated for the benefit of the public, and to secure the respectability of the profession'. This letter, with its reference to the London Society, the taxation of costs, and the respectability of the profession, is the first definite sign of a specifically professional feeling among the attorneys in Bristol.

The minutes of the Law Library Society begin in 1819, and extend to 1870 when the Bristol Incorporated Law Society was founded. There was an admission fee of five guineas, and an annual subscription of two guineas; articled clerks were to pay two guineas a year. The minutes are entirely concerned with the administration of the library and the ordering of books.

The survival of an interesting minute-book recording the foundation and early history of the Yorkshire Law Society makes possible

---

[1] It is hardly surprising that Bristol attorneys should be so ready to support the government. In May 1778 an attorney who had joined the Somersetshire Militia 'for the laudable purpose of serving and protecting his country', and who wanted to maintain his connection with the society, was deemed to be a non-resident member. Perhaps the tavern bill of 31 September 1776 contains a further example of this patriotic zeal: 'pd. for British Herb Tobacco, 1/3.'

a detailed study of its activities during the period 1786–1834.[1] In March 1786 the attorneys and solicitors attending the Assizes at York were invited to attend a meeting to be held at Mr Ringrose's,[2] which was to consider the heads of a bill to be presented to parliament for regulating persons practising as conveyancers—another sign of the importance attached by the profession to this branch of its activities—and to consider a plan for holding regular meetings in the future.

This meeting took place on 21 March, and was attended by forty-one attorneys from all over Yorkshire, some from Durham, and two from London. It was decided that 'as many Gentlemen were of the opinion that such meetings would be of public utility and productive of useful regulations',[3] regular meetings would be held at York every Tuesday evening during the week of the assizes. The rules and aims of the society were formulated in August 1786. It was resolved

That the principal objects of this society shall be to preserve the privileges and support the credit of attorneys and solicitors: to promote fair and liberal practice and prevent abuses in the profession: and to adopt such measures as may appear best calculated to effect these ends and most likely to secure respect to the profession and to be of advantage to their employers.

The company of all the attorneys and solicitors attending the assizes was invited, whether they were generally resident in the county of York or not: members from outside would be considered as honorary members for the occasion of the assizes. There were to be a president, a vice-president, a secretary, and a treasurer. The annual subscription was to be one guinea, with an entrance fee of one guinea. Meetings were to take the form of a supper, and whatever money remained after the expenses of these meetings had been met was to be devoted to such purposes as the majority of members should think fit.

Throughout these years the society paid a great deal of attention to questions affecting the interests and dignity of the profession. It was to protect their interests in the matter of conveyancing that

[1] This minute book was made available for my use by the present secretary of the society.

[2] Ringrose's Hotel, Little Blake Street, 'a fashionable place, frequented by the nobility of the period'.

[3] All quotations are from the minute book of the society.

they had met in the first place. It was resolved that this bill should be opposed, and the chairman, Mr Townend, town clerk of York, was instructed to communicate this decision to the 'solicitors employed on behalf of the profession in London'. Accordingly Townend sent them a copy of the resolutions passed by this 'respectable meeting of attorneys'. The society objected to the bill for a variety of reasons. It was felt that it would increase the number of conveyancers who were not admitted attorneys, opening to them 'the most profitable and agreeable part of the employment now transacted by attorneys'. It was unfair to demand that attorneys should be articled for five years, while conveyancers were allowed to qualify in three, and unreasonable to put attorneys to the trouble and expense of procuring new admissions and further examination 'as to their fitness in that business which they have practised for years'. It was objected that the

clause restraining attorneys etc. from holding courts and drawing surrenders would be prejudicial to the profession in the highest degree and would occasion great inconvenience and a heavy and unknown expense in those parts of the country where small copyhold estates are daily passing from one to another, in some places at the distance of forty or fifty miles from the residence of a barrister, and besides there are not more than three or four courts held by barristers throughout this county whereas some attorneys are stewards of, and hold to the number of twenty or thirty. This would therefore effectually introduce barristers into family business, and by making their clerks admitted conveyancers would enable them to do all the best business now transacted by attorneys.

He concluded by hoping that 'these reasons would have weight with the profession in town, and induce them to prevent a measure so certain to prove detrimental to country attorneys', and asked that a copy of the bill should be sent to him if the business should be proceeded in.

In the following year the society approved the terms of another bill on this subject, with the significant proviso that a clause should be added 'to prevent clerks to counsel employed in any capacity as menial servants during their time of service from being admitted conveyancers, although duly articled pursuant to the directions contained in the said bill'. The Yorkshire attorneys were willing that further restrictions should be placed on the profession for the sake of its increased prestige, and recommended that additional duties should be placed on articles of clerkship, and that the system of taxing costs should be improved.

In 1794 the society suggested amendments in the proposed bill to increase the duty on articles of clerkship and admission fees, but later dropped it when the stipulations of the bill became better known, and when it was discovered that the bill was not being opposed either by the London attorneys or by any others. Ten years later, in 1804, on learning that another increase was proposed in the duties on the profession, the society set up a committee to draft a petition for an increase in fees, which was to work with the London society, and any others that might be interested. The secretary wrote to the London society on 19 July asking for more detailed information about the proposed bill, and to assure him that 'the Yorkshire Law Society will very cheerfully join in any measures that may tend to preserve the interest, respectability, and independence of the profession'.

There were other occasions when the society acted in complete accord with the London society. In 1804 Charles Frost submitted a memorial to the president of the Yorkshire society pointing out the hardships which were often incurred by those seeking the recovery of small sums, owing to the inequitable system of taxing costs.

When a sum of £20 or £30 only is withheld from a person however unjustly it is impossible for any gentleman of the profession conscientiously to advise him to have recourse to the remedy which the law would seem to afford him for the recovery of his due, as the difference between the costs of the suit, and the costs for which on taxation he would be entitled to call upon his opponent would generally speaking, be more than the amount of his debt.

The profession of the law is consequently brought into disrepute and its practitioners whose respectability ought to have every encouragement and support are subjected to the odium of having consumed by exorbitant charges the sum the verdict of a jury had awarded to be the just right of the successful suitor....

Frost was thanked for his concern for the profession, and the society agreed to his suggestion that a memorial should be presented to the judges. In this the judges were told that the society consisted of 130 'of the most respectable attorneys and solicitors practising in Yorkshire', and that its aim was 'the correction of abuses and the promotion of liberal and honourable practice in the profession'. After mentioning that several recent acts had added to the financial burdens on attorneys, the memorial declared that 'effectually to maintain the respectability of the profession so important to the general interests of the country, it is requisite that every branch of it, but particularly that to which your memorialists belong, should be rendered perfectly independent and superior to every temptation'. It was pointed out that the fees of barristers had been raised, while those of attorneys had not, and it was claimed that the memorial was inspired more by a sense of justice towards the country at large than by a concern for the pecuniary interests of attorneys. Their legitimate rewards must be such as to raise them above the temptation to pervert the law to their own ends. Copies of this resolution were sent to the presidents of the other law societies in existence. In the end the fees were raised, and the London society was formally thanked for its exertions, and its Prolocutor, John Kayes, was elected an honorary member of the Yorkshire society.

In 1819 the society expressed its approval of the attempts which the London society made to keep undesirables out of the profession. It was resolved

That to promote this laudable object the secretary of this society be instructed to write immediately on the receipt of every communication from the secretary of the London Law Society with the names of persons applying for admission, and with a copy of the resolution of the London Law Society now read to such members of this society as live at or near the places where the persons so applying for admission shall have served their clerkships.

There were many other matters to which the society gave its attention. Its funds increased, and from time to time substantial sums were invested in the consolidated annuities. In July 1815 the annual subscription was raised to two guineas until such time as the society should hold £1000 worth of this stock, a position which was reached by July 1819. The society made frequent charitable gifts to needy members, or to their widows and young children. The usual method was that a certain sum was handed over to a member who knew the case in question, for him to expend as he thought best, or to pay a weekly allowance. Thus in July 1789 it was resolved

That two shillings and sixpence per week be paid out of the society's funds into the hands of Mr Thos. Holland of Leeds until further orders, to be applied as he shall in his discretion think fit, towards the more comfortable support of Mr John Moxen, an attorney now in the Workhouse at Leeds, either in apparel or other necessaries, without relief to the parish, to commence immediately.

The society also paid the cost of printing lists of members, and of providing them with off-prints of articles of professional interest from the periodicals. In 1797 it voted twenty guineas to Anthony Dawson of Sheffield for his expense in prosecuting one Leander Fawcett who had been admitted without serving a clerkship, and in 1817 £50 was voted to Charles Anderton to help him promote a bill to regulate the practice of unqualified conveyancers—again the solicitude about conveyancing. Sometimes the society was called in to settle disputes between members. In 1797, and again in 1812, it petitioned the High Sheriff and justices to improve the facilities provided for attorneys in the courts at York.[1] A library was started in 1819, and the magistrates were asked to provide a room for it, and in 1828 the subscription was adjusted to make it more attractive for country members. In 1805 it was suggested that the sums allowed to witnesses for their expenses when they were brought to York to give evidence in criminal cases were inadequate —the sum of five shillings being considered 'inadequate even for a common labourer'. The behaviour of barristers towards the profession was closely watched. In 1812 John Pemberton, a barrister of York, was censured for having offered to prepare some conveyancing deeds for £18, and declaring that 'he was quite sure no attorney will transact the business under twice as much'. This, the society declared to be 'contrary to the established rules of liberal practice...and a direct infringement of the business of an attorney'.

The activities of the Yorkshire Law Society were remarkably similar to those of the Society of Gentlemen Practisers, and the resolutions and correspondence quoted amply support the view that in the latter years of the eighteenth century and the early years of the nineteenth, attorneys and solicitors were actively concerned for the 'liberal' and 'respectable' character of their employment. Further support will be afforded by a survey—necessarily less detailed—of the early history of some other provincial law societies.

[1] The Courts were built in 1771. In 1797 the Society complained that the domes at the top made it difficult to hear counsel and witnesses, and in 1812 that there was room for only half the attorneys who attended.

On 2 October 1809 fourteen 'Gentlemen attorneys' met at the Mosley Arms Inn in Manchester, and resolved that 'the attorneys practising in Manchester and Salford do form themselves into a society'.[1] At a dinner held on 20 October, thirty-seven members enrolled, and the constitution was drawn up. There were to be two dinners a year, the cost of which, and other incidental expenses were to be covered by an annual subscription of two guineas. The surplus was to be banked or invested at interest, and 'to be applicable to...charitable purposes in favour of any decayed members of the profession of the law'. This, according to the author of this brief history, was 'little else than a social and benevolent club', and its records end in May 1815. Up to that time six grants had been made to decayed members, of sums ranging from ten to twenty guineas.[2] The Manchester Law Library, evidently an off-shoot of this society, was founded in 1820, at a meeting of seventeen professional men, and was originally housed in two rooms lent by the secretary and treasurer, Robert Kershaw. Another branch of its activities was a Law Students' Society, presumably for the articled clerks of members, which held weekly meetings from 1809 to 1811.[3]

The Law Society at Plymouth began with the formation of a society for 'founding and maintaining a Law Library'.[4] Members were to be barristers or attorneys of Plymouth, Plymouth Dock, and Stonehouse, who were proprietors of, or subscribers to, the Plymouth Public Library founded in 1810. Every member was to give £5 or its equivalent in books, and to pay an annual subscription of £1. Twelve members attended the first meeting held in October 1815. In addition to maintaining the library, the society held an annual dinner at a place appointed by the president.

But the society concerned itself with more strictly business matters as well. In July 1819 a special meeting was called to con-

[1] Information about the Manchester Law Society is derived from a brief history by Alfred Tarbolton, published by the society in 1924, which I was able to see through the kindness of the present secretary.

[2] The existing society began in 1838. Its purpose was declared to be 'to promote fair and liberal practice, to maintain the interests of the profession in relation to general measures affecting it or producing changes of law or practice, to promote the information of its members, to settle disputed points of practice and decide questions of usage, and to prevent abuses'.

[3] Minute Books survive for the periods 27 July 1809 to 29 July 1811, and 1 March 1833 to 26 February 1835.

[4] These details are derived from a lecture on the early history of the society delivered by Sir William Munday in 1923, a copy of which was sent to me by the present secretary. The society's records were destroyed in the late war.

sider the bill before parliament to enable graduates of the universities to be admitted to the roll of attorneys after only three years' service as articled clerks. The meeting decided that 'such a facility of admission into the profession will prove injurious to its members', and drew up a petition to be presented to the House of Commons stating its belief 'that few persons after a residence at college would be found disposed to submit to the confinement and labour inseparable from the office of an attorney, but which your petitioners are perfectly convinced must be patiently endured by such as would become efficient members of the profession'.[1] This is interesting, for it might have been expected that the attorneys, anxious to improve the social status of the profession, would have welcomed into its ranks men drawn from the classes which could afford Oxford and Cambridge. Their motives in opposing this bill were probably mixed. No doubt they thought that men who had been at the universities would not treat the profession with that high seriousness of purpose which they themselves brought to it. They were right, too, in suspecting that the education given at Oxford and Cambridge was less suited to the professional man than that which could be obtained at one of the numerous academies which had been established during the eighteenth century, and which often catered specifically for the man destined for business and the professions.[2]

[1] In 1818 Mrs Munby of York was advised against sending her son Joseph to the University at Cambridge or Edinburgh, if she intended him to follow in his father's steps as an attorney. John Pearson wrote to her on 6 October: '...it would not only defeat all that you had planned for his future introduction into business; but would most probably be ruinous to him. He would learn little or nothing from the professors unless he were accompanied by a private tutor, and it would be next to miraculous if he were not totally corrupted by the profligate company into which he would be introduced....There is a certain measure of attainments in polite learning, which will always be useful in any profession; but great proficiency in learning, accompanied with a fine taste for the classics, will be more injurious than useful to a man of business. They may tend to multiply the sources of his enjoyments, but there is a danger of creating a distaste for the ordinary routine of an office.' Pearson advised sending the young man to some 'respectable academy' where he would receive an education more fitted for one who was to enter the professions. (Munby MSS. in the possession of A. N. L. Munby, Esq., Librarian of King's College, Cambridge. I am most grateful to Mr Munby for letting me look at his family papers.)

[2] It was noted in the first proposals for Warrington Academy that 'It is now become a general and just complaint that some public provision is wanted for the education of young gentlemen designed either for the learned professions or for business' (quoted H. M. McLachlan, *Warrington Academy*, Chetham Society, New Series, 107, p. 11). See also N. Hans, *New Trends in Education in the Eighteenth Century* (London, 1951).

And there was probably also some resentment that they had to share the profits of the profession with men who entered it on easier terms than they themselves had done. This concession was, however, granted to graduates in 1821.[1]

In 1823 a special general meeting was called to consider a proposal that an association should be set up for regulating matters of practice between members. It was decided that the facilities provided by the existing institution were adequate, and the proposal was dropped. Two years later, the society expelled a member who refused to cancel an agreement he had made with his articled clerk 'to credit the latter, as against the premium of £500 stipulated in the articles, with the profits of all business introduced by the clerk to his principal'. In 1835, the society asked Mr J. W. Freshfield, M.P., then chairman of the Incorporated Law Society's committee of management, to draft a petition on their behalf asking for the abolition of the certificate duty. This was unsuccessful, but certain sentences may be quoted from it as exemplifying the feelings of an eminently respectable member of the profession at that date, and to show how closely they echo those expressed by many men some forty years earlier. Declaring that the tax was patently unjust, he went on to say that 'to act unjustly towards members of the legal profession, especially our branch of it, is too popular to warrant an expectation that our application will be favourably received.... It is for the interests of society', he went on, 'that attorneys and solicitors, the confidential advisers of their neighbours, rich and poor, should be sustained in character and in pecuniary circumstances, but the more common course is to depress them to the utmost, so that in the opinion of very many persons, the profession and dishonour are identified.' In essence, these sentiments seem to be exactly those of the Society of Gentlemen Practisers, and the earliest of the provincial law societies.

Three more of the early law societies will be described. The Gloucestershire Law Association began in 1817.[2] There was to be an annual meeting, and each member attending was to pay a guinea; absent members were to pay two guineas to the general funds of the Association. A committee of nine was to meet 'on the Wednesday at each Quarter Sessions at five o'clock in the afternoon for the

---

[1] 1 and 2 Geo. IV, c. 48.

[2] These details are derived from a short history of the society by H. H. Scott (1917), which was lent to me by the present secretary.

purpose of ballotting for members'. There were twenty-eight members at the first annual meeting held at the King's Head, Gloucester. The meeting of June 1819 resolved that 'the objects of this society be the distressed members of it, and also such other distressed attorneys and solicitors who are deserving, resident in this county and city and their respective families'. Other resolutions were passed which were intended to improve the legal services. One was to submit a memorial to the judges asking them to enforce the attendance of special jurymen at assizes, and the secretary was instructed to communicate the terms of this to the other law societies 'in the hope that they will co-operate in the object thereof'. The undersheriff was requested to make special arrangements for attorneys and their clerks in the courts, and the society offered to pay doorkeepers to see that none but attorneys entered by the doors reserved for their use.

The constitution of the society was drafted in December 1819, when it was declared

That the principal objects of the society be to sustain the character of a liberal profession by pursuing and encouraging an honourable course of practice and by discountenancing and repressing whatever has a contrary intent or tendency; and by marking with a becoming regard to what is due to members of the profession at large any unmerited imputation against their character and conduct, and also to afford relief to distressed members of the society and such other distressed attorneys and solicitors who are deserving resident in the said county and city and their respective families.

General meetings were to be held twice a year, and the attendance of members was strongly insisted upon. There were fines for absence and for unbecoming behaviour at meetings, and members of the society who were found guilty of unfair professional practices were to be expelled, and notices of their expulsion were to be published in all the local newspapers.

The society's funds were invested in the five per cents, and from time to time charitable grants were made. In 1821 £20 a year was voted to the widow of a member, and was to be continued until her son reached the age of sixteen. In 1826 the society advanced £120 to pay the stamp duty on his becoming articled to an attorney. In the following year the society appointed an agent in London to scrutinise on its behalf all bills affecting the profession that should be presented to parliament. The society was concerned for the status of solicitors in bankruptcy proceedings, and complained that they were often blamed for delays which were in fact caused by barristers.[1] In the same year—1831—it was decided to oppose a bill before parliament which proposed that a general registry of deeds should be set up. A petition was presented to both houses, and the secretary was authorised to go up to London as often as he thought necessary to consult with the deputations from other law societies anxious about this matter.[2] In 1833 proceedings were threatened against an unqualified person who had prepared a lease, but were dropped on his apologising to the society for his presumption. In the next year, in protest against the recent seizing and opening of parcels sent by the Mail Coach, members were advised to send their parcels for London by the Paul Pry coach, which also was claimed to provide a speedier service. Much publicity was given to this, but the legality of the proposed course was questioned, and the matter was dropped.

There were sixteen founder members of this society, all except one of whom practised in Gloucester itself. By 1835 some eighty-five more attorneys had joined, and by that date members were drawn from all over Gloucestershire and Wiltshire.

The Birmingham Law Society was founded in 1818.[3] There were nineteen founder members, and by 1830 there were some fifty members. The purpose of the society was declared to be the 'promoting and encouraging a correct and liberal course of practice in the profession; and of discountenancing and opposing all practices that may have a tendency to bring it into discredit or to lessen its respectability'. There was to be a general meeting every year, and a basic subscription of £1; the treasurer was to call on members for additional sums when necessary. Members had to be attorneys of at least two years' standing, resident within ten miles of the centre of the city.

The first meeting of the society was held on 3 January 1818, in the Royal Hotel. It was proposed that a Law Library should be set up in a convenient room in the centre of the city,[4] and the committee was instructed to communicate with those 'gentlemen in London concerned to prevent improper persons acting as con-

---

[1] This presumably refers to 1 and 2 William IV, c. 56.
[2] The setting up of a registry of deeds was delayed until 1925.
[3] I am indebted to the secretary and the librarian for permission to examine the minutes of the society.
[4] In 1819 a room was rented from the Birmingham Philosophical Society; it was given up in 1822 as an unnecessary expense.

veyancers'. In August the committee presented its first report. Its members stated that they had watched the progress of the insolvent debtors' bill and the bankruptcy bill 'until they were thrown out of the House of Lords', and had communicated with the members for the county concerning several objectionable clauses in these bills. They had also been in touch with those who were drawing up the conveyancers' bill, and had presented petitions in support of it, and they assured the society that although the bill had had to be withdrawn in the current session, they felt certain that it would pass in the next. They had also corresponded with the London Law Society, and had arranged that they should be sent the names of all those seeking admission at the beginning of each term so that they could inquire into the character of such of them as had served their clerkships in the neighbourhood of Birmingham. The *Law Chronicle* and *Smith's Lists* were to be taken for the benefit of members. Representations had been made to the chairman of the Warwick Quarter Sessions about the inconvenient arrangements of the Nisi Prius Court.[1] It was laid down as a rule of practice to be followed by members that 'except where attorneys are agreed upon by parties, leases shall be prepared by the leasor's attorney unless the lease is in the nature of a sale'.

The society's minutes show that it continued to maintain this energetic concern for professional interests. In 1820 it was resolved to ask all the Inns of Court to supply the society with the names of any persons from the Birmingham area who applied to be admitted as conveyancers—the perennial subject—so that inquiries could be made as to their 'fitness and respectability'. In 1824 an attorney was struck off the Roll at the society's instigation, and the committee was instructed to watch the progress of any bills which might be introduced for the recovery of small debts, in order to prevent the public from being deprived of its right to appear by attorney.

By 1828 the committee's reports show it acting as a fully developed and responsible professional body. It pointed out that it was due to the Birmingham Law Society that the practice of Gray's Inn in admitting unqualified persons who afterwards took out certificates as qualified conveyancers had been stopped, and added: '...if anything were wanting to evince the usefulness of an association of the respectable members of the profession, it is fully estab-

[1] It was reported, in February 1820, that the court had been altered so as to be more convenient for attorneys.

4   R

lished by the benefit that must result to the public at large and to the profession by the measure above mentioned'. The committee expressed its concern at the 'alarming increase in the number of the profession—the applications for admission in Michaelmas Term next are no less than 204, being at the rate of 816 a year'. They felt that this increase could be more effectively curbed by limiting the number of clerks articled to an attorney at any one time to one, than by increasing the stamp duty on articles of clerkship, and impressed upon the society the great importance of this subject for the whole profession.

In October the society, like that in Gloucestershire and Wiltshire, considered the proposal to set up a general registry of deeds. The Birmingham Law Library Society, which was founded in February 1831, amalgamated with the Law Society after only eighteen months of independent existence.

The Kent Law Society was founded with twenty-nine members in 1818, 'to promote fair and liberal practice and prevent abuses in the profession'.[1] Members were to dine together at Maidstone on the day following Commission Day at the Assizes. The early meetings were held at the Rose Inn, Sittingbourne, and were concerned with revising charges for conveyancing. The society heard complaints against members, contributed £10 towards a fund raised in 1822 to assist the widow and eleven children of an attorney of Stratford on Avon who had been accidentally killed, and in 1831 this society also drew up a protest against the proposed bill for establishing a general registry of deeds and instruments affecting real property.

Some remarks may be added about the Sunderland Law Society, which the present society believes to have been founded in 1824.[2] Its principal objects were to 'preserve the privileges and support the credit of attorneys and solicitors, to promote fair and liberal practice, and to adopt such measures as may appear best calculated to effect these ends and most likely to secure respect to the profession and to be of advantage to the employers'. The rules of the

---

[1] This information is derived from a pamphlet published for the society in 1948, sent to me by the secretary.

[2] This information is derived from a copy of the rules of the society sent to me by the secretary.

society were familiar to those of the other societies already described —there is almost a common form of declaring the initial purpose of the societies by this time—but there are two additional rules. It was decided that 'in order to protect and preserve the respectability of the profession no member shall take an articled clerk without receiving with him a fee of One hundred pounds nor shall he give any salary or allowance of any description whatever to a clerk during the time he is under articles nor contract to give him any after the expiration thereof in consideration of his service'. It was further laid down that members who had to appoint commissioners in bankruptcy cases, or any other commissions issued out of chancery, should appoint members of the society only. At a special general meeting held in the same year a scale of charges to be made by members was adopted.

All these societies exhibit very clearly in their constitutions and in their activities those aims which the would-be reformers of the profession were beginning to insist on in the last decades of the eighteenth century. The very language they use is remarkable in its similarity: 'liberal', 'respectable'—these are the key words of these minute books as they are of the pamphlets of the period. The societies are among the first effective and responsible professional bodies to be founded, and they set an example which was quickly followed by attorneys all over the country, and provided a pattern along which other professional societies were to develop in the future. Of course they were neither so numerous nor so efficient as they were later to become: they had no need to be. And while it may truly be said of them, as Sir John Clapham said of the early Chambers of Commerce, established in these same decades by similar sorts of men, that 'although characteristic British organisations, [they] played only a subordinate part in the life of the country',[1] the part they played in the profession then, and as exemplars for the future, was not without importance.

[1] *Economic History of Modern Britain*, 2nd ed. (Cambridge, 1950), I, 310. See also the article by J. M. Norris on 'Samuel Garbett and the Early Development of Industrial Lobbying in Great Britain', in *Economic History Review*, 2nd series, X, 3 (1958), pp. 450–60.

CHAPTER V

THE MAKING OF AN ATTORNEY

IN the education of the attorney the Inns of Chancery played little, and eventually no part.[1] They never performed for the profession those services which the Inns of Court rendered the barristers. In spite of the repeated injunctions of the judges that all attorneys should belong to one or other of these Inns, they continued to decline throughout the seventeenth century, and by the eighteenth century they were of negligible importance in the history of attorneys and solicitors. Those services which they could have performed by giving institutional representation and control to the profession were taken over by bodies specially created for this purpose which have just been described.

There were two general reasons for this decline. In the first place, the profession became too large for the Inns to hold all its members, who were in any case too widely scattered in the provinces for membership of an Inn to be anything more than nominal. This was probably true of an increasingly large proportion of the profession, as the country attorney became an established figure in provincial life, relying on an agent in London to perform those functions for his clients which demanded personal attendance at the courts or law offices in town. In the second place, the Inns of Chancery declined because the sort of education they could provide —occasional readings by some barrister from the Inns of Court which patronised them[2]—was totally inadequate as a training for the sort of work which the attorney was called upon to do. His employment was eminently practical in character, concerned with the forms of legal processes and the application of the laws to a wide variety of situations: he was judged by his acquaintance with the techniques of the law, rather than by his knowledge of its more theoretical aspects.

This being so, the obvious way in which to educate the attorney, the apprenticeship system, was the one adopted. No amount of

---

[1] See above, pp. 7–8; the history of the Inns of Chancery is noticed by Holdsworth, *History of English Law*, II, IV, VI, and XII.

[2] Cf. Holdsworth, *op. cit.* XII, 41.

knowledge of the principles of the law could take the place of that dexterity in its practice which could only be obtained by working alongside an attorney already in business.

This was accepted by most men for perhaps the greater part of the eighteenth century.[1] It was an age realistic in its values, and the class from which in general attorneys were drawn was perhaps notable in its reluctance to indulge in the more useless frills of education. By the end of the century, those who were concerned to increase the respectability of the profession (when respectability had become profitable)[2] were beginning to suggest that this might be done by giving the attorney a more 'liberal' education. But in the meantime, it was the practice of the law, and not its principles, that was held to be the proper concern of the attorney, and for this the apprenticeship system was better suited than any sort of legal university in London.

And the apprenticeship system, found suitable and generally adopted, was that which was insisted on by the act for regulating the profession which was passed in 1729. No one was to practise as an attorney unless he was properly admitted to the Roll, and he would not be admitted unless he had been 'bound by contract in writing to serve as a clerk for and during the space of five years, to an attorney duly and legally sworn and admitted'. Before he was admitted, the judges were 'authorised and required...to examine and inquire, by such means as they shall think proper, touching his fitness and capacity to act as an attorney'.[3]

---

[1] And later. In 1821 Jonathan Dixon wrote to Joseph Munby who was articled to an attorney, and who had expressed dissatisfaction with this mode of education: 'Your making out warrants and copying abstracts is at least as profitable a mode of employing time as my paging the statutes at large, and the only remedy is to acquire as much theoretical knowledge as you possibly can which you will find of the most essential service when a little practice is superadded. Blackstone should be read again and again *nam decies repetita docebit* for the infinite variety of matter and compressive style in which the *Commentaries* are composed render it impossible to retain the many principles and doctrines they embrace unless imprinted on your memory by reiterated perusals. An admirable adjuvant in this respect may be found in Field's analysis of Blackstone in a series of questions to which the student is to frame his own answers.... What has been called copying the trash of an attorney's office is applicable only to the students intended for higher departments of the law, an attorney's office contains nothing that a *cadet* attorney should consider trash' (26 January 1821. Munby MSS.).

[2] Cf. Dr Johnson. 'What is their reputation but an instrument of getting money?' (Boswell, *Life*, Everyman ed. II, 405).

[3] 2 Geo. II, c. 23, sects. v and vi; sect. xv prohibited an attorney from having more than two articled clerks at any one time. The act of 1605 had required that

Some of these stipulations, notably that concerning the examination by the judges, were difficult to impose, and were probably carried out in a perfunctory manner.[1] And without this examination, the obvious fault inherent in the apprenticeship system—that it was too personal in character, varying from master to master— was allowed full scope for development. The attorneys were drawn from a wide variety of social positions, and their practices varied enormously from that of the great London attorney, to that of the small attorney in a country town. In consequence there was little hope that all attorneys' clerks would acquire even a certain minimum of legal education.

An effective examination system would have guaranteed this, but in general all that the judges seem to have required of the clerk seeking admission was an affidavit from his master—or his master's London agent—stating that he had served the prescribed period in articled service. Some attorneys were probably not as scrupulous as they ought to have been in training their clerks and ensuring that they had an adequate knowledge of their profession before signing these affidavits. The critics of the profession often accused them of caring more for the premiums which the clerks brought with them than for the task of teaching them their craft. Indeed, it was more than once suggested that too many attorneys were prepared to forgo a premium altogether in the case of a clerk who would serve them as a footboy or boot-black in return for a promise of his articles at the end of five years.

During the eighteenth century, the attorneys' clerks hovered between the position of being apprentices to a trade like any other, living in their masters' houses and running errands for their wives,[2] and that of the articled clerk, paying his master a handsome premium, no longer living in his household, demanding and receiving a more serious education in his profession. This development is to some extent a chronological one: the type of the modern articled

none should be admitted save those 'brought up in the courts or otherwise well practised in soliciting of causes, and have been found by their dealings to be skilful and of honest disposition' (3 Jac. I, c. 7).

[1] Cf. the admission of William Hickey, Appendix II below.

[2] This is said to have been the lot of Philip Yorke, articled to his father's town agent, Mr Salkeld, 'whose wife, a thrifty woman, frequently annoyed him with household errands. To these, at length, he put a stop, by charging her one shilling and sixpence for a cauliflower, which she had begged him to buy, "as he was going past the greengrocer's":—sixpence for the cauliflower, and a shilling for a sedan chair to bring it home in' (*The Georgian Era* (London, 1833), II, 278).

clerk is a common figure by the end of the century; but exceptions remained. It is, however, a development which is at one with other changes in the profession, and one which is suggested by an examination of the conditions of clerkship during the century.

The Stamp Office registers, giving details of the premiums paid by all apprentices after 1710,[1] provide general information about the attorneys' clerks which is not available elsewhere. They are probably not complete, but they are perhaps full enough to give a correct impression of the sort of premiums which were paid, the length of articled service, and the social background of the clerks. They will be examined in detail at three points during the century.

In the volume recording stamp duties paid to the London office for the period October 1711 to November 1712,[2] some forty-six apprenticeships to attorneys are noted. Of these, thirty-nine apprentices were to serve for five years, three for four years, two for seven years, and one each for the periods of three and six years. The premiums paid vary from £20 paid for the son of an Ipswich clergyman to an attorney living in the Inner Temple, to £250 paid by a gentleman of Bath and £268. 15s. paid by an 'esquire' of the Middle Temple to article their sons to one of the Clerks in Chancery. Only eight premiums were less than £100. Most of the masters mentioned practised in London, many of them having addresses in the Inns of Court and Chancery. The clerks themselves came from all over the country, from London, Surrey, Essex, Kent, Norfolk, Suffolk, Wiltshire, Northumberland, Carmarthen, Berkshire, Hampshire, Rutland, and Cornwall. In thirty-four cases some indication is given of the parents' social standing. Eleven are classified as 'Gents', eight as 'esquires', six as clergymen[3] (including two Doctors of Divinity, one of them the Archdeacon of Lincoln), a victualler, a gun-stock maker, an apothecary, a saddler, a mercer, a drugster, and a watchmaker.

The earliest volume recording duties paid to the country collectors covers the period January 1711 to June 1713.[4] Here some nineteen entries relate to attorneys' clerks. Eleven clerks are

---

[1] 8 Ann. c. 9.   [2] P[ublic] R[ecord] O[ffice], I.R. 1/1.

[3] In his unpublished dissertation (p. 483) Mr Bezodis calculates that out of 610 children of clergymen apprenticed between 1710 and 1720, sixty-one were to lawyers, seventy-two to apothecaries, twenty-seven to barber surgeons, thirteen to surgeons, three to druggists, thirty-three to merchants, mercers, and merchant-tailors.   [4] P.R.O. I.R. 1/42.

articled for five years, five for four, one for seven, one for six, and one for three years. The lowest premium paid was £34, the highest £110; only two were sums below £50. In most cases the entries show the country attorneys taking clerks from the same town or county. The status of parents is not always given, but there are four 'Gents', two clergymen, an 'esquire', a yeoman, a clothier, and several widows among them.

The city register for the period May 1752 to July 1754[1] mentions 241 attorneys' clerks. Again the vast majority are bound for a period of five years; ten are for seven years, six for six years. One clerk is articled for nine years, paying a premium of £10, another is said to be bound for one year only to an attorney of Staple Inn, paying a premium of ten guineas. This last entry, and others mentioning such periods as four months three days (premium £3. 15s.), and two years eight months, may relate to clerks who had been turned over from one master to another; this however is not certain, since there are several instances where this is specifically stated to have happened. Premiums in this register vary considerably from sums of 5s. paid when a clerk is articled to his father, and sums like £20 and £30, to sums such as £260, £300, £315, £350, and £400 (paid to a Middlesex attorney, Robert Jones). There are eighty-two premiums of £50 and under, fifty-nine up to £100, seventy-one up to £200, twenty-three between £200 and £300, and six above £300. Masters and clerks mentioned come from all parts of the country. In all except two cases where the premium is £200 and above, the master is an attorney of London or Middlesex: the exceptions are attorneys in Chelmsford and Stafford. No indication is given in this volume of the status of parents, but it includes references to Roger, the youngest of four sons of Lloyd Kenyon, and brother of the judge, who was articled for five years to James Tomkinson for a premium of £210;[2] and to George Delaval, articled to Arthur Pond in the parish of St Giles in the Fields for five years, giving a premium of £300.

In the country register for October 1750 to August 1754[3] some 108 clerkships to attorneys are noted. Five years is by far the most common period served, though again there are occasional instances

---

[1] P.R.O. I.R. 1/19.

[2] Lloyd Kenyon, the second son, had also been articled to Tomkinson. Roger is said to have 'attained considerable eminence' as a London solicitor (G. T. Kenyon, *Life of Kenyon* (London, 1873), pp. 17–19).

[3] P.R.O. I.R. 1/51.

of clerks who were bound for periods of three, six, seven, and even one of eight years. There are thirty-eight premiums of sums up to £50; forty of sums up to £100; twenty-seven up to £200; and three above £200. The highest sum mentioned in this register is £300 paid to a Clerk in Chancery for a clerkship of five years; and there are again such small sums as £2. 15s., £3, £5, and 10 guineas. There is no indication in this register of the social status of parents.

The last two registers to be examined are those for the years round the turn of the century. The city registers for the period March 1799 to June 1802,[1] mention some 380 clerkships to attorneys. In only fourteen cases is the period served other than five years. Some amounts paid as premiums are only nominal sums, but there is still a fair number of smaller sums which do not appear to fall into this category. The highest sum paid is £525. Sixty-five premiums are amounts of £50 and below; there are fifty-one between £50 and £100, 106 between £100 and £200, eighty-nine between £200 and £300, forty-four between £300 and £400, eighteen between £400 and £500. There are also nine premiums of £525, all of them paid to London attorneys. No information is given about the social background from which these clerks are drawn. Of the premiums between £400 and £500, nine are paid to London attorneys, but the rest are to attorneys in such places as Bath, Bristol, Cheltenham, and Newport, but also at St Austell, Chard, Ashburton, Bewdley, Bridgwater, and Wellingborough.

The country register for the period August 1799 to May 1803[2] refers to sixty-six attorneys' clerks. Nine premiums are of £50 and under; there are four between £50 and £100, twenty-five between £100 and £200, eighteen between £200 and £300, seven between £300 and £400, and there are three sums above £500. Of these last, two are sums of £525 paid to attorneys in Cirencester and Southampton, and the third is one of £551. 5s. paid to a Reading attorney.[3]

These records suggest that many men of humble birth and modest means could become attorneys. For them, a clerkship to an attorney provided the means of surmounting the first—and often the

[1] P.R.O. I.R. 1/38.   [2] P.R.O. I.R. 1/70.
[3] The country registers also include references to the Writers to the Signet in Scotland; in all cases the premium is £100, and the term five years. Parts of these registers relating to certain counties have been published. See *Surrey Record Society*, x (1929); *Sussex Records Society*, xxviii (1924); and *Bedfordshire Records Society*, ix (1925).

most difficult—obstacle in the way of social progress. The professions, in which individual merit may count for more than inherited status, have always been one of the bridges across the gulfs which tend to separate society into classes. For many in the eighteenth century the profession of attorney was an accessible social bridge. It helped a good many men to find a place in society more commensurate with their abilities than that to which they had been born, and one which otherwise would have remained beyond their reach.

There were, of course, those who attacked the profession for just this reason. It did violence to their notions of the perfect and static and hierarchical ordering of society, and raised to an unwarranted eminence many whose birth in no way justified them for it. Complaints of this sort were not always unreasonable. Many attorneys were undoubtedly not over-scrupulous about the sort of men they took in as clerks, nor over-assiduous in teaching them their craft. But not all of those who could afford no premium, and received their articles in return for the performance of menial tasks for their masters were without merit: no more than were the sizars and servitors at the universities.

William Skelton began life as a foot-boy to Bishop Compton of London, and might have risen no further had he not been articled to an attorney as a reward for detecting a plot by the cook at Fulham Palace to poison his master.[1] Skelton is said to have prospered, and so did many others for whom a clerkship provided the opportunities afforded by a scholarship in a more equitable society. Sir John Hawkins, the youngest son of a carpenter, became a prosperous attorney. Bishop Warburton was articled to an attorney, and may have practised for a short time in Newark,[2] and among the judges, Hardwick, Kenyon, Garrow, Somers, Macclesfield, Strange, and Jocelyn all received their early training in an attorney's office.

It is true that some of them went to an attorney's office only to get acquainted with the law in its more practical aspects, and as a preliminary to being called to the bar—the office of Charles Salkeld in Great Brook Street was almost a preparatory school for judges[3]— but there were some like Kenyon and Philip Yorke who were

[1] Dorothy Stroud, *Capability Brown* (London, 1950), p. 44, note.
[2] *D.N.B.*
[3] Robert Jocelyn, Lord Chancellor of Ireland, Macclesfield, Hardwick, and John Strange, Master of the Rolls, all spent some time in his care. Blackstone deplored the practice whereby barristers abandoned a liberal education for the

regularly articled to attorneys, and in the beginning intended to be attorneys themselves.

But the bootblacks on the one hand, and the judges on the other, are the exceptions. In between these extremes there was a broad group of men who never aspired higher than the middling prosperity of the comfortable country attorney. This in itself was something of an attainment for many men, but one of the trends which may be noticed throughout the century is the development of a class-consciousness among attorneys of this sort, which eventually led them to try to exclude social climbers from the lower orders by insisting on higher premiums and higher standards, and social as well as professional qualifications. Or rather, they made a social virtue, respectability, into a professional one.

A further indication of this trend is given by a change in the status of the clerks themselves. At the beginning they were apprentices like any other, commonly living with their master, learning their trade in the intervals of performing more menial tasks for their master's wife. But the position was changing, and in 1760 an attorney could look back on the old days with regret. 'Tempora mutantur', he sighed, 'why, formerly our apprentices would scrape our entries and sweep our shops; why, they will not do that now.'[1] It was complained that attorneys' clerks were under no manner of government; before their times are out, they set up for gentlemen, they dress, they drink, they game, they frequent the

more mechanical training of an attorney's office. Cf. *Commentaries*, Book 1, 1768 (Inaugural Lecture as Vinerian Professor, 1758), pp. 31–2. See also Joseph Day, *An Address to the Attorneys at Law*, etc. (1796), p. 14, where he speaks of the habit of placing young men in an attorney's office 'rather as a check on habits of dissipation than with the intent or expectation that sufficient application would be given to attain a useful degree of professional knowledge'. A somewhat similar position to Salkeld's was occupied by Charles Sanderson, attorney of the Inner Temple. See E. Hughes, *North Country Life in the Eighteenth Century* (Oxford, 1952), p. 77.

[1] *Records of the Society of Gentlemen Practisers*, p. 257. The Society was aware of this development, and decided in 1748 that 'clauses should be offered for the consideration of parliament for the more effectually obliging the clerks of attorneys and solicitors to an actual and menial service of their masters, until such time as each of them were regularly assigned over to another attorney or solicitor' (*ibid.* p. 29). Defoe complained of this development as early as 1715. In his *Family Instructor*, in a dialogue between the father and the master of an apprentice, the father complains that his son has not received proper supervision. To this the master replies: 'Apprentices are not like what they were when you and I were apprentices. Now we get a hundred, or two or three hundred pounds apiece with them; they are too high for reproof or correction' (quoted O. J. Dunlop, *English Apprenticeship and Child Labour* (London, 1912, p. 211).

playhouses, and intrigue with the women;[1] and it is a common thing with clerks to bully their masters and desert their service for whole days and nights whenever they see fit. And indeed, people consider little else at this day in the choice of clerks or apprentices than the sums they are to have with them; one, two, or three hundred pounds are given with a clerk or apprentice, who is looked upon as a boarder rather than as a servant: He takes little care of his master's business, and the master as little to instruct him in the mystery of his profession.[2]

While this may be evidence that the social position of the attorneys was improving, there were some who thought these developments detrimental to the education of the profession. In 1815 William Wright wrote:

Parents who wish to place their sons in the office of an attorney have to lament that very few will now take them into their families. And young men who are articled to an attorney without any guardian over their conduct farther than relates to the duties of an office, and ushered into life without those restraints which are necessary to their happiness, are placed in a situation where they will meet with temptations to vice which many of them will be seduced by, and thus contract habits of dissipation extremely detrimental to their characters and improvement.[3]

And, he went on,

The advantages which a young man receives from proper superintendence are sufficient to turn the scale much in favour of placing him in a respectable attorney's family, in preference to lodgings, where he will be at liberty to act as he pleases, and where he will consider himself conferring an obligation rather than receiving one.[4]

[1] Cf. *Tom Jones*, Book v, ch. 6: 'Will Barnes was a country gallant, and had acquired as many trophies of this kind as any ensign or attorney's clerk in the kingdom.'

[2] Stow's *Survey of London*, ed. John Strype (1755), II, 559, partly quoted in Dunlop, *op. cit.* p. 232. A correspondent to *Felix Farley's Bristol Journal* in 1784 remembered a time when apprentices and attorney's clerks dressed in plain clothes, 'But now, gold laced waistcoats, ruffled shirts, and silk stockings are becoming the ordinary wear of every shopboy in the city' (quoted in John Latimer, *The Annals of Bristol in the Eighteenth Century* (Bristol, 1893), p. 461). In 1794 apothecaries complained that 'while an attorney can easily procure a premium of 3, 4, or 500 pounds...an apothecary, whose profession is of infinitely more consequence, is generally obliged to accept a much smaller sum' (J. M. Good, *History of Medicine* (London, 1795), p. 154; quoted by Dr B. M. Hamilton in her unpublished London thesis).

[3] William Wright, *Advice on the Study and Practice of the Law*, pp. 165–6.

[4] *Ibid.* p. 167. For an attorney who satisfied Wright's standards, see pp. 184–5 below.

The apprenticeship system permitted the widest variety of standards among attorneys and their clerks. Some masters took their task seriously. The apprenticeship of Richard Carre to Francis Sitwell and Thomas Wright, for example, seems to have been closely watched.[1] Carre was given a wide experience in all aspects of his master's business. He spent a great deal of time copying precedents, engrossing deeds, and the like, and was encouraged to study the law books when no other business was on hand. He was probably treated more kindly, and educated more effectively, than Thomas Chatterton, who was articled to a Bristol attorney in 1767. He was kept in the office from eight in the morning to eight at night, given his meals in the kitchen, and made to share a bed with the foot-boy. To the annoyance of his master he spent more time in scribbling verses than in learning the law, and when he eventually ran away to London, Chatterton was 'so ignorant in his profession that he was unable to draw out a clearance from his apprenticeship' that his master had demanded.[2]

Very different from either of these was the apprenticeship of William Hickey. Hickey's father was a prosperous attorney, moving in elegant society in London.[3] Somewhat reluctantly, because he already had two partners, his elder son and Nathaniel Bayley, he had articled William to Bayley in 1765. The practice was a large one, but Hickey was given too much money, too little to do, and proceeded to lead the life of an extravagant and fashionable man about town.[4] For eight months all went well, and Hickey pleased both Bayley and his father, and became popular with many distinguished lawyers. Only Thurlow expressed his doubts about his suitability for 'The dull and irksome drudgery of that laborious profession'.[5] And Thurlow was right. In 1767 Hickey misemployed

[1] See Appendix 1 below.
[2] Chatterton to his mother, 17 May 1770; quoted G. Gregory, *Life of Chatterton* (London, 1789), p. 80.
[3] He figures in Goldsmith's *Retaliation*, along with Garrick, Cumberland, Reynolds and others—company which Sir George Trevelyan considered 'Far too good for him' (*Early History of Charles James Fox* (3rd ed. 1881), p. 143, n. 1).
[4] Cf. Fielding, *Covent Garden Journal*, p. 37, where he says that the word 'fashion' cannot be derived from the French 'façon', 'which is often used to signify affectation. This will extend too far, and will comprehend attornies' clerks, milliners, mantua makers, and an infinite number of the lower people'.
[5] Cf. Cobbett's opinion of the attorney's employment: 'Gracious Heaven! if I am doomed to be wretched, bury me beneath Iceland snows, and let me feed on blubber, stretch me under the burning line, and deny me the propitious

some money entrusted to his care, was discovered, and expelled from his father's house.

The examination which the judges were required to make of the qualifications of clerks before admitting them to the Roll was not conducted in a manner which would have imposed a measure of uniformity on the standards of education among attorney's clerks. Hickey's own examination, when he came eventually to seek admission, may have been exceptional, and his account may be as exaggerated as it is colourful, but it is only an exaggeration.[1] The judges had not the time—some thought they had neither the ability nor the inclination—to conduct a satisfactory examination of all clerks who presented themselves for admission to their courts. And there were, indeed, those who thought that a clerk who had served the required length of time had a right to be admitted without having to submit to the impertinence of an examination.[2]

So it was left to private individuals and to the professional societies to impose what order they could on the education of attorneys by scrutinising the lists of those seeking admission, making suggestions for fresh regulations and an improved system, even occasionally by taking very great pains over the training of those clerks entrusted to them.

One London attorney, Thomas Hood, sent his son who was destined for the profession to school at Sheffield, thinking that Harrow was too near his home and the softening influences of his mother. A local attorney, John Hoyland, kept a fatherly eye on the boy, and the letters exchanged between the two men, mingled with correspondence on professional matters,[3] show how seriously the boy's education was taken, and how concerned his father was that he should never be allowed to forget that he was intended for the law. 'We must not fill his head nor yet his heels with too much music', he wrote, 'it may unfit him for Coke upon Littleton which is of more importance...he must be taught to understand that he

dews,—nay, if it be thy will, suffocate me with the infected and pestilential air of a democrat's club-room; but save me, whatever you do, save me from the desk of an attorney' (quoted Croake James, *Curiosities of Law and Lawyers* (London, 1882), p. 13).

[1] See Appendix II below.

[2] Cf. the attack made on these people by Joseph Day in his *Thoughts upon the Necessity and Utility of Examinations*, etc. (1795), p. 5.

[3] Hood was Hoyland's London Agent.

is not intended for a fine gentleman but for industry. Boys get notions in their heads sometimes which lead, or rather mislead, them to strange consequences.'[1]

Hood's words were prophetic, for when Dick was home at Easter he let fall some opinion about not liking the law, and annoyed his father considerably. 'What he can mean by liking or disliking any-thing', he wrote to Hoyland, in a letter asking that his son's educa-tion and behaviour should be more closely watched in future,

much more daring to speak out, is no small surprise to me. I shall expect him to like what I may think to prescribe to him when the proper time arrives.... I don't take notice to him how much he has disobliged me, but for the future shall watch his motions jealously and desire the like from all under whose care and eye he may happen to be placed. For his education to me will be almost indifferent upon any other plan than the profession of the law. If he should ever defeat my good intentions to him in this pursuit he will forfeit for ever my friendship and affections to him as a parent.[2]

In the event, the behaviour of his clerks forced Hood to take Dick into the office earlier than he had intended. 'I must get him a private master to teach him here', he wrote to Hoyland, 'he will never do any good if he is not a Latin scholar.'[3]

Hood's opinions about the education of attorneys were shared by others. In 1767 Jonathan Dawson of Thorne wrote to Samuel Dawson of Sheffield about a clerk the latter had recom-mended:

Since I had the pleasure of seeing you at Pontefract I have agreed with a writer, notwithstanding which I would also take a clerk and should pay as great a regard to your's as to any man's recommendation, but I really think seventeen years (at this gay time) is rather too old to go out to business, young men then begin to think, and judge for themselves, rather than follow the directions of a master, which to them appear irksome. And this I have so much experienced by the irregularity and misbe-haviour of my late clerk who had a good capacity and was a good scholar, but he had been too much indulged by fond parents, that nothing would induce me to take another whom I had the least ap-prehension of turning out amiss. The fee I expect is 100 guineas in case the young man and I should like each other; but could I meet with a

---

[1] Sheffield City Libraries, T[ibbitt's] C[ollection], 542/1, 20 January 1775.
[2] T.C. 524/35, 18 April 1775.
[3] T.C. 524/39, 4 May 1775.

well-disposed youth who had gone through a clerkship and knew business, I would much sooner make him a handsome allowance than take a clerk, for with my last I took as much pains as if I had been his father, and gave him all the information and instruction in my power, and where a master acts upon that principle, the fee given with the clerk is not much to be considered.[1]

Both Hood and Dawson thought that the clerk's education should be practical in character, strictly subordinated to the demands of his future employment. Others, however, thought that the standards of professional education, as well as the standing of the profession in society, would be improved if it was less 'mechanical' and more 'liberal'. William Wright thought that 'The profession will become more respectable as it becomes more learned',[2] and regretted that clerks were not allowed more time for general study. The accomplished attorney, he believed, should not confine himself to the more practical aspects of the law, but should also be acquainted with history, the law of nature and of nations, the old law books, the classics, and one of the systems of shorthand.[3]

Other writers were also concerning themselves with this problem.[4] Charles Ilsley agreed with Wright that the attorney should receive a 'liberal education',[5] because of the wide range of problems with which he had to deal, canals, turnpikes, enclosures, and the like.[6] Ilsley's opponent on the question of taxing the profession also differed from him on the matter of education.[7] He pointed out that

this word 'liberal' has not a very definite signification, what one man would consider a liberal education would, in the estimation of another of a more liberal turn of mind, be but a confined one. If the word liberal

[1] T.C. 522/257, 22 September 1767.

[2] William Wright, *Advice on the Study and Practice of the Law*; he also thought that those who sought 'honourable distinction' should associate only with those 'distinguished for good sense, good morals, urbanity of manners, and an ardent desire for the attainment of knowledge'.

[3] *Ibid.* pp. 165–6. Wright also had some remarks on the necessity of taking exercise, but discouraged field sports as 'apt to fascinate too much'.

[4] For example, a pamphlet of 1794 which I have not been able to find: *Remarks on the Education of Attorneys, designed to promote a reform in the inferior order of the profession of the law.*

[5] A writer in 1747 thought that attorneys' education should be 'liberal', in order to give them a bias above 'little pettifogging practices' (R. Campbell, *The London Tradesman*, etc.).

[6] Charles Ilsley, *A Brief Inquiry concerning the origin, progress and impolicy of taxing attorneys*, etc. (1804).

[7] In *A Defence of Attornies*, etc. (1804).

be taken in a *liberal* sense, then we must suppose that the writer thinks it necessary for an attorney to imbibe his knowledge from the bountiful bosom of *Alma Mater*,[1] and then to take the Grand Tour, by way of qualifying himself for the mighty undertaking of minuting down a few resolutions respecting the cutting of a canal. But perhaps we are to understand that the writer means a common classical education merely. Still, to prove the necessity of *such* an education, an attorney's liability to be called upon to take the minutes of a public meeting is but a sorry argument, for, surely, nothing further is requisite for that purpose than to have a clear head, and to be able to write grammatically in the vulgar tongue.[2]

Ilsley had suggested that an attorney needed more than a 'smattering in the vulgar tongue', and further, that attorneys should be 'clothed at least with some portion of that venerable dignity and antiquity which Sir Edward Coke has informed us is to be found in our old law books, laws and records'. This the author of the *Defence* took to mean Glanvill, Bracton, Britton and Fleta, Hengham, the Year Books, Statham, Brooke, Fitzherbert, Staund-forde, and many others who wrote before Coke, and asks:

When it is considered that he [the attorney] must spend the five years of his clerkship copying at the desk, or in some other mechanical part of the business, as running to the different offices, attending the different courts, etc., what leisure can he reasonably be expected to have had, for going through a course of study so difficult and laborious? Ten years are not sufficient to enable any man, however bright his talents, to accomplish such a task, even although he should devote to it the whole of his time and attention...the absurdity of the thing is palpable and glaring.

He concluded: 'If an attorney be well acquainted with Coke upon Littleton, Blackstone's *Commentaries*, and the best modern treatises upon practice, together with the determinations upon modern cases, we may pronounce him an able attorney.' Such researches as Ilsley had suggested might legitimately be required of a barrister, but for an attorney they were superfluous.[3]

---

[1] By 1821 graduates wanting to enter the profession were sufficiently numerous to obtain a concession in their favour by which they had to serve only three years in articles. 1 and 2 Geo. IV, c. 48. See above, pp. 45–6.

[2] *A Defence*, etc. pp. 41–2. Joseph Simpson, in *Reflections on the endowments required for the study of the law*, 3rd ed. (1764), recommended a period at the university after clerkship.

[3] *A Defence*, pp. 34–5.

R

In 1846 a Select Committee of the House of Commons in-
vestigated the state of legal education.[1] As far as attorneys and
solicitors were concerned, it was generally agreed that

For the mechanical and almost manual dexterity, which though inferior, is still indispensable, sufficient care...is already taken by the
present practice and regulations. The system of apprenticeship is itself
good, inasmuch as it teaches in the most effectual way, that is by practice,
this portion of the profession....But beyond this it does not appear its
advantages extend.[2]

In 1846, as in certain quarters in the late eighteenth century,
concern was felt at the inadequacy of the general education of
attorneys, and their knowledge of the principles of the law as
distinct from its practice.[3] The aim which Sir George Stephen set
the profession in 1846 was very similar to that of the respectable
attorney of 1800, and even at the earlier date some efforts were
being made to achieve it. In 1807 the Society of Gentlemen
Practisers was considering the foundation of a society 'for the
articled clerks of members and for the purpose of discussing legal
questions'.[4] In the provinces, the earliest Law Libraries were being
established, and at Manchester a Law Students' Society was in
existence in 1809.

These are signs of the ways in which the profession was develop-
ing and of the changing attitudes among the attorneys towards
their calling, and they suggest that already by the end of the eighteenth century men were looking on this as a 'liberal' profession,
and demanding of it standards consonant with this new status.
But for a variety of reasons, among them the very nature of the
attorney's employment, this was not a goal speedily arrived at.
Even in 1846, when the final examination had been in operation
for ten years, there was much to complain of, though it is probably

---

[1] *Reports, Committees* (1846), vol. x.   [2] *Ibid.* p. lii.
[3] Sir George Stephen told the Committee: 'I think that it is most important
that the profession should be so educated as to be qualified for carrying on
intercourse (i.e. with men of every class of society) as gentlemen themselves,
but I apprehend that that qualification cannot be attained except by educating
them as gentlemen, with much greater attention to their *general* endowments
and information than is at present the case.' Stephen believed that not one in
fifty in the profession was educated to the level of the fifth form of a public
school. He may have been over-emphatic in some of his judgments, and he was
not without his prejudices (cf. *D.N.B.*), but his evidence seems generally to have
been accepted by the Committee.
[4] *Records of the Society of Gentlemen Practisers*, p. 29.

also true that by that date society was more generally sensitive and exacting in these matters than it had been fifty years before. The discussion of the problem of making an attorney was carried on at the end of the eighteenth century in language very similar to that employed in 1846, but the evidence placed before the Committee in that year is a salutary warning against any tendency to assume that by 1800 in this, as in other aspects of the history of the profession, all was sweetness and light, and that the pettifoggers were no more.

CHAPTER VI

THE ATTORNEY IN LOCAL SOCIETY

THE country attorney was an important figure in provincial society in the eighteenth century. His professional concerns placed him at the centre of affairs in many localities, and by the end of the century he was often to be found among the more energetic leaders of a greatly enriched provincial life. The evidence for this is scattered through all the specialised histories of the period, histories of families, estates, banking, commerce and politics. Indeed, a large part of the flesh which the local historians are attaching to the bones of eighteenth-century English history is based on documents which have come to the various record offices from solicitors' attics and strong-rooms. Even the catalogue of any one of these deposits gives a very clear picture of the great variety of ways in which the attorneys touched the life of the community in which they lived. The lists of the Tibbitts Collection at Sheffield may be taken as an example.

These are the professional papers of a Sheffield attorney of the eighteenth century, Samuel Dawson, and of his predecessors and successors in the practice. There are a great number of deeds of all kinds, principally relating to Yorkshire, but occasionally to other parts of the country. There are copies of wills, leases and agreements; papers relating to partnerships of linen drapers, runners and casters of steel; a draft agreement of twenty-seven butchers to avoid causing nuisances with the garbage from the slaughter house; appointments of the surgeon of the workhouse; the papers relating to the Earl of Shrewsbury's Hospital in Sheffield; documents concerning the Cutlers' Company of Sheffield, lead mining, turnpike trusts, the Dove and Dearne Canal, the River Dun Navigation Company, and parish business of all kinds—apprenticeship indentures of pauper children, settlement disputes, disputes about rights of way, indictments for not repairing highways. There are papers relating to various criminal cases, and to cases of slander heard in the Consistory Court at York. The concern of Dawson and his colleagues with manorial business is shown in many ways— court rolls, rentals, presentments, maps, plans, and surveys are all carefully preserved. There is evidence of the work of this firm as clerks to the Town Trustees. There are the note-books kept by the articled clerks, a pamphlet describing a plan 'to remedy the great charge and delay of suits at law and in equity', and another relating to the proper conduct to be observed by the apprentice towards 'his master and the world'.

Another Sheffield attorney was James Wheat, who practised at the end of the century.[1] Wheat was a master in chancery, and one of the most important of some seventeen attorneys in the town. He had been articled to a local attorney, John Battie, and when Battie retired, had succeeded to his practice. In 1766 Wheat was clerk to the Capital Burgesses of Sheffield, and in 1778 he became one of the burgesses himself. He was solicitor to the Sheffield General Infirmary and the Charity Schools, and steward of the manor of Sheffield for the Duke of Norfolk. He succeeded Samuel Dawson as Clerk to the Town Trustees in 1777. He had financial interests in the Water Works, the White Lead Works, and the brewery. He was a target for the mob in 1791 because of the part he had played in securing the Cutlers' Act, and also for his concern in obtaining several local enclosure acts. He subscribed to the Tontine Inn, and was the government's agent for the building of new barracks in the town in 1792. Wheat had a large business in putting out his clients' money on mortgage, and occasionally he lent small sums himself: there are several letters from a neighbouring attorney in Paradise Square, Michael Burton, asking for loans of two or three guineas.

Wheat acted as clerk to many *ad hoc* bodies in Sheffield, tithe committees, the committee for building a new poor house, and to those petitioning against the Park Road bill. He was concerned in the Brightside enclosure, and negotiated with Edward Barnell in London about soliciting the bill in Parliament.[2] In 1777 he was appointed clerk and treasurer to the Sheffield–Wakefield turnpike in succession to Samuel Dawson, and for this he was paid an annual salary of £25, in addition to a monopoly of the legal work that

---

[1] Details derived from J. B. Wheat, *Wheat, a Family History* (Sheffield, 1893); and from Wheat's own business and personal papers at Sheffield. See also R. E. Leader, *Sheffield in the Eighteenth Century* (Sheffield, 1901), pp. 190–2, for details of Wheat and other Sheffield attorneys of the eighteenth century.

[2] It was the legal business which enclosures involved, and not so much the fees for secretarial work, that provided the profit in this kind of work. Wheat's fees for the Hallams enclosure were: 1791, £265. 11s. 8d.; 1792, £139. 19s. 0d.; 1793, £15. 1s. 4d.; 1797, £120. 1s. 0d.; 1799, £112. 0s. 0d.; 1800, £214. 14s. 5d. (W[heat] C[ollection], 1240/3).

turned up. Thus he received £93. 16s. 2d. for his trouble and expenses in drawing up a petition to parliament on behalf of the trustees. He sent the accounts of the road regularly to Lord Strafford at Wentworth castle, and dealt in the first instance with all correspondence. He arranged mortgages, collected subscriptions, and paid out the interest due to the trustees.

Wheat had a good deal of business of this semi-public nature, and this, together with that which arose from his private practice, often required the services of a London agent. His bill with one of these, Charles Owen, in 1794 was £111. 5s. 4d., and he also did business with Joseph Allen and Edward Bunn. These men seem to have combined the functions of legal agent with that of a sort of banker in London for their country clients.

All these activities, together with the usual attorney's business of writs, wills, settlements, deeds, sales, and disputes of all kinds, gave Wheat an important place in Sheffield society during the last thirty years of the eighteenth century. The style in which he lived is shown by the household bills which are preserved.[1] He bought wine in the cask from Leeds, damask from Bingley's in London, anchovies, mushroom powder and walnut ketchup from Nobbs and Holland in the Strand, tea from White and Smith at the Golden Canister in Pall Mall. He subscribed to the oratorio in Sheffield, and to many other local societies. He sent his daughter to school in Chesterfield, where she was taught music and French as extras. He organised the Sheffield Hunt Ball at the Tontine Inn in 1786, and rode to town in a chaise painted pea-green with touches of gold, arms, crests, and cyphers. Joshua Sheldon painted portraits of Wheat, his wife and daughter for three guineas each. He bought large numbers of books from Sheffield, Cambridge, and London. These included many law books: Blackstone's *Commentaries* and his *Analysis*, Ruffhead's *Statutes*, Grotius, Bacon, and many manuals of legal practice. He also bought Montaigne's *Essays*, the *Roman Poets*, *Sandford and Merton*, the *Annual Register*, Hastings on the *State of Bengal*, Hastings's *Trial*, and Paine's *Life*. In 1792 he bought the *Rights of Man*, Part II, a small map of France and a map of the Scheldt.

James Wheat may be taken for the type of the prosperous provincial attorney, a figure of some consequence in his society.

---

[1] The bills from 1768–1800 from which these details are derived are in W.C. 1276–87.

He had married the daughter of a Newark attorney, and had at least four children. One of his sons followed him in his practice and was admitted an attorney in 1800;[1] the other went to Lincoln College and then to St John's College, Cambridge, and eventually took orders. His office was in Paradise Square, but he lived at Norwood in a large house he had built for himself outside the town in 1772. He was consulted by London solicitors who were unknown to him as one of the most respectable attorneys in the town, and his advice was sought by many others who had business to do in Sheffield: the proprietor of a travelling theatre asked his opinion on prospects for the coming season.

In many ways, his mode of living was similar to that of two other Sheffield attorneys at the beginning of the century, Thomas Wright and Francis Sitwell. They too played their part in local affairs. One of them, Sitwell, came from a family already established among the gentry of the neighbourhood, and the other founded a gentle family—too gentle indeed to succeed to the practice. These men were followed in their practice by Joseph Banks, who also founded a landed family. He acquired estates in Lincolnshire, became a member of parliament, held the office of clerk of the peace for Nottinghamshire and acted by deputy. He was steward to the Dukes of Norfolk, Leeds, and Newcastle. Banks continued to practise when he was living in London. His son, for whom he bought Revesby Abbey in Lincolnshire, was not an attorney; his grandson was Sir Joseph Banks, President of the Royal Society.[2]

Wheat, however, like many others at the turn of the century, while anxious to live like a gentlemen, was content to found a professional family. Like James Round in Colchester, John Ambrose in Chelmsford, Joseph Hodgson in Carlisle, Charles Potts in Chester, he was the first representative of a family that was to play a continuously important part in local society, a part which was firmly based on his position as a professional man. Several firms that still exist can trace back their origins to an attorney in the second half of the eighteenth century, sometimes directly through members of their own family, sometimes through several changes in the ownership of the practice, but all retaining many links with their

---

[1] He also followed him as clerk to the Town Trustees, and held the office until 1846. Leader, *op. cit.* p. 191.

[2] See *Letters and Papers of the Banks family of Revesby Abbey, 1704–1760*, ed. J. W. F. Hill, Lincoln Record Society, vol. 45 (1952).

founders in the way of estates and local bodies for which, like their predecessors, they are still concerned.[1] Some of them continue to occupy the same premises in a Georgian house which had formerly served their founders for both home and office.

A similar part was played by attorneys in the life of eighteenth-century Birmingham.[2] Most of the attorneys in the town appear in the local newspaper advertising property for sale. Thomas Steward was clerk to the Street Commissioners in 1761. Thomas Cecil received the money due to the weighing machine sold for the benefit of the poor. John Hallam was steward of the Carnation Show in 1775; John Meredith clerk to the builders of the canal from Birmingham to Worcester, to the Trustees for building the new Chapels of St Paul and St Mary in 1772, and the builders of the Coventry and Oxford canal in 1774; he was clerk to the Street Commissioners and the Birmingham Boat Company in 1770. Thomas Brock was secretary to the proprietors of the Birmingham Theatre in 1792; Charles Stuart clerk to the Guardians of the Standards of Wrought Plate in 1778. Thomas Gem acted as solicitor to the Committee of Button Manufacturers; Benjamin Parker was concerned for the Overseers of the Poor; William Smith was clerk to the Street Commissioners in 1791, and secretary to those enclosing Birmingham Heath in 1798, a matter in which Ambrose Mainwaring and Thomas Hunt were also employed. Messrs Barker and Unett were the solicitors to those rebuilding Deritend Bridge, to those opposed to the sale of Comin Square, to the committee of those who opposed the Water Works, and to the committee of Volunteers in 1804. Mr Simpson was Treasurer to the Button Association in 1799; John Brooke to the Church and King Club in 1792, and to the Association for the Protection of Liberty and Property. H. W. Gem acted as clerk and treasurer to the Trustees for enlarging St Martin's Churchyard in 1811; Richard Bird represented the Birmingham Union Fire Office in 1805; William Haynes, George Meredith, and John Meredith were commissioned in the Loyal Birmingham Volunteer Infantry in 1803. Lewis Thompson, who was a partner with Wrightson in the publication of the Birmingham Directory in 1808, had been an

[1] There is one firm which claims direct descent from a sixteenth-century attorney; see Reginald Hine, *Confessions of an Uncommon Attorney* (London, 1945), and *Relics of an Uncommon Attorney* (London, 1951).

[2] Details derived from J. A. Langford, *A Century of Birmingham Life, 1741–1841* (Birmingham, 1868), which is based on Aris's *Birmingham Gazette*.

attorney, and returned to legal work on the dissolution of the partnership in 1812.

The local histories and newspapers of other areas tell a similar story, and show the attorney in touch with local life at a large variety of points, and occupying a position near the head of the hierarchy of the provincial town.[1] There are many examples of this. At Helston families of attorneys intermarried and formed a sort of lesser aristocracy in the town. The families of Grylls, Roberts, Hawkins, Johns, Plomer, Sandys, were town clerks, mayors, stewards of manors, well to the fore in all local affairs.[2] It was commonly believed that attorneys occupied the best houses in town,[3] and in King's Lynn they certainly did occupy residences appropriate to their position in the local community. There the Turners, John Mayer, Robert Underwood, Edward Bradfield, and Philip Case enjoyed such a station.[4] Case, indeed, was a man of outstanding importance in King's Lynn and in Norfolk generally.[5] He had been apprenticed to the town clerk of Lynn at the age of sixteen in 1728.[6] He was admitted an attorney in 1733, bought himself a large house in Lynn, married the daughter of a prosperous

[1] The profession continued to attract a wide variety of men; they were agents only, and ministered to the needs of their community, whatever they might be. William Hall, an attorney of Barnard Castle, advertised in the *Newcastle Journal* that he would take in laundry to be bleached by John Flanders of Crathorne, Yorks.

[2] See H. S. Toy, *The History of Helston* (Oxford, 1936), especially Appendix 30 by J. P. Rogers on 'Families connected with Helston'. See also chapter IX below on Christopher Wallis.

[3]
> 'A Lawyer now was to be found;
> And where's the spot of British ground,
> Where our experience doth not show
> That such a spreading plant will grow,
> And where his dwelling is not known
> As the best house in any town?'

(*Dr Syntax's Tour in Search of Consolation* (London, 1820), pp. 170–1.) On the houses of country attorneys, see also Samuel Foote, *The Orators* (1762) (Foote's Lecture), and Crabbe's *The Borough* (1801), Letter VI, 'The Profession of the Law'.

[4] See H. L. Bradfer-Lawrence, 'The Merchants of Lynn', in *A Supplement to Blomefield's History of Norfolk*, ed. Clement Ingleby (London, 1929), pp. 145–203. For the Turners, see J. H. Plumb, *Sir Robert Walpole: the Making of a Statesman* (London, 1956). There is some correspondence between Walpole and Charles Turner, an attorney, in the Cholmondely (Houghton) MSS. in Cambridge University Library.

[5] Details derived from Bradfer-Lawrence.

[6] His first master, Edward Bradfield, was dismissed in 1728, and Case continued with his successor, Robert Underwood. Of Bradfield it was said: 'His fine Patrimony, And a Profession wherein he excell'd, Gave him Independency, And every Enjoyment that could make Life agreeable: But alas! his accepting

doctor, Walpole's friend George Hepburn, and quickly acquired an exceedingly prosperous practice, numbering among his clients Townshends,[1] Walpoles, Pastons, Turners, Paytons, Wyndes, Spelmans, and Beveys. After serving as deputy clerk of the peace for Norfolk, he became clerk in 1760. He was steward of many manors, and became Comptroller of Customs at Lynn, Wisbech, and Wells in 1754. He purchased his freedom at Lynn in 1733, and was mayor in 1745, 1764, 1777, and 1786. He was deeply involved in politics with Townshend at Lynn and with Townshend's son at Yarmouth.[2] With all this he made a large fortune, and died in 1792 leaving extensive properties in Lynn and the county, and £100,000 in the funds, having from 1745 'virtually controlled the public and social life of Lynn',[3] the valued friend and adviser of Walpoles and Townshends alike.

Similarly at Liverpool it was men like William Roscoe and his kind who took the lead in local affairs.[4] Roscoe was articled to an attorney in 1769, and was admitted in 1774. He went into partnership first with Mr Bannister, and afterwards with Samuel Aspinall, an attorney who had 'long been known for the respectability of his practice'.[5] Roscoe's profession became increasingly distasteful to him, and he left it in 1796, not, however, before he had achieved considerable prosperity by it, and become one of the most prominent citizens of Liverpool.[6]

the Office of Town Clerk subjected him to Servility, And to every Disappointment That could make Death desirable' (Epitaph written by William Brown, printed in W. Richards, *History of Lynn* (Lynn, 1812), II, 915). Bradfield died in 1736 at the age of 47.

[1] One of his brothers, Edward, was agent to the 3rd Viscount; another brother, Thomas, was an attorney.

[2] See the letters printed in Bradfer-Lawrence, *op. cit.* pp. 193–9.

[3] Bradfer-Lawrence, *op. cit.* p. 200.

[4] Dr Chandler quotes a poem from the Roscoe Papers with reference to the part played by Roscoe and his friends in local affairs:

> 'But unluckily then in the Town
> Attorneys were great politicians
> And quakers were men of renown
> And merchants were metaphysicians....
> They'd one family make of all nations
> A state without members they'd rule
> And vote me and a negro relations.'

(George Chandler, *William Roscoe of Liverpool* (London, 1953), p. 52.)

[5] Henry Roscoe, *Life of William Roscoe* (London, 1833), I, 43.

[6] See the letters Roscoe wrote to his wife, printed *ibid.* pp. 205–6: 'I am almost disgusted with my profession as it affords me a continual opportunity of observing the folly and villany of mankind.'

At Bristol the attorneys were closely associated with the trading community in the city, and they were quick to subscribe to the fund raised to assist the king against his rebellious subjects in America.[1] An attorney was clerk to the Merchant Adventurers' Company; another, Henry Bengough, became mayor in 1792. And there were many other eminent attorneys in the city. One of them, Jarrit Smith, was the city's member of parliament from 1756 to 1768. He is said to have been helped in his campaign by Wesley; he became a baronet in 1768, and changed his name to Smythe. Thomas Fane, Distributor of Stamps, Clerk to the Society of Merchants, became heir to the Earldom of Westmorland in 1757, and resigned his practice to his clerk, Samuel Worrall, who was later town clerk and head of a firm of bankers in the city until he went bankrupt in 1819.[2] In contrast to these men, Peter Baynes, an attorney prohibited from practice for non-payment of fees, was employed by one Barry, an unscrupulous inn-keeper on the Quay, to draw up deeds by which sailors who were indebted to him assigned to him their wages and prize-money on their deaths.[3]

The activities of the attorneys reflect very closely the distinctive character of the local history of the area within which they practised. The special problems of cathedral towns, of university towns, of sea-ports and industrial centres all appear from their papers. In Lancashire the peculiar situation of the Roman Catholics provided much work for the profession. Suffering under many disabilities about holding property and the like, Catholics were often forced to rely on the personal discretion of their attorney. Protestant neighbours held their lands for them under trusts arranged by attorneys, and except at critical periods such as those immediately following the '15 and the '45, the relations between Catholics and their neighbours seem to have been amicable. But their position was never secure, and they depended much on legal advice.

[1] See above, p. 37; other details relating to Bristol are derived from John Latimer, *The Annals of Bristol in the Eighteenth Century* (Bristol, 1893).

[2] See L. S. Pressnell, *Country Banking in the Industrial Revolution* (Oxford, 1956), p. 240.

[3] In 1745 a sailor died in Barry's house under suspicious circumstances, leaving a will which made over to Barry £2000 prize money. At the trial Baynes deposed that 'after the privateersman had expired, Barry's wife put a pen into the dead man's hand, and thus made a mark on the blank form of will which was at once filled up in Barry's favour by Baynes himself, who admitted that several hundreds of sailors' wills had been written by him at Barry's dictation after the man had left the port' (Latimer, *op. cit.* pp. 261–2).

The family of Starkie who were attorneys in Lancashire during the century proved good friends to many Catholic families. In 1701 Starkie advised Robert Scarisbrick 'to go into Cheshire or Yorkshire or anywhere else out of the county' to avoid the impending summons for recusancy.[1] Similarly in 1708, another attorney, Nicholas Plumb, wrote to Edmund Blundell telling him of an information laid against Mr Blundell of Ince Blundell by Parson Ellison of Formby.[2] Plumb was able to work things in Blundell's favour at Ormskirk sessions, and again in 1716, when Blundell and his family found it advisable to leave the country, Plumb and his son William, who practised as a lawyer in London, helped them to obtain permission to leave. The family was home again in 1717, and Plumb was advising them about the re-registration of their real estate.[3]

Other attorneys were preoccupied with different aspects of Lancashire life. The precedent book of a Liverpool firm contains, besides the usual references to causes arising from wills and deeds of all sorts, opinions about questions of marine insurance, the

[1] *Blundell's Diary and Letter Book, 1702–28*, ed. M. Blundell (Liverpool, 1952), p. 76.

[2] Blundell, *op. cit.* p. 75. The position of Catholics was precarious, and they were open to the attacks of informers. Charles Butler, an eminent Catholic conveyancer, wrote: 'On an inquiry made in 1780, respecting the execution of the penal laws against the Catholics, he found that the single firm of Dynely and Ashmall, attornies in Gray's Inn, had defended more than twenty under such prosecutions; and, that, greatly to their honour, they had defended them gratuitously' (*Historical Memoirs of the English Catholics* (London, 1819), II, 65). Catholics were not prevented from acting as chamber counsel and conveyancers, and such men as Nathaniel Pigott, James Booth, and Butler himself made a large contribution to the theory and practice of conveyancing. Butler was secretary to the Catholic Relief Committee at the end of the century, and was the first Catholic to be called to the bar after the act of 1791 (31 Geo. III, c. 32) which removed the disabilities on Catholics practising as attorneys and barristers.

[3] There are hints that the Starkies later in the century may have betrayed their trust. A letter from Edward Starkie of 6 March 1760, claiming the Lydiate estate of Lady Anderton under her will (Lancashire Record Office, D/D In 14/35), was endorsed by G. Blundell in 1891, 'Letter from the rascally son of the lawyer to whom Lady Anderton made over Lydiate for her son-in-law's family, the Blundells of Ince'. The estate seems to have been entrusted to Starkie, who then refused to hand it over to the Blundells. But there are further suggestions that Starkie did make a search for the son of Henry Blundell in order to give him some money from the estate (D/D In 14/41 and 44). There was a similar situation in Northumberland in the early part of the century, described by Scott in *Rob Roy*, and Diana Vernon, speaking of the activities of Attorney Jobson, justice's clerk to Squire Inglewood, called him a 'troublesome mischief-making tool', and said, '...it is hard that persons of birth and rank and estate should be subjected to the official impertinence of such a paltry pick-thank as that, merely for believing as the whole world believed not much above a hundred years ago...'.

importing of goods from Ireland, articles of agreement with seamen to sail to Africa, and many other matters which arose in Liverpool at a time when its importance as a seaport was being rapidly established.[1] Another Lancashire attorney, Isaac Greene,[2] was connected with the Corporation of Liverpool, acted as attorney for Lord Molyneux, advised Liverpool merchants about investments, and assisted Richard Norris at election times. He went to London on behalf of the corporation to assist the local members to obtain an act to make the River Weaver navigable so as to open up the Cheshire salt trade,[3] and to obtain payment from the Treasury for the cost of fortifying the town in 1715. Greene made a large fortune, bought up much land in Lancashire, became a landed gentleman—and died intestate.

Another Lancashire attorney of the first half of the century was Alexander Leigh.[4] Leigh had a large practice, and was the attorney and election agent in Wigan of Sir Roger Bradshaigh. 'In 1733 he was steward or clerk of seventeen manorial courts...was deeply involved in the Douglas Navigation project, and thereby concerned in the Lancashire coal trade.' He was mayor of Wigan in 1727 and again in 1737. He was town clerk from 1732 to 1735, was succeeded in this office by his son Robert, who held it from 1735 to 1741, and was in turn succeeded by his nephew and clerk, John Wiswall. With his father-in-law, Robert Holt,[5] Leigh 'formed the channel for appeals from the locality for Sir Robert's patronage'.

In a neighbouring county, the account book of a Chester firm of attorneys, in which Charles Potts was a principal partner, shows them engaged for the clerk of the peace at the sessions, concerned in the usual attorney's business in parish affairs, borrowing money for their clients, collecting their clients' money out on loan; advising

[1] I was able to see this book through the courtesy of the Underwriters' Association of Liverpool.

[2] See R. Stewart-Brown, *Isaac Greene, a Lancashire Lawyer of the Eighteenth Century* (Liverpool, 1921). I owe this reference to Professor H. J. Habakkuk.

[3] Another attorney, William Watts of Middlewich, was employed by those opposing the scheme. Cf. T. S. Willan, *The River Weaver in the Eighteenth Century*, Chetham Society, 3rd series, III (Manchester, 1951), 12–15, 17–18. Richard Vernon, a prosperous attorney of Middlewich, with interests in the salt trade, was one of the undertakers of the navigation named in the Act of 1721 (7 Geo. I, c. 10) (Willan, *op. cit.* pp. 24–6).

[4] See M. Cox, 'Sir Roger Bradshaigh and the Electoral Management of Wigan, 1695–1747', *Bulletin of the John Rylands Library*, vol. 37, no. 1 (1954), pp. 120–64.

[5] Holt was mayor in 1730 and 1736.

about the titles of estates; doing business in Cheshire on behalf of London and Liverpool attorneys; obtaining the conviction of poachers of rabbit warrens and of several persons accused of infringing customs regulations; arranging insurances and enclosures. One client, Mrs Frances Williams, ran up a bill of some £400 with Potts. He looked after her investments, settled her late husband's affairs, paid the land tax, the window tax, and the duty on plate; put out her money on loan and bought Scotch bonds for her; paid certain dues on her Carmarthenshire estates to the Bursar of Jesus College, Oxford.

Potts advised Walter Thomas of Chester in his long dispute with Lady Cunliffe about the obscuring of his windows by the Sugar House, and went up to London to hear a cause relating to his ore mines in Wales. He acted in a dispute between the Dee Company and the Canal Company, and between the Dee Company and the Mayor and Citizens of Chester. Perhaps the most interesting of Potts's clients was the Duke of Bridgewater. It was at this time that he was building the Grand Trunk Canal to connect the Mersey to the Trent, and Potts was employed to do all the conveyancing which was involved.[1]

On the other side of the country, in Colchester, William Mason had a rather different practice. A series of very detailed account books survives and from those for the period 1785 to 1795 a picture of his daily business can be obtained.[2] The overwhelming majority of Mason's clients came to him for advice and assistance in the purchase and sale of land. At times he conducted these negotiations personally from start to finish, but most often he was called in after the bargain had been made, to draw the conveyancing deeds. In most cases also he had the further task of arranging the mortgages that were involved. The sums mentioned in those transactions vary considerably; one is as small as £50: most are much larger. There are several of £1000, three of £2000, one of £3500, and one of £4582. In only one instance does Mason himself seem to have provided the money needed: in 1791 he lent £130 to a client to repay a previous loan on a mortgage which had been called in.

There are a good many instances—they occur regularly at sessions time—when Mason acted on behalf of parish officers or the clerk

---

[1] This information is derived from an account book lent me by Charles Potts's descendant who continues to practise in Chester. Potts was also county treasurer for Cheshire; cf. Willan, *op. cit.* p. 106.

[2] E[ssex] R[ecord] O[ffice], D/DEl B 4–18.

of the peace. Such business usually took him into court, as also did the occasional prosecutions for debt, theft, assault, highway robbery, trespassing, defamation, and perjury. Most of his business, however, did not involve him in court cases, and was concerned with wills, settlements, and deeds of all kinds. There are entries recalling journeys in the middle of the night to make the will of someone not expected to live until the morning. 'You being in an alarming state, journey over to you in the night to make your will.' 'You having sent for me in a hurry to make Mr Keye's will, journey over for that purpose, but he being of an insane mind, after waiting there the night, nothing could be done.'

A regular and profitable client was John Round, himself an attorney, on whose behalf Mason held several manorial courts of which he was steward. His fees on these annual occasions were always substantial: £84. 3s. 0d., £100. 12s. 4d., £75. 11s. 11d., £84. 2s. 3d.[1] Mason also acted for the Frating and Winstree Associations, formed for the protection of the property of their members. The client whose affairs occupy most space in these accounts is the Revd Mr Corsellis of Wivenhoe. His business is carried over from page to page, and from volume to volume: from September 1788 to March 1791 his bill had amounted to £126. 7s. 5d., principally made up of small sums charged for business with a difficult tenant, business which eventually was introduced into the Court of King's Bench. And, after a long series of discussions with counsel, preparing cases for opinions and engrossing deeds, and the like, Corsellis decided not to proceed to trial.

In 1790 he decided to make a new settlement on his wife, and an exchange of his property with his son. This meant going up to London to seek the advice of counsel—Leake and Mansfield—and Mason was given the task of putting his client's papers in order and of accompanying him to London. Mason charged a guinea a day for his attendance in London, in addition to coach hire and other incidental expenses. There were other matters which brought them back to London again in the following year. Corsellis was Mason's most frequent client, but the larger sums among the various items which make up his bill are usually payments for the opinions of

---

[1] When Round died in 1813, Mason's son (who had succeeded his father as town clerk of Colchester) was appointed to several of these stewardships, although Round's successor, his nephew Charles Round, had asked for them.

counsel; Mason's own charges for writing and engrossing and journeying about on Corsellis's business are made up of small amounts of 3*s*. 4*d*. and 6*s*. 8*d*.

Mason's other clients seem to have been farmers and landowners of moderate wealth. There was a sprinkling of professional people and smaller tradesmen—a hatter, a fishmonger. But he did some business for people of a higher status such as Sir William Rowley and Sir Edmund and Lady Affleck. Occasionally he was employed by an attorney from outside the county to conduct cases at the Assizes, but for the most part his clients came from Colchester and the surrounding district of north-east Essex.

The practice of Samuel Meddowes at Halstead was even more limited.[1] His account book for the years 1770–5 has survived, but only some 110 clients are mentioned during this period. By far the largest part of his business was connected with the purchase and sale of land and other property, and with arranging small mortgages —the largest sum he was asked to obtain was £200. Thirteen entries relate to the making of wills and the winding up of estates, twelve to the recovery of debts, thirteen to the administration of estates— serving ejectment notices and making distraints, eleven to mort- gages. Three entries concer nmarriage settlements, one of which was that between the Revd Mr Houghton and Miss Moss, which had to be laid before Charles Gray of Colchester for his perusal, and involved consultations with a broker about investments in the funds. Only two entries relate to parish business. Meddowes's clients were of very humble standing when compared with such men as the Duke of Bridgewater, but they too had their problems which involved matters of law, and could afford a lawyer to look after them. Meddowes's charges may have been more moderate than most; he was not over-exacting in his demands, and left several debts to be collected by his successor, Samuel Alston.

Very different was the career of Thomas Nuthall, the attorney of William Pitt and many other leading figures of the day. Nuthall held many valuable offices in addition to his normal practice. He was registrar of warrants in 1740, receiver-general for hackney coaches in 1749, solicitor to the East India Company in 1765, solicitor to the Treasury in 1765, and secretary of bankrupts in 1766. In 1766 also he had been appointed Ranger of Enfield Chase, a position in which he displayed much zeal in planting and caring

[1] E.R.O. D/DQM.

for the oaks.[1] Chatham employed Nuthall as an intermediary in his attempts to form an administration in 1766, and in May wrote to thank him for his 'unlawyer-like zeal for your friend'.[2]

Nuthall himself had much to be thankful for, and for such a client as Chatham he could hardly be other than zealous. But there are signs of dissatisfaction later. In 1772 there was a dispute about a mortgage of Hayes which Temple and Chatham were inclined to blame on Nuthall. The fault was indeed his, for he had omitted a whole parcel of lands from the mortgage deeds which he had drawn up. 'Here is a story', Chatham wrote, 'of a *mistake* to me quite incomprehensible, had I not often found that lawyers, hurried by variety of business, are the most stupid blunderers imaginable.'[3] Temple's reply was no more complimentary to Nuthall:

At my return to this place (Stowe) on Sunday last, I found your Lordship's letter, together with one of the 4th from that facetious man of business in so many departments, Mr Thomas Nuthall, whose fellow is not easily to be met with: witness your marriage settlement not witnessed, his peremptory and repeated assertions, that your trustees had no power to advance the trust money on mortgage, even though I quoted the very words to him, and his late unparalleled proceedings, which the better to ascertain I send you the copies of the letters which have already passed, leaving the comparison of his letters to you and me, the dates, the contradictions, and the comments to your lordship.... I rely with the fullest security on your lordship's honour, but not at all on Mr Nuthall's law.[4]

In 1775 Nuthall died as a result of an attack by a highwayman, and in July Horace Walpole noted in his Journal, 'Just now the widow of Nuttall, solicitor of the Treasury, who had embezzled £19,000, had a pension of £300 a year to induce her to give up her husband's papers, who had been engaged in many election matters'.[5]

---

[1] Nuthall wrote to Chatham on 21 June 1768: 'I hope I shall leave behind me innumerable proofs, that with care and common honesty in office, the fleets of this land may be supplied from the King's forests and chases only. I had rather this should be written on my monument, than any one compliment that can be given to the last peace' (*Chatham Correspondence*, ed. W. S. Taylor and J. H. Pringle (London, 1840), II, 424-5).

[2] *Ibid.* p. 419, Pitt to Nuthall, 11 May 1766.

[3] *Grenville Papers*, ed. W. J. Smith (London, 1852), IV, 543; Chatham to Temple, 30 August 1772.

[4] *Ibid.* IV, 545; Temple to Chatham, 8 September 1772.

[5] *Last Journals*, I, 469-70.

6

Attorneys of the eminence of Nuthall were clearly exceptional, but there were a few others—John Robinson, Jack Robinson of the Treasury, and Brass Crosby, M.P. for Honiton and Lord Mayor of London in 1770, for example—who held positions of national importance. There was a sprinkling of attorneys in the House of Commons, but the fact that they did not reach the House until fairly late in life suggests that they too, like Nuthall and Robinson, owed their positions to some patron or other, rather than to the fact that they were attorneys, although it was clearly as attorneys that they were useful to their patrons in the first place.[1] But there were many others, like Mr Goodman, 'who lives in Pall Mall and keeps both Chariot and Phaeton, and Fame says has got 20 to £60,000 by Matrimony',[2] who made their mark in the social life of London.

Any assessment of the importance of all this work is difficult, for in most cases the attorneys were only the agents of other men, and a valuation of this sort would perhaps emerge more clearly from a study which viewed the profession from the point of view of society, than from one which looked at society from the attorney's office. Attorneys were often despised because they were merely agents, but such criticisms became less and less apt in a society whose structure was changing so fundamentally, and in which many new pieces of social machinery were being found necessary. In a simple society middle-men may perhaps justly be despised as parasites, but eighteenth-century English society was not simple, and by the end of this period there could be little doubt that its 'agents' played an essential part as a sort of social lubricant. Without them the social changes of the period would have taken place less quickly and less smoothly.

So it was perhaps easier than it had been for attorneys to justify their calling as useful and therefore honourable, the more so since they filled so many places which were later to become the preserves of more specialised professions. And if the profession was found to be honourable, it was also found to be profitable. It certainly attracted a wide variety of men, but the great majority of them

---

[1] Out of some 700 lawyers in the House between 1734 and 1832, thirty-nine were attorneys and solicitors. See G. P. Judd IV, *Members of Parliament, 1734–1832* (Yale, 1955), p. 51; Mr Judd also notices that 'Attorneys and solicitors did not receive their first election until they had reached the average age of 48' (*ibid.* p. 52).

[2] *Verney Letters of the Eighteenth Century*, ed. M. M. Verney (London, 1930), II, 289 (Archdeacon Heslop to Lord Verney, 6 April 1787).

occupied—and maintained—a position in the middle ranges of society, and formed part of what was perhaps a new social class. It was certainly new in its self-consciousness, and in the place it was accorded in society as a whole. As has been shown, these men were already among the leaders of provincial society, and in 1800 they were only entering on a role whose period of major influence lay in the future. But even at that date, they had established themselves in a position of strength, and the respectability of their calling was conceded.

CHAPTER VII

ESTATES AND ELECTIONS

GIVING evidence before the Select Committee on Legal Education in 1846, Sir George Stephen, an attorney and solicitor, said: 'It is quite impossible to define within a narrow compass the nature of a solicitor's business: it extends to anything, it extends to everything: law, I should say, forms about the least part of the duty of a solicitor in a large practice.'[1] What was true in this matter in the nineteenth century was at least equally true in the eighteenth, before the specialisation of activities which resulted in the development of many distinct professions. It was certainly true that the part of the attorney's business which involved him in court cases was a small part of his normal activities. A very much larger part of his time was spent in organisation and administration in many different capacities, and perhaps the greatest single source of business and of profit was his concern with landed property, and all the problems it involved. It was from their work in these important fields that the attorneys derived much of their profit and their prestige. In view of the paramount importance of land at the time, this is not surprising. Land was the foundation of wealth and of many social attitudes and aspirations; it was directly connected with local and political influence.[2] The laws regulating tenures and inheritance were many and complicated, the subject of innumerable treatises and hand-books, and the source, it was alleged by landowners, of much unwarranted profit to lawyers.[3] The buying and selling of even the smallest estate might involve complicated legal problems, prolonged investigations of the title deeds, and the drawing of long and intricate conveyancing deeds. In the case of a major estate, these problems were all multiplied, and they were exacerbated by involved settlements, trusts, and all the rights and duties inextricably linked up with landed property.

All this meant that the services of a legal expert were desirable,

[1] *Reports, Committees* (1846), X, 141.
[2] On this, see Sir Lewis Namier's remarks on land as the basis of citizenship in *England in the Age of the American Revolution* (London, 1930), pp. 20-9.
[3] On the land laws, see Sir Frederick Pollock, *The Land Laws* (3rd ed. London, 1896).

even in matters involving only a few acres of land; in those which involved an estate of any size and significance, they were indispensable. It may be true that the eighteenth-century landowner was more closely acquainted with matters of the law than his successors, but it seems unlikely that many of them commanded either the knowledge, or the time, or the inclination to undertake all the business connected with their property. Thus the lawyer who was entrusted with the purely legal business might also be put in charge of the day to day administration of a great estate as well.

In some cases—and this is perhaps truer of the early part of the century than the later—he did no work save for his immediate employer, and lived in his house. John Fox, for example, the steward to the Russells and their chief agent at the beginning of the century, had his room in the family house in Bloomsbury.[1] He was a bachelor and lived in, and was accorded a respected place in the household hierarchy.[2] Daniel Eaton occupied a similar place in the household of the Earl of Cardigan.[3] In this, as in other spheres, these men were partly paid by a fixed salary, and partly by being given a monopoly of all the legal business which arose from the estate. The fixed sum was not large; John Fox received £10 per annum as legal adviser to the Russells, and £100 as receiver-general. Daniel Eaton's predecessor at Deene received £100 per annum as steward.

Daniel Eaton found this salary inadequate, and supplemented it by doing business outside the Brudenell estate. In 1727 he wrote to the Earl of Cardigan telling him that he had recently got himself admitted an attorney of the Court of Common Pleas, 'an attorney of credit making a certificate of my capacity and producing one of my letters in court, got it done without any manner of difficulty, and with very little charge'. He hastened to explain his reason for taking this step:

[1] G. Scott Thomson, *The Russells in Bloomsbury* (London, 1940), p. 208.
[2] The report of the funeral procession of the Duke of Somerset in the *Newcastle Journal* for 7 January 1749, gives the order of precedence in a large household. Before the coffin 'first went 12 persons in black clothes, then 4 of his Grace's footmen in black, after them 4 Gentlemen in black, then Mr Rhodes, his Grace's Apothecary, and Mr Guidot, his solicitor; next followed the Rev. Mr Barnard, Fellow of St John's College, Cambridge, his Grace's domestic Chaplain, after him walked Thomas Elder, his Grace's principal Steward, bearing a Ducal crown upon a cushion of crimson velvet, supported by Mr Williams, his Grace's Secretary, and Mr Gardner, his domestic Attorney'. Then came the coffin.
[3] Joan Wake, *The Brudenells of Deene* (2nd ed. London, 1954), pp. 210–22.

Your lordship may probably think I have some strange views by the proceeding, but I do assure your lordship that the chiefest inducement to it was that, whereas I have for these seven years past disposed of a great deal of money upon mortgages, etc., to the general satisfaction of all my friends who have entrusted me as well as my own advantage, my just fees have sometimes been denied, and I, having no authority to proceed, could not redeem them by law.

Now that case is altered, for I have an attachment of privilege signed and sealed, and I hope may some time or other be of convenience to your lordship. But I shall not endeavour to practise in any other way, for, as to your lordship's house being pestered by my clients (which might probably be very numerous) must certainly be irksome to you, so, consequently I could never propose any such thing to myself.[1]

The functions of steward, estate agent, and legal adviser, were not clearly separated, and sometimes they were performed by the same person, who seems very often to have been an attorney. It has been suggested that it was in the eighteenth century that the specialised estate agent first appears, being needed to cope with the increasing complexity of estate administration, and the geographically scattered nature of the estates of the great landowners.[2] There are important examples, however, of estate management being carried on by men who had attorneys' practices.[3] Indeed it would have been surprising if they had not been found performing a duty for which they had so many professional qualifications. The management of the scattered parts of a large estate seems frequently to have been entrusted to a local attorney, and even the central

[1] Brudenell MSS. F iii 123; quoted Wake, *loc. cit.* The second edition of Miss Wake's book contains a portrait of Eaton.

[2] E. Hughes, 'The Eighteenth Century Estate Agent', in *Essays in Honour of J. E. Todd*, ed. H. A. Cronne, T. W. Moody, and D. B. Quinn (London, 1949), pp. 188–9.

[3] This of course antagonised those who were anxious to keep attorneys out of this business. In 1727 Edward Laurence wrote: ' I cannot forbear here to take notice, that Noblemen and Gentlemen lie under great Evils and Inconveniences, when they suffer themselves to be persuaded to employ *Country Attorneys* for their Stewards; because it seldom happens that they are well Qualified for that Trust....A Steward's Business is not such as may be done as it were *by the by*: 'Tis his *whole* Employment, and a full one too;...the Attorney, if he has any Character, has business enough of his own, of the Law, and therefore should not undertake the Office of Steward....I have known Instances where a Country Attorney has been Steward to seven or eight Noblemen, and others, and has yet done nothing else but attend the Court-keeping and collecting of Rents; by which means the Tenants have taken the Advantage of doing what they would with their Farms, quickly lessening the Value of the Estates by *Over-Ploughing*, etc....' (*The Duty of a Steward to his Lord* (1727).)

direction of an estate as large as that of the Rockinghams was entrusted to a Yorkshire attorney, Richard Fenton, and his successor, Charles Bowns, both of whom did similar business for other landowners, and some normal attorney's work besides.

Fenton corresponded with Rockingham on all matters relating to the estates, especially those in Yorkshire, and to politics in Yorkshire. He occupied a position of great responsibility and trust: between 1760 and 1765 he received more than £60,000 in rents from the Rockingham estates at Badworth, Malton, and Wentworth, out of which he financed the running of the estate and the household, and remitted large sums to Rockingham in London. In the years immediately after Rockingham had succeeded, however, the annual rents were not sufficient to pay all the demands on the estates, encumbered as they were by debts and annuities, and Fenton had to borrow money to keep things going. He wrote to his master in 1765: 'I do assure you, my Lord, I have at several different times borrowed sums of money in my own name and security, and which I still owe, to discharge demands at Wentworth, which could not reasonably be deferred longer.'[1]

Fenton reported regularly about estate matters. On 14 November 1765, for example, he wrote to tell Rockingham about the purchase of two estates, and sent an account of his receipts and payments since his last letter. He discussed arrangements for paying debts incurred at Wentworth for hay and other things, and asked that money should be sent to the household steward to tide him over till the Christmas rents came in.

The taking away the hill,[2] and the turnpike work have been very expensive jobs. Were all the present demands cleared off, things might probably be kept for the future on an equal footing—but this I found not possible to be done—because there were some large bills standing out when Mr Evans[3] left your lordship's service, and because I have since at different times had orders from your lordship for several considerable extra sums; when the bills are now discharged, which most certainly would only be right to have done immediately, I should think that the common disbursements, including what I pay for interest money, etc. would not exceed the rents there.[4]

---

[1] W[entworth] W[oodhouse] M[uniments] R 171/5, 3 November, 1765. Fenton was also a receiver of the land tax. He lived at Bank Top, Barnsley.

[2] Wentworth Woodhouse, the largest house in England, was begun in 1740; this presumably refers to the laying out of the park.

[3] Presumably Fenton's predecessor.   [4] W.W.M. R 171/4.

There are signs that Fenton did not think himself adequately rewarded for his devotion to Rockingham's interests. On one occasion he asked Rockingham to use his influence to get him appointed clerk of the peace. What his salary was does not appear, but the connection was a valuable one, and he remained in this position for some thirty or forty years. He retired about 1790, and was replaced by Charles Bowns, who seems to have taken over his practice as a whole.[1] Bowns acted as Fenton had done, and like him, thought himself underpaid by Rockingham's heir, Fitzwilliam. It was not until 1811, however, that he asked for an increase in his salary. He wrote on 4 June, describing his affairs, and giving interesting details about his relations with other landowners for whom he acted as agent.

The agencies I hold have necessarily occupied so much of my time that it has not been in my power to pursue the profession of a solicitor to that extent which is sufficient to enable me to answer the growing expenses which I experience, and which my limited income has not been equal to, on which account I have been obliged to request an increase of salary from Colonel Beaumont and Mr Tullerton which they have granted, and must inevitably have made the like application to your lordship four years since had I not been favoured with your lordship's professional employment, for which I take this opportunity of tendering my most grateful thanks. I have also been desirous of deferring the application until such time as an advance should take place in the rents of your lordship's estates in my collection.

The salary which Colonel Beaumont allows me upon the amounts of the rents, etc., which includes the auditing the accounts of the House Steward at Bretton and of the principal head agent at Newcastle, where I go annually at his expense, but all incidental business not relating to the estate is paid for as professional, being too uncertain to compound for.

Mr Tullerton makes me the like allowance of 4%.

The annual amount of the rents and produce of your lordship's farms, tithes, mines, woods and canals under my collection is little if anything short of £40,000 and the quantity of land exceeds 15,000 acres, the cultivation and cropping of every close of which, as well as the state of the buildings thereupon must be attended to every year, in consequence of the mode of management prescribed by the intended articles with the clients;[2] to which must be added, the auditing of Mr Birnam's

---

[1] Bowns was undersheriff for the county to Sir George Wombwell, and appointed Joseph Munby his deputy in 1809. Letter of Attorney in Munby MSS.

[2] Improvement clauses in the leases granted to tenants were increasingly popular, and their insertion and proper operation called for a good deal of expert knowledge on the part of the agent.

(steward at Wentworth) accounts—the accounts of Law Wood and Elsicar Collieries, and likewise those of the Irish, Malton, Higham, and Harroden estates; for all of which I take the liberty of humbly requesting your lordship will be pleased to make such augmentation to my present salary as your lordship may think proper, upon consulting with any professional gentleman acquainted with business of that kind, and to whom I beg leave to refer your lordship, in order to ascertain what sum may now be fair, reasonable, and adequate compensation for the management and attention required upon an estate of the magnitude and nature of that which your lordship is pleased to entrust to my care.[1]

Fitzwilliam seems to have received this request sympathetically. He consulted Mr W. Baldwin of Brook Street about it, who suggested that Bowns should be given £1200 per annum, and added: 'I do verily believe that by his £400 per annum he has not been much benefited.'[2]

Not all agents were held in such high esteem. The position offered scope for cheating and some agents were not able to resist the temptation. Thomas Carter, an attorney of Leicester, was steward to Mrs Brent, and in 1725 the Revd Mr Robertshaw was asked to investigate his affairs on Mrs Brent's behalf. He discovered that Carter had been claiming sums for repairs which had never been done, and he asked Carter to come over to Amersham to sort out affairs before they became publicly known. 'He was', Robertshaw wrote, 'fool enough to offer me a sum of money to get the vile affair hushed up.' Carter blustered and threatened for some time, but Robertshaw was able to obtain conclusive evidence against him. 'He then began to change his note, and confess that he had done wrong, and that it was in our power to ruin him with all his other clients, many of whom were persons of great quality and distinction.' In the event, 'he gave bond to refund Mrs Brent six hundred guineas in a year and a half's time, viz. £105 at each quarterly payment; which he actually performed within the time limited, and was contented to be turn'd out of his stewardship into the bargain'.[3]

---

[1] W.W.M. F 106 a.

[2] In the same year Heaton, the agent of the Duke of Devonshire, who had been with the family for more than forty years, had his salary of £1000 increased, and was given £1000 besides. On this occasion Lady Bessborough recommended to Lord Granville the method of paying an agent by allowing him a percentage on the rents in his collection. See Hughes, *loc. cit.* p. 193.

[3] *Shardeloes Papers*, ed. G. Eland (London, 1947), pp. 64–7.

It is probable that many landowners harboured suspicions that all attorneys and agents would behave in this manner whenever they had the occasion. Certainly Lord Shelburne did. In a memorandum which he drew up on the problems of the management of land in Ireland and England, the principal burden of which was contained in the rules 'put yourself in the power of no man', and 'see with your own eyes', he showed himself no friend to the professions, and suggested that the natural interests of landowners and those of their agents were necessarily in conflict.[1] He had no great opinion of the abilities of the generality of professional men, and thought that 'want of time and application are the real causes of the perpetual blunders, which are to be found in every transaction of business (and I believe there is not a settlement in the kingdom without some),[2] much more than the policy which is supposed to prevail in all trades, of making business for their own endowment, or any positive dishonesty among agents'.[3]

Shelburne went on to suggest that a closer supervision ought to be exercised by landowners in person—'The eye of the most ignorant owner operates upon his agents like witchcraft'[4]—and that they could do much of the work themselves that they were used to entrust to others.[5] When landowners neglected their estates, and left them in the hands of agents, both they and the society which depended on them were bound to suffer. 'Though the rich may in some respects set a bad example', wrote Shelburne, 'yet upon the whole they soften and liberalise, excite industry, and make society by bringing men together, who polish themselves, enforce a due administration of justice, and keep down the professions, whose employment is to rob every country, and if left to themselves, naturally produce upstart manners and yet a total want of principle.'[6]

It was just this development that was responsible for the profits of attorneys, and for their increasing importance in society, along with other kinds of professional men. Those who could afford to engage an

---

[1] This memorandum is printed in Lord Fitzmaurice's *Life of Shelburne* (2nd ed. London, 1912), II, 336–7.

[2] Cf. the views of Chatham and Temple, p. 81 above.

[3] Fitzmaurice, *op. cit.* pp. 340–1.   [4] *Ibid.* p. 341.

[5] Cf. *ibid.* p. 347: 'Of all the follies the greatest is that, which formerly was practised and is still continued in some great families, that of having some considerable lawyer or some eminent man of business at a considerable salary to audit your accounts. There is a family whose fortune was entirely made by the father's auditing the accounts of different estates, which many of the owners were infinitely more capable of auditing.'   [6] *Ibid.* p. 361.

agent to perform those functions which they themselves found too irksome or too complicated, and in doing so, allowed the attorneys to prosper, and to develop into a professional class with its own interests and its own powers. And the attorneys on their part exploited the possibilities of being—or of being thought to be—indispensable.

All agents were liable to be plunged into hectic activity at critical periods in the affairs of their employers. The prolonged dispute between Sir James Lowther and the Duke of Portland over the right to the Forest of Inglewood kept many lawyers, great and small, busy for ten years.[1] At an advanced stage in this dispute, in 1771, the *London Packet* noted that the 'suit (is) in such favourable train that the bar may reasonably expect that a three years' crop will yet be taken by the lawyers on both sides before a final decision can possibly be obtained'.[2] In fact the dispute lasted from 1767 to 1777, and the attorneys who prepared the way for the barristers, and who gleaned the field after the bar had taken its crop, profited greatly. Lowther bought up many of the attorneys in Cumberland, and in 1770, 'Legions of attorneys, accompanied by all the sheriffs and bailiffs they could lay their hands upon, were informing all whom they thought they could terrify that they must be prepared to quit their tenancies immediately'.[3] In the end, Portland's claim to the land was established, and Charles Howard, writing to congratulate him, wished him a 'Lasting deliverance from Lawyers, Doctors, and Sir James Lowther'.[4] Certainly the lawyers gained much from this struggle, and if trials of strength of this magnitude occurred only once in a century, in everything but size it was typical of scores of disputes over property rights which were fought out in the eighteenth century, disputes which were caused and invigorated by the great prestige and influence which attached to landed wealth at that time.

---

[1] See A. S. Turberville, *A History of Welbeck Abbey and its Owners* (London, 1939), II, ch. 6.

[2] Printed in *Newcastle Journal*, 25–30 November 1771.

[3] Turberville, *op. cit.* p. 122.

[4] 10 February 1777, *Letters at Welbeck Abbey* (Roxburgh Club, 1909), p. 181. One of Lowther's agents in Cumberland at this time who assisted him in the election of 1768 was John Richardson, a Penrith attorney. He was the son-in-law of another attorney, Thomas Whelpdale, and had succeeded him as steward to Portland. He was dismissed in 1763, and in consequence had espoused Lowther's cause. For his part in the election of 1768, see C. R. Hudleston's article in *Transactions of the Cumberland and Westmorland Antiquarian and Archaeological Society*, new series, XLIX (1950), 166–79.

This was reflected, too, in the care which was devoted to the drawing up of marriage settlements, a task closely linked with the management of a landed estate, and a further source of profit for lawyers, barristers and attorneys alike. These settlements were commonly documents of great length and intricacy, and in the case of the most complicated of them, the services of a London expert would be needed. It is well known that marriages between people of any standing in the eighteenth century were very frequently matters of interest rather than affection, 'just like other common bargains or sales, by the mere consideration of interest or gain, without any love or esteem, of birth or of beauty itself, which ought to be among the ingredients of happy compositions of this kind, and of all generous productions'.[1] Temple considered that this was a recent development—it is certainly an arrangement of this kind that Hogarth depicted in *Mariage à la Mode*; and Professor Habakkuk, while he disagrees with Temple about the novelty of the custom, considers that marriages of this kind were more frequent in the early eighteenth century than they had been at earlier periods.[2] And whatever may have been the harmful results to society which Temple complained of, arrangements of this sort were a source of immediate gain to the legal profession. There may have been some loss of profit to them since will and settlement disputes were perhaps fewer in the case of property so closely tied up in strict settlements, but the making of the settlement in the first place, and the supervision of trusts which was subsequently needed, left much scope for the lawyers. And it may be suspected that the life tenant of an entailed estate was more in need of legal advice about what he could do than was an owner outright. The more closely an estate was bound up the greater was the challenge it offered to legal ingenuity to get round the entail.[3] Most collections of attorneys' papers appear to contain draft settlements of this kind, and even

---

[1] Sir William Temple, *An Essay on Popular Discontents* (1701), p. 77. Cf. Fielding's *Love in Several Masques* (1727), ii, vi, where Sir Positive Trap described the preliminaries of his own marriage: 'why I never saw my lady there 'till an hour before our marriage. I made my addresses to her father, her father to his lawyer, the lawyer to my estate, which being found a Smithfield equivalent —the bargain was struck.'

[2] H. J. Habakkuk, 'Marriage Settlements in the Eighteenth Century', *Transactions of the Royal Historical Society*, 4th series, xxxii, 24.

[3] It was certainly a popular belief with the critics of the profession that many estates were eaten up by lawyers' fees, and the lawyers in *Bleak House* had no cause to complain of lack of business from wills and settlements.

when they concerned persons of no great social standing the law charges were likely to be substantial.[1]

A further position of trust and responsibility which an attorney was commonly called upon to fill was that of trustee of an estate during the minority of the owner, or during his absence. John Ambrose, who was the founder of a family firm in Essex, was appointed steward and receiver of the rents of the estate of Richard Rigby after his death, and during the minority of his heir, his nephew, Francis Hale Rigby.[2] He held this position until 1802, when he was succeeded by his son. The administration appears to have been completely in Ambrose's hands, and the confidence placed in him was justified, and was rewarded by substantial fees and by the respect of the owner.[3] He was responsible for making all payments—thatching, painting, plumbing, bricks, coals, poor rates, and land tax. He had to deal with all the bequests made by Rigby, and to receive the rents and profits of the estates. For the year ending Michaelmas, 1798, for example, the receipts from the estates in Essex, Suffolk, Warwickshire and Bedfordshire amounted to £4573. 4s. 9d. and the disbursements to £638. 3s. 0½d., including a salary of £150 paid to Ambrose himself. Richard Rigby had died in 1788, leaving it was said almost half a million pounds of public money to be refunded, so great care and economy were needed in the administration of the estates left in Ambrose's hands. Some had to be sold, and Mistley Hall had to be let. All this was negotiated by Ambrose in the last years of the century, and in the years following, when young Rigby was away from home in the army, his efforts had to be continued.

---

[1] There is an account of the negotiation of a marriage settlement in 'Sir Walter Calverley's Memorandum Book', *Surtees Society*, vol. 77 (1886), 113–15.

[2] Richard Rigby was paymaster to the Forces 1768–84. Ambrose was admitted an attorney in 1769, and practised at Manningtree. He died in 1805, and was followed by his son, admitted attorney 1795, and his grandson, born in 1798. The papers of his firm are deposited in the Essex Record Office (E.R.O. D/DHW).

[3] Ambrose II was jealous about his reputation, and indignant when a defaulting tenant insinuated that he was only turning him out to stir up a law suit. He wrote: 'I do assure you so far from *preferring a few law suits* there's nothing upon this earth I would use more endeavours to avoid; for I would not have my soul rent therewith in the manner some people are, or I think must be, upon any account whatever' (E.R.O. D/DHW C 2, Ambrose to Francis Smythies, 20 November 1792). A Francis Smythies was town clerk of Colchester at the end of the century. If it was he who was giving Ambrose this trouble, it may have been that there was some professional rivalry behind this correspondence.

All these were responsible positions, and the men occupying them or desiring them were very anxious to cultivate a reputation for professional ability and integrity. It is small wonder that they and their kind were anxious to make it plain that they did not share the attributes which society had been only too ready to bestow on the profession by its largely undiscriminating abuse. They were also valuable positions, both from the actual salaries and legal fees which they carried, but also because they placed their holders in an important position in local society as the intermediary between the landowner, on whom social obligations still lay heavily, and his tenants. Some glory was reflected from their employers on them, and when their masters were absent in London or in the army, they had to fill their places at the head of the local hierarchy.

For these reasons such positions were anxiously sought after, and for the same reasons landowners were scrupulous in choosing their agents. Some of the factors taken into consideration appear from the correspondence about filling the post of agent to Earl Fitzwilliam at Malton, made vacant by the death of James Preston in 1787. On 15 June 1787 Daniel Lambert wrote to Fitzwilliam soliciting the place and giving such an account of himself as he thought would recommend him.

I am an attorney and have resided many years in this borough, and I flatter myself with credit and honour. I am now employed to receive near £10,000 per annum rents for the gentlemen of the neighbourhood, and being upon the spot, I could transact your lordship's affairs here as well as any man.... I am well aware of the importance of this charge and that your lordship's prudence will suggest the necessity of inquiring into the character and situation of any person soliciting the honour of so respectable an employment under your lordship.

He then gave a list of the people who would answer for him, and mentioned that he had lived nearly twenty years in York and was known to most persons of account there.

If your lordship should think proper to direct an enquiry concerning me, I have the greatest confidence that your lordship will find that I am not unworthy of the trust, but on the other hand, if industry, experience, responsibility, and the well-earned character of an honest man may be recommendations to your lordship, my mind tells me that you will find me to be the very man your lordship ought always to have resident here. Mr Burke and Mr Weddell (our worthy members) both personally know me. I will only add my Lord that the honour I solicit to serve your lordship (in case you should approve of me) will crown the utmost of my ambition.... I can give any security for fidelity and to account that your lordship may require.[1]

Several letters were written to Fitzwilliam in support of Lambert, including one from Burke. On 17 June he wrote that he did not know what the position required, but that he would pass on such applications as he received. In what he said he was naturally enough concerned primarily for the political importance of Malton.

Mr Lambert is a man of character and resides in the town of Malton, and I believe is much esteemed there. I cannot think any place circumstanced like Malton can be totally out of danger, at a time when no money will be spared and when no principle or even foresight of possible inconvenience stand in the way of receiving it. Your lordship will therefore trust your concerns with him who with an attention to your estates is best in a situation from his residence and connections as well as his general activity and influence, to prevent the entrance of competition into the only place which you can properly call your own. I believe application will be made to you on the part of very respectable persons in York. But as security is better than hope anything that will remotely shake Malton or risk it in the smallest degree ill be will-compensated by any friends made for York or the county.

Several other persons applied for the position, and Fitzwilliam insisted on having someone who was resident in the borough. Among these applicants was one Hastings who had been Preston's clerk, and had been disappointed of the office of deputy clerk of the peace which Preston had promised him. Having no other appointment, he claimed that he would be able to devote the whole of his attention to Fitzwilliam's affairs.[2]

His application was supported by several of the tenants, and he was eventually appointed, and held the office until 1818. Lambert, however, seems to have remained in favour, for in 1794-6, when there was a dispute among local attorneys as to who should solicit the Malton enclosure bill in parliament, Fitzwilliam considered that Lambert had claims which could not be overlooked.[3]

[1] These letters are contained in W.W.M. F 78 a.
[2] From other letters it appears that Hastings had at one time been butler to Josiah Maynard, but he must have been admitted as an attorney subsequently if he envisaged acting as deputy clerk of the peace.
[3] By 1807 Lambert had gone over, and was supporting Fitzwilliam's opponents in the election of that year. (W.W.M. F 72). See p. 100 below.

Calculations of political interest such as Burke had made were natural in appointing an estate agent, and the majority of the struggles between landowners were fought, like that between Lowther and Portland, for political reasons. The activities of attorneys as estate agents cannot be separated from those as political agents, because of the close connection between the right to vote and the possession or tenure of landed property, in addition to the importance of the landed gentry in the structure of society in the eighteenth century. Thus Richard Fenton and Charles Bowns were very closely involved in the political activities of Rockingham and Fitzwilliam. Once again, in the absence of a fully articulated professional system, it was to the attorneys that men turned to perform these duties; and, indeed, the professional political agent may perhaps be said to have sprung from among the attorneys themselves, rather than to have replaced them.

The management of the local political interests of men as influential as Rockingham and Fitzwilliam was a serious responsibility, and at election times, all other work had to be pushed into the background. Contested elections were rare, but it was not always clear until the last moment whether there would be a contest or not, and the election agents had to be prepared for anything.[1]

The task of the main agent was to organise the election campaign, and to marshall the forces of voters and canvassers in the localities. Richard Fenton appears to have organised the by-election at York for William Thornton in 1758, and his account with Rockingham on this occasion was written with extreme care in a large leather-bound volume.[2] Here are recorded the sums which were subscribed by thirty-six persons to Thornton's election expenses, which came to £2978. 10s. 0d. The amounts paid for 'Treats, entertainments, and other incidental charges' are also meticulously

[1] On Yorkshire politics in the eighteenth century, see the following articles by C. E. Collyer in *Proceedings of the Leeds Philosophical and Literary Society (Literary and Historical Section)*: 'The Yorkshire Election of 1734', VII, i (July 1952), 53–82; 'The Yorkshire Election of 1741', VII, ii (October, 1953), 137–52; 'The Rockingham Connection and Country Opinion in the Early Years of George III', VII, iv (December, 1955), 251–75; and in *Thoresby Society Miscellany*, XLI, iv, no. 99 (1951, published 1954), 'The Rockinghams and Yorkshire Politics, 1742–61'. There is some correspondence relating to the county election of 1734 from George Phipps, attorney and agent to the Earl of Strafford, and predecessor of Fenton and Bowns, in *Wentworth Papers, 1705–1739*, ed. J. J. Cartwright (London, 1883). Fenton is mentioned several times in this correspondence.

[2] W.W.M. E 219.

noted down: they amounted to £8388. 8s. 7½d. The sums paid to various helpers in the election campaign are recorded; five guineas to Mr Joliffe to distribute among the mob; payments for freedoms; payments to messengers and chairmen; sums of 10 guineas each paid to three champions; 1 guinea to Henry Varlow, 'a hero'; £2. 4s. 0d. to Christopher Warton for the interest on £300 borrowed for the election. Fenton's own travelling expenses are noted, as are the sums paid by him when canvassing votes, and to poll clerks and attendants. The first statement of the election put the cost at £11,408. 14s. 7½d., and the subscriptions came to £10,923. 10s. 0d., leaving £485. 4s. 7½d. due from Rockingham to Fenton. Later in 1759 and in 1760 further claims were made for expenses from others who had assisted, and by the end of July 1760, Fenton still wanted £547. 13s. 9½d. from Rockingham.

Fenton was also concerned in the preparations for the county election of 1784 when a contest seemed likely up to the last moment.[1] There are many letters from those who acted as agents on that occasion, putting forward claims for payment, and there is a list showing the amounts claimed by each agent and the amount which the committee finally decided to give him. Many of the agents were local attorneys—Daniel Lambert, Jonathan Danser, Fenton himself—but they were assisted by many others, chosen as were the attorneys for their local influence and connections. When the polling had begun, the attorneys among them could be more profitably employed at the booths, scrutinising the voters' franchises, supporting those on their own side, and objecting to those on the other.

There are records of the sums paid to the clerks of the peace of the Ridings, of £25 paid to the London agent, Joseph Allen, of sums paid to four 'advocates'—Fenton himself was paid £77 in this capacity—of fees to the undersheriff, counsel, and clerks. Robert Lakeland, an attorney of York, complained that his claim for expenses had been reduced from £10. 7s. to 8 guineas. 'The allowance of a guinea and a half per day', he wrote, 'may be reasonable to such attorneys as canvassed only a small circle in their own neighbourhoods and could of course sleep at home and attend to

---

[1] 'Foljambe and Weddell were nominated, but declined to go to a poll the evening before the election' (W. W. Bean, *Parliamentary Representation of the Six Northern Counties* (Hull, 1890), p. 657). Wilberforce and Duncombe were returned (W.W.M. E 21).

other business; but I beg leave to represent to you that with respect
to myself it is inadequate both as to time and expenses; as I was
under the necessity of being from home both day and night, totally
neglecting my professional business which would have paid me
better, and at an expense which (including horsehire) half a guinea
a day will not reimburse.' Thomas Plummer, another York attorney,
who was also dissatisfied, declared that parsimony of this kind
would 'recoil upon the cause itself', discouraging men from assisting
in the future, and he went on to maintain that 'the fees of electioneering agents, etc., should not bear an exact ratio to the service
or other mode of charging in private business for the employ ceases
with the election but their zeal and activity may be long remembered
by and give offence to some of their friends who are inimical to the
cause and on the other hand any particular attendance in private
practice must have a previous or a consequential employ if not both
and probably secure a client for ever'.[1] He claimed that he had
wholly neglected his own practice for over a month, and had broken
an agreement with the city candidates in order to attend more
closely to the concerns of those for the county. He thought 60
guineas too small a reward to him in his 'peculiar position as a
confidential agent'. Plummer occupied an important position in
the running of this election—many of the requests for payment
from other agents are addressed to him—and he was obviously
concerned that the committee did not put the same value on his
services that he did himself, and hinted that they were taking
advantage of his known adherence to 'the cause'.

Another correspondent wrote from London: 'I could have
wished that 50 guineas instead of 30 guineas had been given to Mr
Law, this being a lawyers' harvest, they estimate wages pretty high,
but I have seen him and he expressed to me no dissatisfaction at his

---

[1] Some attorneys felt they could not risk losing clients by being on the
wrong side in an election, even to oblige a man like the Earl of Strafford. William
Ingram, a Wakefield attorney whose vote and interest Strafford had sought in
1733 replied explaining that they were already promised to Sir Rowland Winn,
and which, he added, 'I could not tell how to deny him, since hee is one of my
best clyents and I am under great obligations to that family. Besides if I had
denied him I should have disobliged several of his friends who are my best
clyents, and truly, my Lord, I cannott live as I do without businesse, wherefore
I hope your lordship will pardon me if I cannott oblige your lordship herein;
and I hope Sir Rowland will bee for the interest of the country, and never
prevailed on to accept of a pension or place...' (Ingram to Strafford, 26 October
1733; *Wentworth Papers*, p. 485; quoted Collyer, 'The Yorkshire Election of
1734', *loc. cit.* pp. 60–1).

fee.' Thomas Barstow, an attorney of Leeds, thought that agents should be paid 2 guineas a day, 'myself and two clerks being solely taken up with that business all the time and a great part of the time two of my own horses and frequently a servant employed therein.... The other part of the bill', he explained, 'is for money paid for distributing and putting up papers, cards, and circular letters, searches into the Land Tax duplicates, copies and abstracts and remarks thereon, amounting the whole to £3. 7s. 2d.'[1]

Richard Fenton's successor as agent was Charles Bowns, who was employed in the election of 1807.[2] By then agents' fees had been increased.[3] Mr Hall, a solicitor of Barnsley, who was asked to assist as deputy to the sheriff, was told:

> The sheriff's deputies will receive the same compensation per day as the respectable professional men who are engaged on behalf of the candidates in canvassing etc., and we understand this to be at five guineas a day. Should you have been engaged in canvassing for any of the candidates, it will not be urged as an objection to your acting for the sheriff.[4]

Between elections, it was the duty of the local attorney who acted as agent to look after the political interests of his employer. In 1792, on the advice of Charles Bowns, a tenant was evicted from one of Fitzwilliam's farms near Doncaster because he was suspected of belonging to the Constitutional Society at Sheffield.[5] In 1807 William Hastings, the agent at Malton, supplied Fitzwilliam with a list of the tenants who had voted against the family interest, and suggested that they should be evicted. He also reported that among those most active in canvassing for the opposition were four

[1] The 1784 election was disastrous for the 'Whigs'; this same agent wrote to Bowns: 'I am sorry the world is so bewitched; Pray God mend them or make new ones, whichever's the less trouble.'

[2] James Wheat was concerned in this election on Wilberforce's behalf at Sheffield, and was paid £133 (*Wheat Collection*, 1236).

[3] According to Oldfield this was 'the most expensive election contest that ever distinguished the annals of electioneering'. Polling went on for fifteen days, and the candidates were said to have spent nearly half a million pounds (T. H. B. Oldfield, *Representative History* (London, 1816), v, 267). See also W. W. Bean, *op. cit.* 657–9. Professor Gash states that the election cost the Lascelles and Fitzwilliam families over £100,000 each (*Essays Presented to Sir Lewis Namier*, edd. R. Pares and A. J. P. Taylor (London, 1956), p. 280).

[4] W.W.M. E 178/44.

[5] W.W.M. F 71. The tenant was subsequently reinstated. He belonged to the Society for Constitutional Information, not to the Sheffield Society, and even the latter he claimed was more repectable than Fitzwilliam thought.

attorneys, including Daniel Lambert and Edward Leefe, and he suggested that some mark of resentment should be shown them. This was not easy, since both had been employed by Fitzwilliam in the past, and in the recent election, Leefe had been canvassing on behalf of Fitzwilliam's candidate. In the following year, Hastings reported that there was a house for sale in the borough which carried a vote and asked whether he should buy it. He was instructed to do so, but to pay only the real, not the election value of the property, and only if the freeholder whose property adjoined did not want the house.

Matters of this kind were not always arranged as scrupulously as this, though clearly Fitzwilliam felt no great anxiety about his position at Malton. There are many examples of the illegal or barely legal practices adopted by attorneys during elections— arranging fictitious conveyances, splitting burgages, questioning the right of an opponent's supporters to vote, and all the rest. No special blame need be assigned to the attorneys for this. They were expected to do their best for their employers, and in the tangled undergrowth of the electoral system of the eighteenth century there was ample opportunity for legal quibbling and chicanery.

Details of these practices can be gathered from many of the local political histories and from the *Journals of the House of Commons*. Many are given by Oldfield who was himself an attorney and was certainly a reformer, anxious to clear away many of the survivals which others of his profession found so profitable.[1] It will be convenient to take some examples from the borough of Horsham, the scope for attorneys' activities being clearer in the boroughs, and Horsham being one which was hotly contested on several occasions.[2] In the election of 1715 John Linfield, an attorney, was found guilty of illegally procuring votes and was ordered by the House to be taken into the custody of the serjeant at arms on 16 June. On 2 July he petitioned for his release, acknowledging his guilt and claiming 'that it being term time, and an issuable term, if his confinement should be continued it may prove very prejudicial as well to the affairs of his clients as his own'.[3] His friends were able to get a

---

[1] He is said to be an attorney in *D.N.B.* but 'unknown to the Law List'.

[2] There is a very detailed account of election matters there in W. Albery, *The Parliamentary History of Horsham* (London, 1927).

[3] Albery, *op. cit.* p. 68.

majority of the House to vote in his favour, and he was released after paying his fees and apologising to the Speaker.

In 1790 another Horsham attorney received a request from Alexander Williams of Chichester to use his influence with Lady Irwin to procure a 'quiet seat' for a friend.[1] Lady Irwin, however, was not in a position to offer anyone a 'quiet seat'. In 1791 she herself wrote to a neighbour Mrs Bridge: 'As I learn that I am again to be attacked by the Duke of Norfolk, I hope you will have the goodness to assist me by conveying over your property to some friend of yours you can trust and who will vote for my friends when the time comes, and I will order my steward to pay your attorney all the expenses attendant thereon.'[2] Prolonged struggles for political influence like this one between the Duke of Norfolk and Lady Irwin, provided many pickings for attorneys, and as was the case here, were only brought to an end by the sale of the borough, itself likely to be a long business, profitable to lawyers.

The Duke of Norfolk's attorney in this dispute was Thomas Charles Medwin. In 1786 he was appointed steward of the Duke's Court Baron, and in 1787 Norfolk bought out the town clerk and steward of the Court Leet, William White, who was a supporter of Lady Irwin, for £1000, and installed Medwin in his place. Medwin, who already had a considerable practice, was an expert on manorial law and custom, and an appropriate assistant of the Duke's in this strategic position. As steward of the Court Leet he was able to reject the votes of all Norfolk's opponents, and from 1788 the attack on Lady Irwin proceeded. Burgages were bought, faggot votes created, the court and burgess rolls manipulated in the Duke's favour; the burgages were conveyed to Medwin or another agent 'to preserve appearances', and the *Sussex Advertiser* noted that as a result of the determination of the Duke to oppose Lady Irwin, the prices of houses with votes had 'increased near a thousand per cent in their value'.[3] Between 1789 and 1802 the tussle continued, with *quo warranto* proceedings being instituted against faggot voters on both sides. The defeated candidates in the election of 1790 petitioned against the result, alleging that there had been illegal practices on the part of the bailiffs and the returning officer whom Medwin as steward had appointed, and who in their turn

[1] Albery, *op. cit.* p. 247.
[2] *Ibid.* p. 248.
[3] *Sussex Advertiser*, 8 September 1788; quoted *ibid.* p. 130.

had appointed Medwin as their poll clerk. In this capacity, Medwin had refused to accept any votes on Lady Irwin's side.

The uncertainty about electoral proceedings at Horsham was shown by the tactics adopted by both sides in 1806. Medwin, acting on the determination of the House of Commons in 1715, adopted the practice of splitting burgage holdings into as many parts as possible. The other side, acting on the basis of the act of 1696 which held that the right to vote depended on the possession of a whole burgage, adopted the method of piecing split parts together. When the election came on the bailiffs held that the matter was one in which they could use their discretion, whereupon Lady Irwin's agent declared: 'Then it will be my duty to go and get a wheelbarrow full of new conveyances.'[1] Naturally, in these circumstances, the Duke's candidate was again successful. Lady Irwin's agents objected, and the bailiffs, remembering the penalties which had been imposed for a false return in 1790, made a double return and left the issue to be decided by the House of Commons. After the election which followed the fall of the All Talents Ministry, the bailiffs refused to make a double return, declared the Duke's candidates elected, but had their decision reversed in the House. In 1808 the Duke's candidates were again successful at the polls, and were again unseated on the petition, and it was not until he had bought the borough from Lady Irwin's heir for £91,475, that the Duke was successful in getting his candidates into parliament, and keeping them there.

There were as many examples of attorneys acting in these ways as there were attorneys acting as political agents, men like John Butcher, the Duke of Rutland's agent at Cambridge,[2] and John Robinson himself, who began life as an attorney, became Lowther's attorney and agent, and, after many years as Secretary to the Treasury under Lord North, ended his career in charge of the preliminary organisation of the election of 1784.[3] These are examples of the more famous of the political managers and agents, whose successors in the nineteenth century, in a field of electoral management rendered perhaps more fertile by the Reform Act and the

[1] Albery, op. cit. p. 200.

[2] See H.M.C. Rutland MSS. III.

[3] Robinson had been articled to Richard Wordsworth, William's grandfather; he was town clerk, and subsequently mayor, of Appleby. There is a short account of Robinson's career in I. R. Christie, The End of North's Ministry, 1780–82 (London, 1958), pp. 32–3.

Voters' Register, were men like Joseph Parkes in Birmingham and John Coppock.[1] But there was a multitude of lesser men, the local attorneys all over the country, who found in these transactions a 'lawyers' harvest' indeed.

There is another aspect of political life from which the attorneys could profit. This was the business of soliciting private bills in parliament. Because of enclosures, turnpikes, canals, and many other matters of this kind, there was a very large number of such acts in the Commons in the second half of the century, and there was much competition among local attorneys to do this work. This, too, was an employment that was eventually taken over by specialised parliamentary agents, but in the meantime it was done by the country attorneys, often with the help of their London agents, some of whom were coming to specialise in work of this kind.[2]

[1] In 1844 James Heywood wrote to the president of the Anti-Corn Law League: 'In the warfare of the registration the solicitors rise to the rank of Generals, and the policy of the government of the country greatly depends on their talents and energy in the right formation of the constituencies on the register.' I owe this reference to Dr Norman McCord. There are many examples of such men in Trollope's novels; see also Norman Gash, *Politics in the Age of Peel* (Oxford, 1953).

[2] O. C. Williams, *The Clerical Organisation of the House of Commons* (Oxford, 1954), p. 186. For the dispute between the Society of Gentlemen Practisers and the clerks of the House who claimed a monopoly of certain types of parliamentary agency, see p. 26 above.

CHAPTER VIII

ADMINISTRATION AND FINANCE

In their concern with estates and elections, the attorneys were only agents, filling—perhaps exploiting—situations which they had not created. The same was true of their work in the administration of local government. Much of the burden of government was placed on the shoulders of lords lieutenant and the justices of the peace in the counties, and of the varied courts and corporations in the towns and boroughs. It was passed on by them to their assistants and subordinate officers, the clerks of the peace, town clerks, clerks to corporations, stewards of manors and the like. It was these posts that were habitually filled by attorneys, and which provided yet another way in which they could enhance their position and add to their influence in eighteenth-century society.

Local government in the period before 1835 was studied by the Webbs, and from their work some idea can be obtained of the part which attorneys played in it. In the first place they held the office of clerk of the peace, or performed its duties as a deputy for some protégé of the lord lieutenant. In Cumberland, for example, in the last decades of the century, the clerk of the peace was J. B. Garforth, Lord Lonsdale's agent and attorney, and one of his members of parliament. Garforth practised in London, lived in Yorkshire, and spent only part of the recess in Cumberland. The routine business of the office was carried on by another attorney, Joseph Hodgson of Carlisle, who had to report regularly to Garforth about county business, and go up to London whenever occasion demanded.

Hodgson was succeeded by his brother William, who became clerk of the peace, the first of his family to hold an office they were to monopolise until the twentieth century. This seems to have been a common situation. The Webbs noted it, and remarked: 'We find in practice the post of Deputy Clerk of the Peace held, almost as a hereditary possession, by the principal firm of solicitors in the county town, one of the partners of which personally attended the justices' meetings, drafted their formal resolutions, and advised them in matters of law, but left all the work to his clerks. Under these circumstances it was with the utmost difficulty that he or his clerks could be got to perform any official duty out of which they could extract no fee from some person or other. Everything beyond the crowded business of Quarter Sessions, the orders desired by private suitors, and those absolutely required by law tended to be neglected.'[1]

These are the opinions of reformers, judging the eighteenth century by standards appropriate to the twentieth. There may have been a tendency to neglect business which was unlikely to be profitable for that which brought in handsome fees, but these offices were mainly paid by fees. It is perhaps surprising that so many officials of this kind were able to keep up an extensive private practice at the same time as they coped with the growing number of administrative duties, but Hodgson's correspondence at least does not suggest that these duties were always neglected.

It would have been more surprising if they had been, for so long as the lord lieutenant continued to be a friend of the existing government, it seems unlikely that any negligence on the part of the clerk of the peace would long be tolerated. The bonds which held society together in the eighteenth century were different from what they were later to become, and perhaps they meant that a system which would certainly have broken down in 1900, could still function with some success in 1800. This is not to say that the system was completely efficient. It was not, and its deficiencies were beginning to be noticed. But it bore the burdens of wartime administration, in a period when the central government was unusually concerned about what went on in the localities, and was impinging ever more closely upon them.

Of course patriotic zeal may have operated to ensure that the system worked more smoothly than it would have done normally. In December 1795, for example, Garforth wrote to Hodgson:

I was yesterday told that a requisition was intended to be made to the Sheriff to call a county meeting to hear petitions against the two bills for the preservation of his Majesty and to prevent seditious meetings— I hope the sheriff will have prudence enough not to do it, but if otherwise, that the friends of the constitution will not only put a negative thereto but will make a Declaration similar to the Declaration of the Merchants etc., at the County Meeting on Tuesday last at York.[2]

[1] S. and B. Webb, *English Local Government: The Parish and the County* (London, 1906), p. 504. For a succession in office such as that the Webbs complained of, see *Wiltshire Quarter Sessions and Assizes, 1736* (ed. J. P. M. Fowle 1955, Wiltshire Archaeological and Natural History Society, Records Branch, vol. xi).

[2] Hodgson MSS. File A, bdle 3; Garforth to Hodgson, 5 December 1795.

Fear of Napoleon may have caused an unusually large proportion of the people to rally to the support of the government and the constitution, but even in quieter times, those who owed their positions to their avowed friendship to the existing administration would not be over-hasty in putting those positions in jeopardy by neglecting to carry out the wishes of the government.

In the absence of more specific organisations of local government, a great deal of the legislation passed to cope with the conditions at the end of the century had to be put into effect in the localities by the magistrates and county officials. In January 1793 one of the Cumberland justices wrote to Hodgson, asking him to order several volumes of statutes needed to complete the series, and he added: 'as a few years last past has made a wonderful addition to the laws respecting magistrates and the sessions business, I think it will be proper to order the last edition of Burn down with the statutes.'[1]

What all this 'wonderful addition' implied in the case of Joseph Hodgson can be briefly indicated from his correspondence. The Overseers of Rockliffe were fined for not making a return of those who were fit to serve in the forces; the Duke of Portland wrote for the names of the officers of the Militia in order to insert them in the *London Gazette*; the Lord Lieutenant wanted lists from the constables of all men between the ages of 55 and 60, and of wagons, carts, etc.; arrangements had to be made for the release of prisoners on condition of joining the army or navy abroad; meetings of the justices were held to raise men for the navy; there were riots at Brampton to be dealt with; Portland wrote again for a list of all the friendly societies in the county. New acts such as the Hair Powder Act imposed fresh duties on the clerk; men objected to having to find a cavalryman and a horse, and complained that their incomes had been overestimated; James Graham of Netherby was unable to accept the offer to recommend him to the Lord Lieutenant as commander of the Volunteer Troop at Carlisle; Portland wrote again in 1803 about finding men to serve in the navy, and in the same year the proclamation against aliens had to be published throughout the county.

[1] Hodgson MSS. File L, bdle 22; J. C. Satterthwaite to Hodgson, 23 January 1793. The extent of this 'wonderful addition' is shown visually by the increase in the size of Burn's *Justice of the Peace*. The first edition was contained in two volumes: the nineteenth edition, published in 1800, was in four volumes, each of which contained on the average more than 800 pages.

These were some of the duties which were the result of the war. In addition to these, the normal sessions business went on.[1] The county was indicted for not repairing Blennerhasset Bridge, and Hodgson had to go up to London on the matter. Garforth had to be kept informed of all county business, and routine matters about land tax duplicates, sessions precepts, jury lists, had all to be communicated to him. Hodgson kept him informed about politics in Carlisle and the county, and took up the necessary details to London when there was a petition against the election return, as in 1796.

In 1792 the Society against Vice and Immorality sent an account of how the prisoners in Dorset Gaol were employed, and asked Hodgson to distribute copies to the magistrates. In 1794 the Board of Agriculture asked him to circulate a questionnaire about cropping to the more intelligent farmers in the area. The secretary of the Society for Bettering the Condition of the Poor wrote about visitors for cotton and woollen mills. The Lord Chancellor wanted lists of all persons discharged under the insolvent debtors act. There was the regular business with game certificates, ale house recognisances, hair powder certificates, reports from the Grand Jury about the state of the county gaol, and all the day to day matters of appeals, settlements, roads, bridges, and the like.

Added to this was Hodgson's private practice, his agency for the Paisley Bank, and local business for Lord Lonsdale. Towards the end of the century Hodgson was joined in Carlisle by his brother, William, who eventually succeeded to his practice and his offices. As clerks of the peace, some functions were denied them: they could not, for example, practise in the county courts, but they could

---

[1] The following lines from the *Ladies' Magazine* for 15 December 1750 describe the business of a country quarter sessions:

'Three or four Parsons, three or four Squires,
Three or four Lawyers, three or four Lyars,
Three or four Parishes bringing Appeals,
Three or four Hands, three or four Seals,
Three or four Bastards, three or four Whores,
Tag, Rag, and Bobtail, three or four Scores;
Three or four Bulls, three or four Cows,
Three or four Orders, three or four Bows,
Three or four Statutes not understood,
Three or four Paupers praying for Food,
Three or four Roads that never were mended,
Three or four Scolds,—and the Sessions is ended'
(quoted in L. J. Redstone and F. W. Steer, *Local Records, their nature and care* (London, 1953), p. 120).

carry on the business right up to the appearance in court, and then, if necessary, get a partner or another attorney to do the court work. Here again the Webbs take the profession to task. They quote the opinion of James Bland Burges, M.P., who considered that the county court was 'an engine of the most nefarious oppression' leading frequently to the 'necessary ruin' of one or both litigants,[1] and, they continue, 'the profit of rapacious attornies, in collusion with one of their number acting as Undersheriff, aided by venal jurymen serving for the shilling fee. The cases cited appear to support this indictment. But Burges became a permanent civil servant, and dropped the Bill he had contemplated.' The fees of the clerk of the peace were limited by an act of 1755,[2] but the office continued to be sought after, for apart from the fees and the salary, the position brought in much profitable legal business of which the clerk had the first picking.[3]

Since the administration of justice and of local government was so largely left in the hands of amateurs, they had to rely very heavily on the professional advice of lawyers, clerks of the peace and under-sheriffs. And since the justices were not uniformly upright and public-spirited, there were many complaints both of their negligence and of the deceits which they practised. As one critic pointed out, 'the ignorant magistrate...not infrequently degenerated into a passive and mischievous instrument in the hands of a rapacious attorney or some other discarded underling of the law'.[4] In the case of the trading justice, intent only on his own profit, this might develop into a formidable conspiracy between justice and clerk. Certainly this was the opinion of many observers.[5] But if there were

[1] J. B. Burges, *An Address to the Country Gentlemen of England and Wales* (1789), quoted Webb, *op. cit.* p. 290, n. 2.

[2] 26 Geo. II, c. 14.

[3] Struggles between attorneys for offices of this sort were not new in the eighteenth century. Cf. J. J. Bagley, 'Kenyon *v.* Rigby: The Struggle for the Clerkship of the Peace in Lancashire in the seventeenth century', *Transactions of the Historic Society of Lancashire and Cheshire*, vol. 106, 1954 (Liverpool, 1955).

[4] Thomas Gisborne, *Enquiry into the Duties of Man* (1794), p. 288; quoted Webb, *op. cit.* p. 349, n. 5.

[5] There are many instances in the works of Fielding; see, for example, *The Justice Caught in his own Trap* (1730). The trading justice is described in a farce quoted by the Webbs as 'An old fellow, qualified with ill nature and avarice, by the help of a little money and some interest, gets into the commission. He entertains a clerk, some broken attorney (for they make the best clerks)...and for their honesty they are generally on a par. The fees are divided into four parts; the justice has two, the clerk one, and the favourite constable the other' (*The Perjuror* (1717); quoted *ibid.* p. 329, n. 1).

attorneys ready and willing to indicate to their employers ways of getting round the law, there were others who, again inspired by motives of gain, might keep a very close watch on the activities of those whom they disliked.[1]

The increasing importance of special sessions and the growth of petty sessions which the Webbs noted meant that some local attorney would be recognised as the clerk for all these occasions by all the neighbouring justices, and his office would become the clearing house for all problems to be heard by them. 'The justices' clerk, attending or residing at the private house of the country gentleman, in this way gradually ceased to exist. When any person importuned a magistrate at his private house on any business requiring a warrant or other instrument, he was generally referred to the office of the attorney in the market town, who took the fee, and prepared the necessary document to be signed by the magistrate when he rode in to attend the divisional sessions.'[2] In this way, the office of the clerk became almost the headquarters of local and county administration, and what were in fact official papers have thus been submitted to the fate of private property, so that records of these activities survive in many cases only by chance.

A similar situation existed in the boroughs, in which the attorneys perhaps stood out more clearly as a sort of urban élite.[3] Their political activities have already been described, but there were other sources of profit, legitimate and otherwise, many of which were revealed by the municipal corporations commissioners in 1833. Their standards in dealing with corporation property were no higher than those of the corporations themselves, and John Butcher, who profited greatly from his post as attorney to the corporation of

---

[1] 'When a Justice of the Peace, inspired with a true public spirit, meets with inferior officers of courage and intrepidity, and sets about a reformation of the unlicensed houses, he finds himself surrounded with numbers of pettifogging attorneys and solicitors, who watch his steps, and if there happens the least flaw in the method of drawing up and managing the proceedings, he finds himself obliged to attend a certiorari in the King's Bench' (*Distilled Liquors the Bane of the Nation* (1736); quoted Webb, *op. cit.* p. 336).   [2] Webb, *op. cit.* p. 415.

[3] The importance of attorneys' families in one borough is very clearly indicated in H. S. Toy, *The History of Helston* (Oxford, 1936). Shelburne thought that the benefits which owners could derive from boroughs were exaggerated. The demands on them for subscriptions, etc., were heavy: 'add to this livings, favours of all sorts from government, and stewardships, if there is an intriguing attorney in the town, who under the name of your agent will deprive you of all manner of free agency upon your own property, and sometimes of the property itself, if it is a small one' (quoted Fitzmaurice, *Life of Shelburne* (2nd ed. London, 1912), II, 357).

Cambridge, cannot have been unique.[1] More legitimate were the profits they gained from holding such offices as town clerk, as well as various others in the borough courts. At Oxford there were three places in the city government which were habitually filled by attorneys, those of town clerk, city solicitor, and coroner, in descending order of importance, and which seem frequently to have been held in succession.[2] The fees obtained from suitors in the city courts seem generally to have been declining and at both Oxford and Cambridge there were complaints that the courts were being neglected by the more respectable attorneys in the town.

There were many other capacities of a semi-official nature in which attorneys could act. They played an important part on all the various committees which were an increasingly common feature of urban life. They were often collectors of the stamp duties which were charged on apprenticeship indentures.[3] Occasionally they appear in the lists of those who administered the land tax, although there was a certain prejudice against employing them in this—as in other capacities—lest, getting too close a knowledge of other people's affairs, they should be tempted to 'set them by the ears'.[4] They were, however, usually clerks to the commissioners in the localities. Occasionally also they were receivers of the income tax, such as Christopher Pemberton, receiver-general for Cambridgeshire. He had succeeded his father as receiver-general of the assessed taxes, was clerk of the peace for the county, and colonel of the Cambridgeshire Militia.[5] Attorneys almost always acted as clerks to the boards of general commissioners of the income tax.[6]

[1] Cf. *Digested Report of the Evidence taken before the Corporation Commissioners at Cambridge* (1833), p. 44. See also the articles by Helen Cam, 'Quo Warranto Proceedings at Cambridge, 1780–90', *Cambridge Historical Journal*, VIII (1946); 'John Mortlock III', *Cambridge Antiquarian Society Proceedings*, XL (1944).

[2] Cf. *Oxford Council Acts, 1701–52*, ed. M. G. Hobson (Oxford, 1954), *passim*; and the account of the town clerkships of the Heyricks, father and son, and of William Burbidge, in Leicester, in A. T. Patterson, *Radical Leicester* (Leicester, 1954). See also R. W. Greaves, *The Corporation of Leicester* (Oxford, 1939).

[3] *Surrey Record Society*, XXVIII (1924), 'Surrey Apprenticeships', Introduction, p. xxiv.

[4] W. R. Ward, *The English Land Tax in the Eighteenth Century* (Oxford, 1953), pp. 88 and 159. By 22 Geo. II, c. 2, no attorney was to act as a commissioner for the land tax unless he possessed property to the value of £100 per annum.

[5] A. Hope-Jones, *Income Tax in the Napoleonic Wars* (Cambridge, 1939), pp. 51–2. On a number of occasions Pemberton was also clerk to enclosure commissioners in the county. (L. S. Pressnell *Country Banking in the Industrial Revolution*, p. 353, n. 1; see also *ibid.* pp. 61–2).

[6] Hope-Jones, *op. cit.* p. 63.

There were many other semi-official positions commonly filled by attorneys. The great number of enclosure acts,[1] the turnpike trusts, the companies of canal builders, and of industrial enterprises of all kinds—all these bodies had greater or lesser amounts of secretarial and legal work to be done, and in most cases the attorneys were the only persons available with the necessary qualifications.[2] Acting as clerk to one of these bodies, the attorney would only be given a nominal salary, but he was given a monopoly of the legal work to be done, and in the case of an enclosure act, for example, this might be a great deal. These were considered desirable jobs, and there was much competition for them. In the case of clerkships to guilds, schools, charities, and the like, the position was often filled by successive members of the same firm, or it was taken over with the practice when it changed hands, but in such matters as enclosures there was often much dispute among attorneys representing the different landowners concerned about soliciting the necessary bill in parliament.[3]

Once again, in the case of country banking and in financial transactions of many kinds, the attorneys in the eighteenth century are found filling the places which were later to be occupied by men exclusively concerned with these matters. They were in an

[1] Attorneys formed a good proportion of enclosure commissioners; cf. W. E. Tate, 'Oxford Enclosure Commissioners, 1737–1856', *Journal of Modern History*, XXIII (1951), p. 145. Between 1760 and 1800 1479 enclosure acts were passed; cf. W. G. Hoskins, *The Making of the English Landscape* (London, 1955), p. 143. Such acts were a source of much profit to lawyers, and they naturally opposed the passing of a general enclosure act. Lord Ernle, *English Farming Past and Present*, 4th ed. (London, 1927), p. 251.

[2] In only one year, 33 Geo. III, some 114 local acts were passed, principally concerned with roads, canals, and enclosures (*Chronological Table of the Statutes*, 1955).

[3] In 1805 the Registraryship of the Bedford Level fell vacant, and the post was disputed between Edward Christian, Downing Professor, and William Saffery, an attorney of Downham, in Norfolk. Each of them claimed the majority of the votes, but Christian took possession of the Fen Office in the Temple, where the records were kept, and barricaded the doors and windows. Saffery, however, got into the office in the absence of the clerks, and when Christian returned he was refused admission. On the following day Christian asked permission to take away some private papers from the office. This was granted, but Saffery's clerks, suspecting a trick, opened the door cautiously, saw three men behind Christian, closed the door again hurriedly so that Christian was only able to get his hat inside. Saffery refused to return the hat, and kept it as a trophy. Christian claimed that the chief justice of King's Bench held him to be in the right, but when he applied to court, judgment was given in Saffery's favour (Henry Gunning, *Reminiscences of Cambridge* (2nd ed. 1855), I, 194–5). I owe this reference to Mr John Saltmarsh.

advantageous position for undertaking work of this kind. As the confidential advisers to men of property it was part of their business as attorneys to be acquainted with the financial world. They were in contact with those who either had money to lend, or who wanted to borrow, and in many normal occasions of their practice as attorneys—in connection with marriage settlements, the making of wills—they were liable to have money left with them to dispose of, or to be asked to find those willing to lend and to take up mortgages. With their unrivalled professional knowledge of local society, the attorneys were the most obvious men to resort to for help in matters of this kind. Some of these functions were to remain characteristic concerns of the profession, but by the end of the eighteenth century, the development of a more intricate and complete banking system meant that much of this work was performed by others who were not attorneys.

For these reasons, attorneys are found to be one of the main groups of those involved in the foundation of country banks. Along with industrialists and those responsible for the collection of taxes and duties of all kinds, they were most suitably situated to assist in this development and specialisation. Because of their convenient situations and their wide professional connections, they were also employed as agents by banks which were already established. But above all else, they appear to have filled an extremely important place in the financial life of the country in the business of arranging loans and mortgages. This is an aspect of the business of the attorney in the eighteenth century which is confirmed by all the professional papers which have been examined.

The part played by attorneys in founding country banks has recently been shown by Dr Pressnell, and will not be dealt with here.[1] But the activities of Joseph Hodgson as agent to the Paisley Bank in Carlisle may be described in some detail, for he was a salaried agent only, not a partner in the bank. It is not clear when his connection with the Paisley Bank began, but by December 1790, he was sufficiently well established to be consulted, rather in the capacity of the head agent of the bank in the area, about the character of a man seeking the post as agent in Penrith. His function was to circulate the notes of the bank as widely as possible. The bills bought by him were sent to the London agents of the Paisley Bank, Messrs Smith, Payne and Smith; an account of these was

[1] L. S. Pressnell, *Country Banking in the Industrial Revolution*, pp. 36–44.

sent to Paisley, and the sums placed to Hodgson's credit there. The usual method of sending the notes to Carlisle was by the carriers' cart which travelled between Carlisle and Glasgow, a method not without its hazards from weather and from the rivalries between the two firms of carriers which operated on that route. In winter months when the carts could not get through, notes were remitted by the post, but as only £150 could be sent under one frank, this was not a satisfactory method.

Hodgson's salary was paid every six months. In 1792 he was paid £100 together with travelling and other incidental expenses, and in the following year his salary was raised to £105. Naturally the bank was anxious that its agents should not use the company's money for their own purposes. In 1792 Hodgson was asked about the activities of the agent at Penrith, which had aroused the suspicion of Hog, the manager of the bank with whom Hodgson corresponded. In 1794 doubts were apparently felt about Hodgson himself: certainly Hodgson had the impression that the bank suspected him of dishonest dealings. On 13 April 1794 Hog wrote to assure him that there was no ground for suspecting him, and told him: 'I know full well that you are above such a thing.' The following day Hog wrote at greater length to explain the letter which had caused Hodgson this uneasiness, but he added:

Allow me to add that I did think some of your customers were making forced transactions to support their credit which is a losing game to us and dangerous to you, and I still think the way some of the notes returned had that appearance.... I thank you for the communications as to your private fortune which were quite unnecessary to mention— it is indeed very handsome and much may it increase.... I am obliged to you for the benefit you mention we have derived from your own money but we had no expectation of such a thing, nor wished for it.[1]

These suspicions seem not to have been entirely allayed, for in October Hodgson wrote again on this point, and claimed,

I can with confidence assert that no agent ever made it his study more to advance the interests of his employers than I have done in regard to the agency I have transacted for you which I am convinced every banker in Carlisle well knows, and as to money I can only inform you I have upwards of two months had from seven to £900 by me belonging to my clients and which I was liable to be asked for at a moment's notice. Therefore I made no use whatever, except permitting you to have the interest of it.

[1] Hog to Hodgson, 14 April 1794; Hodgson MSS. File C, bdle 7.

8   R

As to the mode of issuing your notes it has not in the least degree altered except for the better at Carlisle—I have always since I began given your notes to persons going to buy cattle in Scotland with which no fault was found till lately and how the circulation is altered in that respect I cannot say, tho' I can say it is the worst we have....As to your suggestion of paying value for part of the notes issued here I cannot say how I can answer that further than my opinion that it is very improbable: to be sure a case may arise of that kind, but I hope it is seldom....When I give your notes for English those I receive I lay by me till the Monday or Tuesday following whatever day I may receive them....As to my receiving any emolument either directly or indirectly from your money I can assure you no such thing exists. I am not like a person in trade for it seldom happens I lay out more than £10 at a time and that very seldom—indeed my income is and has been such for years back that I might have lived, had I thought proper, in a very different style. My office of clerk of the peace alone produces more than £200 exclusive of my professional practice....You may therefore easily form an idea of my situation but if you still have any idea of my using your money I hope you will have the candour to say so at once, and I will as soon as possible settle all accounts between us. The idea of being suspected I hate— when I first saw your letters I made up the balance of cash in my hands.[1]

Here the letter breaks off, but the connection appears to have continued for some time, and was kept up by William Hodgson when he succeeded to his brother's practice.

The Paisley Bank and the Paisley Union Bank were rivals, and both had agents in Carlisle. Each was concerned that the other's agent should be prevented from poaching on what they considered to be their special preserves, though they were not above encouraging their agents to do this if it could be done with impunity. These activities caused some bitterness at Paisley, but so long as each found them profitable, they were not likely to stop.[2]

The bank kept a very close watch on Hodgson's activities, even to the extent of pointing out a discrepancy of eightpence. From time to time Hog wrote long and intricate letters advising him on the method of circulation to adopt, and on the course he was to adopt at critical times such as that of the crisis in 1793. The bank partners were not entirely satisfied with the way Hodgson's notes circulated, as has been shown, but he seems to have been held in some esteem. He was often asked for his advice about extending

[1] Hodgson to Hog, 10 October 1794; Hodgson MSS. Paisley Letter Book.
[2] Cf. the letters from Hog of 24 March and 18 May 1792; Hodgson MSS. File C, bdle 7.

the business of the bank by appointing agents in other towns in the border counties, a matter in which his professional connections were of some help. The bank was prepared to allow him to undertake all aspects of banking business, provided that he fitted up an office solely for this purpose, and they sent a clerk from Paisley to help him with this. Like all eighteenth-century business correspondence, this one contains references to many other matters. Hodgson supplied Hog with salmon, and on one occasion sent him a greyhound. Hog in his turn suggested that there might be money to be made in exporting coals from Cumberland to Dublin in 1792, and advised Hodgson about the possibility of setting up a cotton manufactory in 1793.

Most attorneys had no such direct connection with the banking world, but all of them seem to have played an important part in transacting financial business. The negotiation of loans was a major part of their business, and in most cases the money they dealt with was that of their clients, but occasionally they put out their own. William Adams, a Sheffield attorney at the beginning of the century, seems to have lent his own money to clients, in sums of £60 and £100, and also in sums of £2 or £3. Most of the money he handled, however, belonged to others.[1]

Samuel Dawson, another Sheffield attorney, had a more extensive business of this kind. In his case the sums involved were much larger. John Bright wrote in April 1747 for a further loan of £1000.[2] Another client, Thomas Hinckesman, wrote in August 1754 thanking Dawson for his offer to put out £500 for his mother.[3] In 1765 Dawson was asked to procure £2000 for William Howley on the security of land worth £3000.

I have it in my power to make the security better, perhaps as good again, but I hope there is no need of it. The gentleman need not fear the sum increasing by an accumulation of interest, as I will sooner lose my head than forfeit the Equity of Redemption. Of my lands I may

[1] Diary and Account Book of William Adams, MS. Sheffield City Libraries. Joseph Hunter, *Hallamshire* (ed. Alfred Gatty, London, 1869), p. 432 n. 1, quotes the following lines about Adams by Henry Parke, curate of Wentworth:

'Adams the wealthy, good, and mild,
He builds his house and tills his field;
But amongst all attornies he
A miracle is sure to be
Who follows law with honesty.'
[2] T[ibbitts] C[ollection], 522/16, 30 April 1747.
[3] T.C. 522/99, 19 August 1754.

perhaps sell some for which reason I shall not engage them. Before the matter goes much further, I must beg to know who the lender is. I should not care to come into the hands of a money scrivener that lets out his own money in others' names, and twice a year renews the securities. . . .[1]

The lender was not a money scrivener, but a Lieutenant-Colonel of the Queen's Dragoons of Mansfield, 'of as good a temper and as much integrity as any gentlemen in the country; he is now retired and out of the army, and proposes to live upon the income of what he has, and if his interests be duly paid will have no thought of calling in his money. . . .'[2]

This loan was negotiated by Dawson through Charles Bellamy of Mansfield. Dawson seems to have been widely known as an agent in these matters, and in December 1768, another attorney, Jonathan Dawson, wrote to him: 'I have at present 5 or £600, shall have £900 or £1000 in a month or thereabouts. Also £2000 the 1st May and £2000 the 12th May next but would wish to have the two latter sums go in three securities of £1000, £1000, and £2000 or thereabouts. If these or any of them suit or are likely to suit, I shall be glad to hear from you and to divide the profits as usual. Also several sums of £100 and £200 at present.'[3] Dawson was still conducting business with this correspondent in 1772, when he told him: 'Within a fortnight past I have lent £1000 at £4–10 and £2500 at £4–5 on as good security as is in Yorkshire, and it is with difficulty now to be procured at £4–10 which is the interest expected for this money.'[4]

Dawson was in business at least until 1776.[5] He had an extensive practice. He had been articled to John Battie whose daughter he had married. Some indication of one side of his business, the problems it involved, and the kind of person it meant dealing with, is given in this correspondence. In this, as in other branches of the attorney's work, it is very clear that the slightest suspicion of improper behaviour would have a disastrous effect on a man's practice. When so much depended on a reputation for honest dealing and a respectable connection, the anxiety of the attorneys to be thought respectable is very understandable, as also is their indignation at the undiscriminating abuse to which they were sometimes subjected.

---

[1] T.C. 522/246, 27 September 1765.   [2] T.C. 522/247, 4 October 1765.
[3] T.C. 522/270, 7 December 1768.   [4] T.C. 522/319, 13 July 1772.
[5] He died in 1777.

Certainly the position had its temptations. Benjamin Rogers noted in his diary on 26 June 1733,

I heard a month or more ago that Mr Thomas Binkley, attorney at law of Eynsbury, was gone off 4 or £5000 in debt. He was a man of good credit in his profession, by which means he had the putting out a great deal of other people's money, and it is said he has carried with him most if not all of the above mentioned sum and I now hear he is gone beyond the sea. *Cave cui credas.*[1]

Many of the critics of the profession noted less respectable financial dealings among attorneys than those of Samuel Dawson. Robert Holloway's strictures are highly coloured, but they are perhaps merely exaggerated statements of real practices. He censured the custom

where attorneys make a trade of discounting small bills of ten or twenty pounds, that do not hold out a probability of prompt payment, for a bill upon the house of Child or Drummond *would not* answer their purpose; four times out of five the bill is not paid when due, which *does* answer their purpose. The next morning process is sued out, and £15 or £16 costs in proportion to the number of endorsers, either real or fictitious, is added to the debt of a less sum: this lays the foundation of judgments upon judgments, and a vast accumulation of costs, the dreadful proceedings we reprobate. And we know several instances where an attorney has contrived to make £100 cost upon a debt of £10 within twelve months.

Let any man read the daily papers, and notice the great number of advertisements offering sums of money upon notes, bills, or other securities of respectable tradesmen; who are these reptilized sprigs of Croesus? the diabolical jackals of more diabolical attorneys.[2]

He adds, 'We know of an attorney who, in 18 months sued out ninety tailable actions, all grounded upon small bills, that came into his hands from similar means; this is what they call made business, and, to say the truth, much is made of it.'[3] Financial transactions of this sort were clearly not beneficial to the community, and there was another which Holloway also censured, which was that he ascribed to Mr Gregory Bateman, whose 'parents kept a second-hand clothes shop at the end of Monmouth Street. At a very early age he was admitted an attorney; and, without fortune, family

---

[1] *Diary of Benjamin Rogers*, Bedfordshire Historical Records Society, xxx (1950).

[2] Robert Holloway, *Strictures on the Characters of the most prominent practising Attornies* (1805–11), p. 88.

[3] *Ibid.* p. 89.

connexions, or a capacity above mediocrity, he soon acquired some monied connexions, which gradually increased, until he found himself able to command vast sums, and become, as it were, banker to most of the distressed men of fashion in town. His house was the *depot* of title-deeds, and other permanent securities, upon the credit of which he procured pecuniary accommodations to an immense amount, and his notes passed with a currency and credit almost equal to the national bank—insomuch, that it became a proverbial saying—"Guineas at BATEMAN'S at two pence a bushel".[1]

[1] Robert Holloway, *op. cit.*, p. 67.

CHAPTER IX

TWO ATTORNEYS

I. CHRISTOPHER WALLIS

THE Journal of Christopher Wallis, attorney of Helston in Cornwall, gives a vivid picture of the life of an attorney in the period
1790–1815.[1] Wallis was the eldest son of a schoolmaster.[2] He had
been articled to William Sandys, a member of a prominent family of
attorneys in Helston,[3] and was admitted to the Roll in 1769. His
Journal is extremely detailed, and must have been a labour of several
hours every week. All the work he did is recorded meticulously,
together with long and interesting accounts of the state of the tin and
copper mines and of agriculture in Cornwall during these years. At
the beginning of each volume there is a survey of the main events
of his year, and at the end there is usually a passage in which he
reflects on events in Europe in this crowded period, and he has
much to say about that 'frantic, eccentric, clever fellow, Napoleon'.
There are occasional gaps in the Journal—he did not always record
his business journeys to London—but for the most part it is very full,
and when it is not, there is usually an entry in which he rebukes himself for his failure, and resolves to be more painstaking in the future.
And, in addition to this account of a large and varied practice, there
are many passages which reveal Wallis's attitude to his calling, and
show him to have been eminently, and self-consciously, respectable,
the very type of that élite of attorneys which was more and more
deciding the character of the profession at the end of the century.

Wallis's assiduity in compiling his journal is a reflection of the
attention he devoted to his work. He rose very early—at 5, 4,
even 3 o'clock, and after dealing with some correspondence at his
home in Trevarno, went in to his office at Helston, and stayed there
until 9 or 10 o'clock at night.[4] On Sundays and holidays the pace

---

[1] This Journal, only portions of which survive for the period 1790–1815, is
preserved in the library of the Royal Institution of Cornwall at Truro.

[2] Nicholas Wallis, master of the endowed school at Madron. See H. S. Toy,
The History of Helston (Oxford, 1936), p. 301.

[3] See Toy, *op. cit.*, esp. pp. 601–2.

[4] In August 1810 he copied into his Journal an extract from the Cornish
Gazette which calculated that 'The difference between rising every morning at

was only slackened, not halted. Indeed, such is the impression of unremitting labour that the Journal leaves, that it is hardly surprising to find him writing on 28 October 1792:

> Owing to very attentive business, and by too much for one person to manage, I had greatly impaired my intellects and memory, and carried on business rather irregularly, so that no perfect Journals or accounts have been kept by me for near three years last past, but by retiring to Trevarno using exercise and quiet, I am restored, but now find the want of regularity, and I shall be a considerable loser thereby, however to make amends, I have determined to be minutely regular from this time, and with patience all will get right again.[1]

Wallis had an extensive practice in Helston and the surrounding country, together with much business that took him further afield to Exeter, Bodmin, Truro, Falmouth, Launceston, and Penryn, and occasionally for weeks at a time to London. There was the usual business of wills, mortgages,[2] bankruptcies, leases, insurances, parish affairs; cases in the Archdeacon's Court, the Admiralty Court, the Stannary Court. He did much conveyancing, and was steward for the Cornish estates of Lord Arundell.[3]

He was deeply interested both as owner and as lawyer in the copper and tin mines, and was involved in the disputes about patent rights between Boulton and Watt and the Cornishmen. He was attorney for Edward Bull, one of the principal antagonists in this long-drawn-out conflict, and gave much of his time to this matter from November 1792, when Bull asked him to undertake his defence along with two other attorneys, Messrs Grylls and Borlase, until Bull died in 1798 with the question still unsettled.[4] He followed the matter from the court of Common Pleas to the court of Chancery,

six and eight o'clock in the course of 40 years—amounts to 29,000 hours or three years and 121 days and 6 hours, so that it is just the same as if ten years of life were to be added, to which we might command eight hours every day for the cultivation of our minds in knowledge or virtue or the dispatch of business'.

[1] On 28 October 1816 he noted in the margin of his Journal: 'On reading the above. . . I find that I have kept perfect Journals for 24 years last past, and have preserved them, and hope to continue them.'

[2] He himself held a mortgage of £5000 on Lord Clifford's manor of Tresithney.

[3] For an account of the profits which Wallis derived from the different parts of his practice, see Appendix III below, which also contains a transcription of one week's entries in his Journal.

[4] Cf. J. Rowe, *Cornwall in the Age of the Industrial Revolution* (Liverpool, 1953), esp. chapter III, 'The Years of Conflict, 1775–1800'. Dr Rowe mentions that one of those who challenged Boulton and Watt, Jonathan Hornblower, was driven into the debtors' gaol by the expenses of litigation at this time (*ibid.* p. 109).

and spent much time in London consulting barristers and hearing cases—in 1794, for example, he was in London from January until July, and he was back again for the hearing in the Hilary Terms of 1795 and 1796.[1]

In addition to all this, Wallis devoted much attention to his property in the mines and in land. He was extremely interested in questions about agriculture, and owned a considerable amount of land, some of which he farmed himself, and the remainder he rented to tenants over whom he kept a close watch. He kept a precise record of crops and prices and prospects for the season, and was much given to reflections on the theory and practice of agriculture in Cornwall.[2] He derived a useful income from his lands,[3] but was more deeply involved in the mines, having large shares in many, and owning some of them outright. These were difficult years in the mines, due both to legal disputes, and to the fluctuating prices of tin and copper, and they demanded much care and attention. No one could have been more assiduous or have displayed more anxiety than Wallis, and in a rapidly increasing fortune he reaped the reward of this devotion to detail.

In October 1794 he reflected:

On maturely considering my present situation in the world, I cannot but admire the providence which has conducted me through life. In 1769 I was scarce worth anything, and I had my doubts where to settle for a livelihood. However by mere chance I fixed at Helston and in 1785 I was worth upwards of £20,000.

His professional income suffered during his illness brought on by overwork, but it very quickly recovered, and rose from £560 in 1794 to £2130 in 1804.[4] And in December 1805 he recorded that

---

[1] Wallis usually stayed at 131 Strand, and did business for other clients during these visits.

[2] In 1793, when he was considering farming more of his land himself, Wallis reflected: ''tis impossible to do any good without Norfolk or Suffolk ploughmen and also a Kentish ploughman, as the Cornish husbandmen are only fit for harvest men, and nothing else.'

[3] In 1794 his freehold lands produced £130 per annum, and his leasehold lands £580, and he was anxious to convert them all to leasehold.

[4] The estimated profits from Wallis's business are given in Appendix III below. Seeing the hand of Providence everywhere, Wallis believed that even the loss of income during his illness had been beneficial, since it meant that he was not pestered with suitors seeking his daughter's fortune when it appeared that it was declining. He was thus able to choose a suitable husband, who benefited from an income which quickly increased after Wallis's recovery. See p. 124 below, n. 2.

he had made a clear saving of £13,763 in the preceding six years. Indeed, almost everything he touched turned to gold, and in 1797 he wrote:

Having for three months last past given some attention to business and 'tis wonderful to see how it increases, having during that time got on an average full twenty guineas a week, but should I give way again to business, I cannot refrain giving it more thought and attention than would be consistent with my constitution, which I am well persuaded would be very soon impaired, and therefore perhaps 'twould be better to fly from business than to seek it—but remember that Chancery and Exchequer suits are easily and in general profitably conducted, and 'tis Common Law business that perplexes and requires much attention—conveyancing is pleasant, amusing, and profitable.

A month later he was estimating the relative profits to be gained from his business as an attorney, and from his mining interests, and came to the conclusion that while the income from his business might be more reliable, the present appearances in the mines gave him grounds for thinking that they would yield at least a thousand pounds a year for some time to come. And in addition to this, he added that the exercise he gained in looking about the mines 'will be more conducive to my health, than the perplexing thoughts and agitations of conducting law suits'. On this occasion as on some others, he admitted to some doubts about the life he had to lead as an attorney. His profits from business averaged about £500 a year, but he wondered whether it was worth the anxiety involved.

There is [he wrote] a very great deal of perplexity and uneasiness, and much attention is required in the conduct thereof, and many charges made, which tho' conformable to strict law, yet I hold these charges not to be justified in conscience, and much chicane, with reflections on persons, are absolutely necessary to feed the vanity or rather perverseness of those concerned in law suits, and these proceedings often hurt me when I come to recollect them and all the circumstances attendant thereon in order to complete my Journal.

In January 1796 he had decided that in future he would not engage in business regarding wrecks: the charges for the labours of himself and two clerks for the previous three weeks he reckoned would not amount to £60, and that would be paid reluctantly. This he considered an inadequate recompense, especially as these matters generally terminated 'very unpleasingly'. A similar fastidiousness in his business had led him to dismiss Mr Pearce Rogers in November 1794. He was, he said,

no service at all to me, he is expensive, negligent, and made up of trifles—will extort from a poor man half a crown and immediately spend a crown, in what can be of no use to him—his sentiments are low, his abilities not sufficient to discover when 'tis for his interest to be liberal, and what is very extraordinary, I scarce ever sent him about any business that he succeeded in—so that I have made up my mind to part with him.

Clearly Wallis was well able to forgo business which would have been unpleasant to him, and he was under no necessity of stirring up trouble for the sake of settling it, in the way that so many of his profession were accused of doing. But however much he might reflect that he was able to live comfortably 'without meddling with trifling troublesome suits, and perplexing myself with a variety of suits and business', he allowed himself no respite, and his income continued to mount. On 31 December 1813 he noted at the end of his Journal for that year: 'Making up, casting and balancing cash account for the year 1813 the Dr and Cr amounts to £33,446, yet not a farthing mistake or omitted, but all perfectly right.'

Other entries in the Journal leave a similar impression of this rather high-minded, and perhaps rather self-satisfied attorney. There are hints of it in his dealings with his clerks. When James Borlase went up to London in November 1805 to get himself admitted as an attorney, Wallis wrote:

He came to me nine years since, when after a short trial 'twas thought his health would not permit him to attend to writing, and he continued to come to the office till 12 November, 1800, when he was articled to me for five years—in the first year he spent his leisure in a fruitless courtship, and the latter three years he has bestowed on the volunteers, of which he is adjutant.

'He writes well', Wallis added later, 'and at times has been a useful clerk to me; is not read in Law (because of time spent with Volunteers) and has retained little theory or practice, however I think will do well in life.'[1]

Wallis adopted a similar attitude towards the affairs of the nation,[2] his tenants, and to political affairs in the borough of Helston

---

[1] Borlase apparently practised at Helston. He was made an Alderman in November 1816. For the Borlase family, see Toy, *op. cit.*, esp. p. 593.

[2] Reflecting on the fortunes of England at the end of 1810, Wallis noted that 'she seems to be at peace tho' at war with all Europe, her trade is beyond all example great, and her credit unbounded her funds are very high, and money

during a lively period in its history.[1] After holding his manorial court at Trevarno in 1797, he confessed that he was 'much soured and hurt at the innovations made and which have been creeping into use for several years past'. The innovations of which he complained were a much larger consumption of punch and beer, the replacement of 'good beef pudding' by 'geese, turkeys, hams, and other dainties', and the addition of a fiddler, to the entertainments which accompanied the court, 'so that instead of the day being a refreshment to the tenants, it becomes debauchery in every point of view', whereas formerly the 'company broke up in good season and went quietly home to their families'. Wallis was not prepared to countenance this, and decided to miss holding the court for one year, and afterwards to provide the tenants with two shillings to pay for their dinners at a public house, and nothing further.

Until 1813, when he became a freeman, there is not much indication in his Journal that Wallis played any part in the political life of the borough, but he must have been closely aware of what was going on, in the disputes about the charter and about who was entitled to vote, the more so since his partner, Joseph Roberts, was the attorney and election agent to Sir Christopher Hawkins, who headed the opposition to the Duke of Leeds at Helston, and eventually succeeded him as patron.[2] Wallis confessed that he disliked the charter of 1774, 'because 'tis unconstitutional and unjust, a gross innovation on the liberties of Englishmen yet I perceive the present opposition thereto is in very slovenly hands, therefore I will not trouble myself any further on the subject'. Two years later, however, in 1815, this opposition had been removed from these 'slovenly hands', and was being managed by Wallis himself. In that year he was up in London, arranging for the presentation to the House of Lords of a petition in favour of the bill inspired by the supporters

very plenty her industry is not equalled and her merchants are very enterprising, her revenues are large her navy equal to all the world combined her sailors full of life and spirit, and their commanders the best informed, zealous and rather too much courage, so as to border on insolence; her soldiers are all heart and her statesmen are learned and some have had much experience and many are patriots, but the struggles between Ins and Outs are contemptible'.

[1] On this period at Helston, and the disputes about the charter and the representation of the borough, see Toy, *op. cit.* pp. 246–321.

[2] Roberts was born about 1779 (Toy, *op. cit.* p. 303, n. 3). Wallis married Philippa Roberts of Helston in 1771 (*ibid.* p. 301, n. 3). His wife died in 1807, but Wallis lived until 1826. His daughter Philippa married Captain Joseph Lamb Popham, and carried Trevarno into that family.

of Sir Christopher Hawkins, and which was supposed to 'secure the freedom and purity of elections in the borough of Helston'.[1]

In all this, Wallis is characteristic of the respectable attorney of the end of the century—even in the doubts which may linger in the mind about the complete sincerity of some of his pronouncements. But it is easy, and not always just, to criticise those who are ready to commit themselves in speculations which the more circumspect avoid. If the opinions of Wallis and others among his colleagues sound high-minded, it may mean that their authors were high-minded, sharing this quality with men who were having an increasingly powerful effect on their society. Wallis saw clearly what were the better things, approved them and endeavoured to follow them. And when he fell short, it was all confessed in his Journal. He went on buying state lottery tickets—and successfully—after noting that 'gaming is an odious and disgusting passion, which condemns men to ignoble sensations'. He was a devout churchman, and hated the Methodists who 'make a show of sanctity of manners, are certainly devoid of true religion, loyalty or true morality... altogether intolerable in their dealings, advancing the greatest falsehoods in their bargains, and must in every point be guarded against'. He often reflected on the 'mutability of all sublunary things', and time and again recorded his conviction that he had been singled out for divine favour. All his projects prospered, even though he claimed no special aptitude or inclination for them, and almost in spite of himself. 'I am of opinion', he wrote, 'that Providence has thrown mines in my way for some peculiar purpose, as my inclination is much against such adventures, but by some unaccountable ways, I have been led to the mines.'[2]

The last Journal to survive is that for 1815, and at the end of the year Wallis closed it with these words:

Thus ends the year 1815. O Almighty and Just God of Heaven and Earth, accept my most grateful thanks for thy great mercies bestowed

---

[1] Toy, *op. cit.* p. 299. Toy seems mistaken in saying that Wallis had not been resident in Helston for twenty years (*ibid.* p. 307).

[2] In thanking God for his health and prosperity at the end of 1805, he wrote: 'I daily perceive his providential care over me and over all my serious affairs, and I entirely attribute my prosperity to divine protection and tho' my income this year in business is less upwards of £500 than last year, the reason is that I was nearly half the year in London, and there employed on several government matters, for which no gratuity has yet been received, but I doubt not of its producing to me at a future day, twice £500 and make ample amends for the loss of time.'

on me through a long life of seventy-two years, constantly guarded by providential care, and when I trace back all my days, and count the many fortunate events thereof, thy goodness to me appears in every moment thereof and in all my transactions; I beseech thee O Lord for thy protection thro' the remainder of my life in truth, justice, and in a deliverance from evil.

Christr. Wallis,
31 December, 1815.

Such sentiments, recorded by an attorney in his business journal, would probably have come as a surprise to many who had been accustomed to think of the profession as a race of pettifoggers. And if it be pointed out that Wallis, like so many of those seeking to reform the profession at this time, was well able to afford honesty and high principles, it may be replied that this does not make these qualities less meritorious or less beneficial to society. It may mean that, backed by the strong motive of self-interest, they had a greater chance of being generally established.

2. WILLIAM HODGSON

The opinions of Christopher Wallis on his professional standards are drawn from the years of his prosperity. To a young man with his career to make, and without any material advantages to begin with, things may well have appeared differently. William Hodgson, the younger brother of Joseph Hodgson, deputy clerk of the peace for Cumberland at the end of the century, spent the early years of his career in London, and the letters he wrote to his brother describe his life as a clerk in the office of a London attorney.

He wrote on 30 January 1795 to say that he had been admitted an attorney by Lord Kenyon the preceding Saturday, and he asked Joseph to employ him from time to time on legal services in London. He had met Garforth, his brother's superior as clerk of the peace, and had been civilly treated by him.[1] Having decided to seek his fortune in London, he wrote:

I went to Messrs Ellison and Nares, Crane Court, Fleet Street, on Tuesday only for trial until the expiration of this term when I'm to enter into pay if we can agree, for as I could not suit myself as to my

[1] John Baynes Garforth, steward and agent to the Earl of Lonsdale, clerk of the peace for Cumberland, M.P. for Cockermouth 1780 and 1790–1802. Garforth did Joseph's agency business in London, so that Joseph could hardly neglect him to feed his brother.

mind and this being a respectable office, I thought it better to be improving myself tho' without emolument for the present than sitting idle at home.[1]

His letter to Joseph in March described the character of his work:

Messrs Ellison whom I'm with have a great deal of all kinds of business, except agency, the conveyancing has been allotted to me, at which I'm kept very tight for this month past, under the eye of Mr Ellison who is a very sulky man, not saying much, but when any of them does anything that does not please him one would imagine from his countenance that he subsisted upon nothing but crab pudding; there is another clerk who takes the Common Law under the inspection of Nares who is a pleasant man enough, but of this branch of the business I expect to have a part ere long. The other four do nothing but copy who are the wickedest dogs I ever met with, consequently I've enough (. . .)[2] keep them under. We are kept very hard at it and (. . .)[2] office is by no means an agreeable one, but with this I can put up, as the variety of business transacted therein must be of very great advantage to me, for I think I've learnt as much since I came to London as I did the whole of my time in Carlisle. I think I could have a more agreeable situation with a better salary but will not be in a hurry to change so long as they behave decently to me, tho' they've had about eight clerks within this year.[3]

William performed occasional services for his brother, both legal and otherwise, and Joseph was anxious about his financial position, and more than once offered to send money to help him out. But William felt obliged to get along without aid until it was absolutely necessary, being already conscious of a large debt to Joseph. In April he wrote to reassure his brother who had heard rumours that William was unhappy in London.

I recollect telling Mr Jackson when in Town that I was not partial to London, which most certainly is the case, though I'm well enough satisfied, and can live very contented in it; but it is natural to every person at first leaving home to feel somewhat awkward and find a vacuum now and then, though ever so close employed and I'm sure mine is pretty tight, for my leisure hours (which are few indeed) I employ in reading, which daily comes more and more habitual and I feel a secret satisfaction in thinking it no more than a transitory labour in full assurance of receiving the advantage thereof at a future time. It would have been a

---

[1] Hodgson MSS. (Cumberland County Record Office), File H, bdle 16.
[2] MS. torn.
[3] Hodgson MSS. File H, bdle 16 ; 16 March 1795.

great benefit to me had I been sent from home sooner for my connections were such as directed my attention entirely from business; and London is the place to learn industry especially when a person has time enough to discover that which is for his own interest; however I must now endeavour to make up here by assiduity in business what I lost in Carlisle by my own negligence.[1]

For some months, however, William's financial situation seems to have continued to be very precarious. He was doing some legal business on his own,[2] and was undertaking some discounting of bills for Joseph,[3] but later he wrote to say that 'A little money would be acceptable tho' I'm not in immediate want, *but not from you*, as I look upon myself as equally bound to pay you as any indifferent person: therefore if my father should think me extravagant, don't urge him as *I can do without it*: by your offering me in the manner you have done you only heap more obligations upon me than I shall ever be able to extricate myself from, as all I can do is to thank you for your goodness.'[4]

But his legal business was evidently not enough to support him, and in June he wrote to his brother about an opportunity of supplementing his income by entering into a partnership with a Carlisle man named Batey in the commission business.

In consequence of your intimating to me before I left the country that if I could get into a concern you would stand my friend and which I have not had the least reason to dispute since I came to this grand Emporium of Revolutions. I now take my pen to address you on that head, to request your friendly advice and assistance, having at present an offer to embark in a concern which if I may judge from appearances holds out the most flattering prospect.[5]

Batey was connected with two Glasgow firms, and had agreed to take him into partnership if he could find £500. He asked Joseph whether he and his father would be prepared to advance this sum, and went on:

I have no doubt we might do very well being careful and industrious and not extending our trade beyond our capital, and without prejudice

[1] Hodgson MSS. File H, bdle 16; 1 April 1795.
[2] He hastened to assure Joseph that his masters knew nothing of this, and that on admission he had entered himself as living at a different address from that of Ellison and Nares.
[3] Joseph was the Carlisle agent of the Paisley Bank.
[4] *Ibid.* 7 May 1795.
[5] *Ibid.* 17 June 1795.

to my profession; on the contrary it would certainly be the means of introducing business as Batey's connections are extensive and respectable....I cannot think of staying more than this year in my present obscure situation and where I'm to settle next God only knows: I've long been meditating what I am to do, every place is overstocked with our profession.[1]

Joseph and his father seem to have agreed to advance the capital, but on 14 July William wrote to say that further acquaintance with Batey had led him to abandon the plan.

I still continue to conduct all the conveyancing business in the office [he went on] taking part of the common law (but not so much as I wish). I attend all the commissions of bankruptcy we have. Nares and me are all in all, and when I want to go any way he always lets me. Ellison is much the same as he was, only an extraordinary circumstance took place one day last term: by appointment I met him at Westminster Hall, and as soon as the business was done he asked me into a coffee house, gave me a cup of chocolate and bid me take a coach home!!![2]

By September he was considering giving Ellison a month's notice of his intention to leave, although he had doubts about obtaining another situation. In October he had revised his verdict about Batey, and had agreed to go into partnership with him after all, under modified conditions. Ewing, the Glasgow merchant, had undertaken to pay him £100 per annum for transacting his business here, which I am to be admitted an equal share of on becoming partner. That no advance (or at least very trifling) is to be made, but to be confined solely to executing consignments for the first year. That the business to be transacted and managed under his name if I think proper. That I am to be at liberty to transact my own professional business at my direction, and to apply the rest of my time to the business in the warehouse. That I am to be admitted to an equal share with him. And that I am to be at liberty to withdraw myself from the concern at the expiration of the first or third year. He has taken a warehouse and two rooms ready furnished over it, at £50 per annum (clear of all taxes) one of which I am to have (being a large one) and is to be divided into two, one for a sleeping room and the other for my private business. Such are the outlines of the terms proposed, which I think advantageous to me, for I don't imagine I can spend a year better, than seeing into such business, joined with an opportunity of having a good deal of leisure time for study. I don't say I mean to quit the concern the first year, but supposing I was to do so, I should be in no worse situation than I am at present, on the

[1] Hodgson MSS. File H, bdle 16; 17 June 1795.
[2] *Ibid.* 14 July 1795.

9   R

contrary better, for I should have a more extensive knowledge of the world and my connections consequently much increased. In my opinion harm cannot well be done, as the £110 *certain* will cover rent and other incident expenses.[1]

He asked his brother to lend him £40 or £50 to cover initial costs if he approved the plan.

In the meantime, William remained with Ellison and Nares, and went on doing small legal jobs of his own as opportunity offered. In December, however, he wrote to say that he was giving up his connection with Batey, saying that he would prefer to remain where he was 'than rise to fall'. He did not approve of Batey's behaviour, but thought he could leave him without losing his good offices.

At present I am totally undetermined (until I hear from you) what course I must steer. I could 'tis true get a situation tomorrow in an attorney's office, but really I don't think of again assuming that capacity, clerks here not being looked upon as somewhat inferior, but abject slaves. You may perhaps think I should remain here and try for myself by not having full employment it would give scope to idleness, but I may with confidence assert (and without being accused of vanity) that the tenour of my conduct since I came here has been a continued attention to business and study carefully avoiding everything that might lead on to excess or excite my passions to debauchery and intemperance, which I trust I shall have resolution enough and gratitude enough to continue.[2]

On 30 December he assured Joseph that there had been no formal agreement with Batey, and added: 'rather than be a common hack clerk here, I would prefer trying my fortune in another country: not that I dislike work, but I cannot submit to the treatment.'[3] In January he was still undecided as to his course, and did not know whether to take out his practising certificate or not.

Sometime in May he seems to have decided to set up as an attorney on his own account in London, for he wrote to his brother:

I should like to be down at Carlisle Assizes but my prospect seems a little clouded at present, however, I shall with calmness relinquish the idea if business requires my presence here. We are full of electioneering here—my little brass plate has attracted the notice of the canvassers, there has been a set here this morning soliciting my vote and interest for Curtis.[4]

[1] Hodgson MSS. File H, bdle 16; 2 October 1795.
[2] *Ibid.* 13 December 1795.   [3] *Ibid.* 30 December 1795.
[4] *Ibid.* n.d. (sometime in May).

But his business cannot have been very pressing, and he seems to have spent the summer at Carlisle. He was back in London at the end of October, and early in November he wrote:

My situation at present no doubt is awkward but what can I do? I must rub on until I get to my *Chambers* which are at No 9, Clement's Inn; but I expect to be there in the course of 10 days. You must send all my papers and books of every description—indeed I expected they would have been off before now. The desk and bed send by sea immediately putting into the desk and drawers such books as you think I shall least want, and put the other up in a box and send by the coach. I am in great want of them.[1]

On the following day he wrote again:

If I was only settled in Chambers[2] I think I shall do very well; attention and industry must bring a man through, and though when in the country I was threatened with a relapse of youthful inclinations I hope it is now removed, and sobriety and steadiness filled the chasm which I trust will remain prominent features in your very affectionate brother.[3]

He asked Joseph to send at once certain books which he wanted urgently—Sellon and Impey's *Practice*, the *Modern Pleader*, *Chancery Practice*, Cook's *Bankruptcy Laws*, 'and as many more as will cost no more than 3s.',[4] and asked him to recommend him as agent to the local attorneys and to John Robinson.

By the end of the year William's business was still not enough to take up all his time, and he wrote to his brother suggesting a scheme for helping him in his banking business, which he thought would bring in about £100 a year.

All bills sent here by you [he wrote] if dishonoured are returned through the Bank with about 4% charged thereon, of which you have not one farthing but all the risk. Now if I could raise as a standing stock about £200 and give Smith, Payne and Smith notice that all dishonoured bills bearing your endorsation would be paid by me for your honour it would have a two-fold good attending it, viz. the principal one of pocketing the regular and fair charges and then the bill will reach you two days sooner than usual.[5]

---

[1] Hodgson MSS. File H, bdle 16; 7 November 1796.
[2] The rent of his chambers was £15 per annum.
[3] *Ibid.* 8 November 1796.
[4] *Ibid.* 11 November 1796.
[5] *Ibid.* 26 December 1796. Smith, Payne and Smith were the London agents of the Paisley Bank.

He recommended the plan strongly to Joseph, and said it would be worth while even if it meant borrowing money to supply himself with the necessary capital.

Only a few other letters from William survive. They show him trying still more ways of making money. In 1797 he was selling hams which had been sent to him from Carlisle. The trade was good in July, but flat in September and October. On 24 October he wrote:

The sale for hams is slow, but I keep rubbing on—all the bacon is gone except two hlds[?]—if the hams had been small the difficulty of effecting sales would have been trifling, but on the contrary they are in general great ugly ill-shaped Scotch dogs weighing 50–70 lbs each.[1]

These letters end in 1797. Although they suggest that William's position was still far from secure, and no doubt leave much unsaid about the ways in which he obtained a living, it comes as something of a surprise to find that he is one of the attorneys most savagely attacked by Robert Holloway in his *Strictures on the Characters of the most prominent practising Attornies*, published between 1805 and 1811.

Mr William Hodgson [wrote Holloway] is a man in whom *virtue, modesty, humanity, chaste practice*, and amiable endowments are un-questionable; in him nature seems to have erected one of her proudest banners on which is emblazoned all the virtues we meet with in the heathen mythology—all the piety we are taught in the Apocrypha, and the morality bequeathed to the roll of attorneys by the Settlers at Botany Bay!...It is said charity covers a multitude of transgressions:— whether this gentleman's transgressions have any covering at all we know not; but in mercy to decency, it is time they had.

He goes on to accuse him of brow-beating a debtor who was desperately ill, and of writing to him in terms 'such as might naturally have been expected from a baptised wolf. "Is it to me that you come for mercy? Thrust your hand in the fire and pray the flames not to burn you!"'

The attack continues in the most violent language, and concludes:

We do not impeach his abilities as an attorney, or his want of assiduity for the interest of his client; and if a little swearing should be necessary, it is no more than what Edw. Barnet,[2] or any other *conscientious attorney*

---

[1] Hodgson MSS. William Hodgson's Letter Book, 24 October 1797.
[2] Another attorney attacked by Holloway.

is ever ready to do for the benefit of his client, and we dare say Mr Hodgson never swore anything extra-judicial, or neglected to make his own affidavit an article in his bill of costs;—we shall only say, we were very lately requested to draw an indictment arising out of a squabble about this gentleman's veracity, which we declined, and we trust our reasons for declining it were such, as will do honour to our liberality, even towards an enemy.—To conclude, we wish Mr Hodgson and men like him to bear in mind, that the most feeble insect that is wantonly trod upon today, may gain strength again tomorrow to sting its oppressor to the heart.

N.B. We understand he has lately taken a partner, and a wife; we sincerely hope the breed at Carlisle, and the practice in Clement's Inn, will both improve.[1]

William survived this blistering attack, and enjoyed long years of prosperity at Carlisle. He became clerk of the peace for Cumberland, an office which was held by his family throughout the nineteenth century. He became a justice of the peace, deputy-lieutenant of the county, and was five times mayor of Carlisle. He died in 1850 at the age of 77 in circumstances very different from those which had surrounded him in his early years as an attorney in London.

[1] Holloway, *op. cit.* pp. 277 *et seqq.*

CHAPTER X

THE ROAD TO RESPECTABILITY

In his play *Pasquin*, first performed in 1736, Fielding wrote:

Religion, law, and physic, were designed
By Heaven the greatest blessing on mankind;
But priests, and lawyers, and physicians made
These general goods to each a private trade,
With each they rob, with each they fill their purses,
And turn our benefits into our curses.

This was typical of the general belief in the earlier part of the eighteenth century that professional men were merely parasites. They were not engaged in productive labour; they made their living out of other people's misfortunes. The doctors and the lawyers especially, and among them, the apothecaries and attorneys more particularly, were subjected to the almost universal abuse of the satirists and commentators of the time, in plays, pamphlets, and novels. They were quacks and pettifoggers; they exploited the mysteries of their craft for their own ends. What they did for their clients had largely to be left to their own judgment, and this judgment was assumed to be exercised primarily in their own favour. They were expected to be hypocritical, selfish, and cunning, and were liberally abused for doing what was expected of them. It certainly gave a man no special prestige to be an attorney: rather was it a social handicap he had to overcome. Tom Clarke, in Smollett's novel Sir Launcelot Greaves, 'never owned himself an attorney without blushing'.

This does not mean that men of gentle birth are never found as attorneys in this period; Thomas Fane, a Bristol attorney, succeeded to the Earldom of Westmorland. Nor does it mean that a man never achieved gentility by means of the profession. On the contrary, it provided a social stepping stone for a good many people of humble birth. But the profession was merely a stepping stone to gentility in these early stages, and men who had exploited the undoubted possibilities of gain presented by the profession were not usually content to remain attorneys, nor to found merely professional families. They got into the landed gentry as quickly as they could for their profession as such conferred no particular dignity. Sir Joseph Banks, for example, the President of the Royal Society at the end of the century, owed his social standing to an attorney grandfather who had bought himself an estate and a seat in parliament, which he passed on to his son who was not an attorney.

For those who were not sufficiently prosperous to buy themselves into the gentry there was no escape from the abuse which was hurled at the profession. Much of this was of the type that is habitually reserved for professional men on the grounds that all professions are conspiracies against the laity. Professional men were also attacked in the way that middlemen are often attacked, and as exploiting the complexities of society—in this case the undoubted complexities of the legal system—complexities which they had a vested interest in preserving and augmenting. Certainly the profession offered very real temptations to the unscrupulous, and since so little was expected of it, perhaps its standards were not especially exalted.

They were, in fact, the standards more generally observed in the early eighteenth century. Social commentators of this time found much to complain of, but their attitude towards what they saw was very different from that of later critics: they were satirists, not reformers. Fielding and Hogarth described the contemporary scene meticulously, not without some delight in its chaotic and unscrupulous character. There was not much confidence that anything could be done about it—things were what they were—and if it was to be judged at all, it was by standards which had long been accepted. Nor were there lacking those who considered the social order, like the constitution, to be perfect, and blamed any faults on mankind. They thought that social abuses might be corrected or punished—they could scarcely be cured, and they were more often causes for satirical amusement than for high moral indignation.

Certainly parliament and the judges tried to regulate the attorneys, in the corrective, punitive, fashion of most social legislation of the time, but their efforts met with no very conspicuous success until the attorneys themselves, and society generally, began to demand higher standards of behaviour. In the meantime the popular attitude was one of 'comic toryism'[1] which conceived of society as

[1] The phrase is Professor Basil Willey's; see *Eighteenth-Century Background* (London, 1940), ch. 3.

being static, and of its standards as being fixed. Some, like John Brown, seemed almost to despair of mankind.[1] They believed that selfishness and luxury were rife; they saw no signs of public spirit and few of private morality.

No one believed that attorneys at any rate exhibited either of these qualities. There were perhaps special reasons why lawyers should be abused. Physical ills, which were the source of the profits of the medical profession, were accepted as the lot of mankind, and it was possible to be grateful to those who could alleviate them. The lawyer, on the other hand, was made necessary only by the depravity of men—or of other men—and by the increased complexity and artificiality of society. A defeated client would abuse his own attorney for his ineptitude, and his opponent's for his chicanery. His successful antagonist would resent having to pay for what he believed to be his rights, and would harbour a grudge against his adversary's attorney for having subjected him to unnecessary expense and delay. Further, lawyers were agents and nothing more. They were, in the opinion of many besides Swift, 'A society of men bred up from their youth in the art of proving, by words multiplied for the purpose, that white is black, and black is white, according as they are paid.'[2] It was assumed that they were not over-fastidious in accepting cases and clients, or very seriously concerned that justice should prevail. As one writer remarked in 1747, 'Attorney and knave are very near become terms synonymous'.[3]

The increasing complexity of the laws and the legal system is in some measure an indication of the increasing complexity of society. New situations demand new laws, but the old are reluctantly, and often belatedly abandoned. This has, perhaps, been true in a special degree of England, where the legal system has been based on an historical foundation. The doctrine of precedent and the reliance on case law had become so firmly established as to make English laws a by-word for abstruseness. Not that this was always deplored. Montesquieu considered that the multiplicity of English laws was the price of the Englishmen's liberty. But it afforded ample opportunity for lawyers who wanted to exploit this situation for their own ends. It did not mean that Englishmen did not resent having

[1] John Brown was the author of the popular *Estimate of the Manners and Principles of the Times*, published in 1757.

[2] Cf. Junius's belief that the profession was supported by 'the indiscriminate defence of right and wrong' (Letter of 22 June 1769; Bohn ed. I, 165).

[3] R. Campbell, *The London Tradesman* (1747).

to pay the price of their liberty. Some were dissatisfied with the legal system; many more thought that it was sadly perverted by the lawyers. For all of them, the attorneys provided a suitable target at which to aim their shafts of resentment. They were without professional bodies to defend them, and they did not share the social prestige of judges and barristers.

Elsewhere, declared and statutory law had provided the basis of the legal system: the distinction is between those countries with a common law system, and those in which it is based on the Roman civil law. Some critics thought that codification and simplification were desirable, and that the laws could be made readily understood by all. So long as they remained buried in the Rolls and Case-Books, relevant to the limit of legal memory, so long would the opportunities for legal abuses remain, so long would droves of lawyers flourish. Some, too, tended to overlook the necessarily complex structure of society, and to sigh in vain for a return to a state of rural simplicity, in which neither laws nor lawyers would be required.

These themes can all be discerned in the satirical and critical writing of the period. The adjective habitually—almost inevitably—applied to attorneys was 'pettifogging', one who was not over-scrupulous, and given to stirring up trouble in order that he would be employed to settle it.[1] He was described by Ned Ward as 'an amphibious monster that partakes of two natures, and those contrary. He's a great lawyer both of peace and enmity, and has no sooner set people together by the ears but is soliciting the law to make an end of the difference.'[2] Robert Holloway, later in the century, portrayed many such men in startling colours. Of one of the most notorious of these he wrote: 'Right and wrong claim no distinction but as they severally serve his interest. Justice and injustice have the same *convenient* quality. His penetration is superior to most men's; the first fee enables him to pronounce the cause *just*, the second amounts to *inspiration*, and a third shall

---

[1] The word has been used in this sense since the sixteenth century. Its origin is uncertain. *O.E.D.* suggests that it may be a combination of 'petty' and 'fogger', 'fogger' being derived from Fugger, the name of the Augsburg financiers, and used to imply one who used on a small scale the dishonourable devices popularly attributed to great financiers.

[2] Quoted at length in J. C. Jeaffreson, *A Book About Lawyers* (London, 1867), pp. 324–5. See also E. B. V. Christian, *Leaves of the Lower Branch* (London, 1909), for further strictures of Ned Ward.

decree the client the kingdom of Mexico, if he wants it. Find but money, and he will find title.'[1] Others felt that 'When a lawyer is just, 'tis because he has no temptation to be unjust; that is, where he has so much money to plead the cause of his client, that 'tis out of the power of the other side to bribe him'.[2] Even Johnson, who 'seldom encouraged general censure of any profession', and who was 'willing to allow a due share of merit to the various departments necessary in civilised life', was not above sarcastic reference to members of the profession.[3]

A pamphlet published in 1749 pointed out that in the hands of the lawyers the law was a source of oppression rather than of relief, and was profitable only to the lawyers themselves.[4] 'Some...inferior practitioners not only instigate the unwary to unjust and unreasonable litigations, but, whilst their money lasts, dissuade them from amicable and equitable accommodations; and instead of being peace-makers, are promoting the breach thereof, even among the best united friends.'[5] Existing laws on several matters—bankruptcy[6] and debt were notorious examples—offered wide scope for the chicanery of lawyers, and even the employment of an honest lawyer in such matters was likely to prove an exorbitant expense. The law so bristled with jargon and technicalities that clients could neither control the actions of their attorneys, nor check their bills.[7]

Such technicalities were not unwelcome, however, when they could be employed to defeat an opponent in the law. Indeed, the *Gentleman's Magazine* went so far as to claim in 1733 that 'The retaining so many strange and undefined and technical expressions in our laws, is not owing to Gentlemen of the Long Robe, as imagined, but to the client, whose avarice, and eager desire of conquest, together with the artifice, ignorance, and knavery of his under-agents, multiply cases, and add to the increase and bulky burden of our laws, and to the dilatoriness of the proceedings in

---

[1] *Letter to John Wilkes*, c. 1771. See also *Strictures on the Characters of the most prominent practising attornies* (1805–11).

[2] *An Essay in Praise of Knavery* (1723).

[3] Boswell, *Life of Johnson* (Everyman ed.), I, 393, and II, 536.

[4] *Animadversions on the present laws of England*, etc. This pamphlet is only known to me from a notice in the Monthly Review for 1749.

[5] *Ibid.*

[6] Cf. Samuel Foote's play *The Bankrupt* (1773).

[7] See, for example, Arbuthnot's *Law is a Bottomless Pit*, ch. IX, and Foote's play, *The Englishman returned from Paris* (1756), especially Mr Latitat, attorney of Staple's Inn.

our courts'.[1] Some attorneys were assumed to be cynical enough
to believe that their clients needed to be impressed with the complexity of the system, lest they should doubt whether they were
getting their money's worth, John Bull thought the law 'a pretty
science', with 'a prodigious number of learned words', until his
wife pointed out that he had paid handsomely for 'every syllable
and letter of these fine words'.[2] And it was clearly special pleading
to suggest that 'obscurity and darkness are the darlings of mankind.
... Men may pretend what they please, but they are never pleased,
nor part with their money more readily, than when their intellects
are puzzled, and their senses reduced to a state of confusion.'[3]

And if there were too many laws, there were too many lawyers.
For, as one critic explained, 'It is not here as in mechanical
mysteries, the fewer operators, the more beneficial the operation.
Here one makes work for another; experience demonstrating that
whenever a lawyer is wanting, peace is undisturbed. Even the
catchpole is looked upon as a member, and encouraged, because he
brings grist to the mill.'[4] Pettifogging was inevitable since there
were far too many lawyers for them all to make an honest living;
some indeed would have denied that it was possible to be both
honest and an attorney. But some who criticised the excessive
numbers were more realistic than others. In the absence of any
very stringent or effective regulation of the profession there were
undoubtedly many men who practised as attorneys who were in
no way fitted to do so. But many complaints ignored the fact that
an increasingly complicated society required the services of more
and more agents of all kinds, so that comparisons between the
unproductive character of the employment of attorneys and the
enriching labours of merchants and honest handicraftsmen were
becoming less and less apt.[5]

One critic suggested that there should be councils of commerce
in the larger cities to settle commercial disputes, and that suitors in
chancery should be given the opportunity of having their costs

---

[1] *Gentleman's Magazine*, March 1733.
[2] Arbuthnot, *Law is a Bottomless Pit*, ch. ix.
[3] *Law Visions; or, Pills for Posterity* (1736).
[4] *Plain Truth, by way of a dialogue between Truman and Skinall* (1736).
[5] Similar complaints were heard about domestic servants, 'agents' of another
kind, 'drones in the hive, consuming the produce of other men's labour and
industry without contributing anything thereto'; see J. J. Hecht, *The Domestic
Servant Class in Eighteenth Century England* (London, 1956), p. 178.

settled by two merchants, instead of by a taxing master, that is, by a lawyer.[1] But if the merits of such a suggestion are doubtful, it is clearly a good deal more realistic than that made by another writer much later in the century when he asked

Whether a board or committee of healing and mitigation, between adverse parties to be composed of neighbouring gentlemen, clergymen, sensible farmers and burghers, might not be appointed in every market town and borough throughout the kingdom; a quorum of which might sit for an hour or two every market day, and endeavour to reconcile and compose small differences and misunderstandings among neighbours, and thereby prevent vexatious and expensive suits at law so that those who met in enmity might return to their homes in friendship; to the country's peace, the salvation of families, and the utter disappointment of fleecing attorneys?[2]

It is always possible to believe that problems are capable of solution by simple means if their complexity is ignored, or the effectiveness of regulations is exaggerated. Many ideal solutions to these problems were suggested from the earliest times, but since they tended to be of the type which claimed that the results of the dishonesty of attorneys would be avoided if attorneys were not dishonest, none of them were specially helpful or important. At best they were anachronistic in their proposals. The suggestion made by William Sheppard in 1657 that lawyers should be paid by the state, according to their abilities, and not by fees, which this last pamphleteer quoted with approval, was clearly such an idealistic solution.[3] And while there may perhaps have been grounds for supposing that legal expenses and delays were greater in England than elsewhere, it was probably an exaggeration to say that some nations of Europe 'at this day, carry their code in their pocket, with

[1] *Animadversions on the Present Laws of England*. The same writer maintained that 'The decrease of the number of lawyers would increase our national wealth without diminishing theirs, since they could be diverted to productive employment'.

[2] *Speculations upon Law and Lawyers* (1788). Another suggestion that the number of attorneys in each county should be limited to twelve, and that 'lawyers should be obliged to testify that they thought their clients to have an equitable right to the claims they were making, was condemned by the *Monthly Review* in 1785. It would only mean that 'the greatest business would be in the hands of the person who possessed the most callous conscience. Like the oaths invented to protect religious establishments, they may sometimes drive away honest men, but knaves never' (*A Free Inquiry into the Enormous Increase of Attornies*, noticed in *Monthly Review*, 1785).

[3] William Sheppard, *England's Balme* (1657); quoted in *Speculations*, etc.

the same ease as we our Common Prayer, or Court and City Register', and to imply that England could profitably follow this example.[1] John Corry, writing in 1801, may have underestimated the value of the services which professional men rendered to society, but when he asked himself when the evils of quackery and superstition in medicine and law would be abolished, and answered by saying: 'When mankind prefer temperance to excess, and exercise to indolence, health will be promoted. And when the natural beneficence of the human heart is directed by prudence, men will not involve themselves and their families in want and ruin by law suits', he was probably not over-confident that this millenium was at hand.[2]

Nor had attorneys in the eighteenth century at least any grounds for supposing that such a drastic, and for them disastrous, reformation of human nature was imminent. The frequency of the complaints that whole estates were eaten up by lawyers' fees may equally well be taken as an indication that the English landowner was a litigious animal, as for a proof of the wickedness of attorneys. But those who were prepared to denounce the attorney as the paid and hypocritical agent of other men, prepared to do or say anything for money, did not care to excuse him as an agent merely, and turn their attack on his principal. It was convenient to blame the attorney when anything went wrong, and when it went right, he was not in any special sense praiseworthy: *then* he was only an agent, *then*, justice had prevailed. When it was claimed that

> A Plaister for a broken head,
> When made by Law, if 'tis thick spread,
> Before is healed the outward Sore,
> Will cost at least Ten Pounds or more[3]

it was apparently forgotten that without the law, the wound might have remained unhealed.

The attorney was used as a scape-goat also by those who found it easier to criticise him than the laws themselves. Just as it was commonly suggested that the constitution was perfect, but that it could be perverted by politicians, so many believed that the laws

---

[1] *Speculations*, etc.

[2] *A Satirical View of London at the Commencement of the Nineteenth Century*, by an Observer (i.e. John Corry), p. 130.

[3] *The Pettifogger, a satire in Hudibrastick Verse*, etc. (London, 1723).

also were perfect, but perverted by lawyers. This was noticed in
Foote's play the *Lame Lovers*, performed in 1770:

> As Farquhar has observ'd, our English Law,
> Like a fair spreading oak, the Muse should draw,
> By Providence design'd and wisdom made,
> For honesty to thrive beneath its shade;
> Yet from its boughs some insects shelter find,
> Dead to each nobler feeling of the mind,
> Who thrive, alas! too well, and never cease
> To prey on justice, property, and peace.

It was common enough in the eighteenth century to appeal to some
far distant golden age for criteria of behaviour; it was even suggested that 'the law was formerly an honourable situation in life,
but (is) now degraded'.[1]

But if there were those who followed Coke in appeals of this sort,
and in their worship of the common law of England, there were
also those who suggested that the system was iniquitous, profitable
only to lawyers, and quoted Bacon in their recommendations of
codification and simplification. 'Dim Sasson', in his *Law Visions;
or, Pills for Posterity*, published in 1736, set himself the task of
cleansing the 'more than Augean stable' of English law and its
practitioners. He noticed Bacon with approval, and claimed that
more recently Hales and Holt had also declared themselves to be
in favour of codification, but that they had been defeated by the
machinations of the common lawyers. He referred to the great
increase in the volume of the laws, but maintained that 'voluminous
as our Laws had become, the Locust race are increased to almost
the number of lines in the Laws'.

Critics of this sort were more inclined to favour parliamentary
intervention to reform the abuses of which they complained. It
was, they thought, naïve to suppose that the law would punish the
lawyers. As one who had suffered from the law's delays and expenses
asked: 'If a dishonest attorney should think fit to betray his clients,
sell them to their adversaries, do anything in their cause that is
contrary to their interests, pray what remedy have they? Why, to
employ another attorney to call him to account, who will do the
very same, ad infinitum.'[2] It was from such critics, too, that

---

[1] *The Present State of the Practice and the Practisers of the Law*, etc., n.d.
(after 1729).

[2] *An Apology for the Conduct of Mrs T. C. Phillips* (1750), pp. 111, 188.

suggestions came for regulating entry into the profession, and for imposing a time limit in which all causes should be decided.[1]

But it was more usual to respect—even venerate—the law; those deficiencies that were noticed were ascribed to those who perverted it for their own ends. It was only men like Bentham, who were not at all impressed by the force of arguments based on historical precedent and the wisdom of ancestors, who perceived that popular criticism of attorneys might be no more than superficial in character, ignoring the fundamental fault, which lay in the legal system itself. Many people in this profoundly legalistic age were ready to agree that they were 'lawyer ridden', as other ages had been 'priest ridden';[2] but perhaps fewer were prepared to suggest the abolition of an instrument which one day they would probably want to use themselves. So instead of attacking the law, they attacked the lawyers, and among the lawyers, not the Bench and the Bar, but the attorneys and solicitors, a manifest unfairness which roused Bentham to indignation. 'How long', he asked, 'shall the inferiors in power and opulence—the inferiors who are but instruments—be execrated, and the superiors, who are the authors of it, adored? Attorneys, solicitors—were they the makers of the system of technical procedure?—were they the makers of the law of evidence?'[3]

The English legal system undoubtedly attracted many men to become attorneys whose standards of conduct were not high enough to enable them to resist the temptations it offered, and the standards of society were low enough, and the system complex enough, to

---

[1] *Animadversions on the Present Laws of England* (1749), suggested that England should emulate Prussia, Russia, and other countries, in decreeing that all cases should be finished within a year.

[2] See, for example, Alexander Grant, *The Progress and Practice of the Modern Attorney* (1796).

Another writer believed that 'The virtual Death's wound of our Laws, which are, in general, the Master-piece of human wisdom: is but too evidently inflicted in their perverted and rapacious process'. He distinguished a distressing pattern in the history of the English Nation, which 'has continued by some strange Fatality, even from the obscure times of its Druid Thraldom, ever under the Influence of some oppressive *Incubus.*—It was for many Centuries prior to our first William's Invasion, Conquest-ridden.—Very soon after that famous period it was still more heavily priest-ridden.—Under the Tudor Family it was most egregiously Tyrant-ridden. For a short space it was pretty roughly ridden by Fanatics.—and I am sorry to observe that its present Inhabitants, have but too long groaned, under the ruthless Load and the oppressive Lash of Lawyers' (*A Free Inquiry*, etc. 1785).

[3] Jeremy Bentham, *Works*, ed. J. Bowring (Edinburgh, 1843), VII, 188 (*Rationale of Judicial Evidence*).

allow them to sin with a considerable measure of impunity. 'Now', it was complained, 'every little pitiful tradesman, that can just make up enough money to put his son out clerk, is for making him a lawyer, and consequently as he thinks, a gentleman.'[1] It was people such as these who were responsible for the scandalous practices in the profession, coming as they did 'of some abject, paltry race, born and bred in want, and having but very indifferent principles on the one hand, and pressed by great necessity on the other, they stick at nothing, but do incredible mischief in the commonwealth'.[2]

Many such criticisms suggest that their authors resented the fact that the profession could be used as a means of rising in the social scale, and thus doing violence to the prevailing notions of an ordered, static, hierarchical society. Complaints about those who had 'scraped gentility out of attorney's fees' were at least as old as the seventeenth century.[3] The professions were, indeed, one of the most powerful solvents of this traditional structure, but while it persisted, there was some truth in the assertion that those who came from obscure families would be less well educated, more needy, and therefore perhaps less scrupulous than others. Of course there were the exceptional men, 'men of genius and integrity, from whatever class they may have originated', but many shared the view that 'the probability is exceeding strong against a low-bred youth exercising with honour...a profession replete with unavoidable opportunities to harass his fellow creatures'.[4] Attorneys could hardly deny the justice of many of these complaints about their profession; but they were not always fair, and some of the more affluent members of the profession were roused to the only course open to them which was to insist that there were some at least who were concerned for the 'love of justice, the cause of truth, and the honour of the calling', who did not 'debate for fees only',[5] and to drive the 'vile and needy pettifoggers' beyond the pale.

By the end of the century much more was expected of the

---

[1] *Proposals Humbly Offered to the Parliament* (1707).   [2] *Ibid.*
[3]   'Lord what a broking aduocate is this?
                He was some squir's scriuenor, that hath scrapt
                Gentilitie out of aturney's fees;
                His bastard actions prove him such a one,
                For true worth scorns to turn chameleon.'
(John Day, *Law Tricks* (1608); Malone Society, vol. 87 (Oxford, 1949), act ii.)
[4] *Observations on the Use and Abuse of the Practice of the Law* (1786). There are similar complaints in *Animadversions on the Present Laws of England* (1749).
[5] *Speculations upon Law and Lawyers* (1788).

profession than had been in Fielding's day. Attorneys appear very frequently in his plays and novels, very much at home in the rough and tumble world he described. Their standards of conduct, like those of the society in which they lived, were low, careless, and devoid of any concern with social responsibility. They, like other men, were individualistic and acknowledged few duties except to themselves. If they were hypocritical, selfish and cunning, this was exactly what was expected of them. Jane Austen's world is very different from Fielding's, and so are her attorneys: so also is her esteem for the professions.[1] For her, a profession provided an opportunity for a man to acquire moral dignity, and a new individual worth. A man owed a duty to society and himself, and his profession was the way in which he could perform it. His worth was proved by his actions, not by his inherited status. Mr Gardiner, in trade at Cheapside, is a more worthy man than Mr Bennett, content simply to enjoy his tenure of an entailed estate, with no thought that he ought to prove that he deserved it. Sir Walter Elliot might be flattered to be told—even by his attorney's daughter —that his face was that of a gentleman, innocent of any of the distinguishing features with which his profession marks a man, but Sir Walter is portrayed as a fool, whose standards of what makes a gentleman are certainly not those of Jane Austen.[2]

Nor were they the standards which were coming to be insisted on in society generally. Formerly gentility had been inherited: now it was to be earned, and a man acquired it by recognising his duties to society and performing them. This was the keynote of much social criticism in the age of the evangelical revival, and it was powerful enough eventually to influence the whole of society, and to bring about a social revolution of far-reaching importance. The contrast between the old world and the new, in those aspects which most nearly affect this study, is, in brief, the contrast between the system of patronage and influence, and the examination system. There can be discerned a novel concern with individual worth and

---

[1] For a discussion of this, see Lionel Trilling, *The Opposing Self* (London, 1955), p. 215.

[2] 'Wentworth? Oh! ay,—Mr Wentworth, the curate of Monkford. You misled me by the term *gentleman*. I thought you were speaking of some man of property: Mr Wentworth was nobody, I remember; quite unconnected; nothing to do with the Strafford family. One wonders how the names of many of our nobility become so common' (*Persuasion* (1818), ed. Chapman, p. 23). See also Sir Walter's views on the naval profession (the one specially dear to Jane Austen), *ibid.* p. 19.

tested ability, which in many ways was significant of wider changes taking place at this time.

This new preoccupation with moral worth is shown in many ways. Gentleman was now a title to be earned, and had a specific moral connotation which was absent from the earlier concept which took the possession of coat armour and of inherited landed wealth as its criteria. Of course, certain of the old characteristics remain—and the title still implied a certain economic status. But it came to be accepted that a professional man, even an attorney, could be a gentleman. Gentility had often been obtained in the past through the professions, now it was conferred by them, and enjoyed in them. And, with the example of the judges and barristers before them, a determined effort was made in the last years of the century by a section of the attorneys to get themselves genuinely accepted as gentlemen. In view of the contemporary estimate of the attorney which has been summarised above, their task was a difficult one, but it was made easier by social and economic changes which allowed the development of a large and wealthy body of attorneys, conscious of their common problems as never before, and conscious too that the particular problem which they had to solve was only a smaller version of that which confronted the larger social group to which they belonged.

This social group was the 'middle class', and the way the problem was solved in both cases was by insisting on their 'respectability'. That there had always been a group of people of middling economic importance can hardly be denied, but it is also true that the size and the influence of this group was greatly enhanced by those changes which are summarised as the industrial revolution. And, as they come to realise more and more fully their improved economic position, these people gained self-confidence, became more aware of their common interests and opinions, created their own standards, and stopped looking to the old aristocracy for their rules of conduct. In these years round the turn of the century, the 'middle sort of men' became the 'middle class'—it is then that the term is first used with a more than economic meaning—and it was not long before Brougham was eulogising them as 'by far the most wealthy order in the community...the genuine depositories of sober, rational, intelligent and honest English feeling'.[1] And so soon were

---

[1] Brougham, *Speeches* (Edinburgh, 1838), II, 600; quoted A. V. Dicey, *Law and Public Opinion in England* (London, 1905), pp. 184–5. Cf. Beckford's speech on the 'middling people of England, the manufacturer, the yeoman, the merchant,

they established as a moral force in society that Shelley could attack them in 1820, in words which would often be echoed in periods more commonly associated with class conflict, as a new aristocracy of 'attornies and excisemen and directors and government pensioners, usurers, stockjobbers, country bankers, with their dependents and descendants...a set of pelting wretches in whose employment there is nothing to exercise even to their distortion the more majestic faculties of the soul'.[1]

The standard of morality most commonly associated with this class is that of respectability, 'the state, quality, or condition of being respectable in point of character or social standing'.[2] For the middle class, respectability was at once the quality which distinguished them from those they thought beneath them in the social and moral scale, and the claim to recognition which they advanced to the established upper classes. It was, too, an attitude for which they were frequently condemned: in the eyes of men like Melbourne it was nothing more than 'affectation and conceit and pretence and concealment'.[3] Such condemnations are not always just: they are often

the country gentleman, they who bear all the heat of the day...', delivered in the Commons in 1761 (Add. MSS. 38334, ff. 29 seq. 13 Nov. 1761), quoted in L. S. Sutherland, 'The City of London in Eighteenth-Century Politics', in *Essays Presented to Sir Lewis Namier*, ed. R. Pares and A. J. P. Taylor (London, 1956), p. 66). See also, Asa Briggs: 'Middle Class Consciousness in English Politics, 1780–1846', in *Past and Present*, No. 9 (April, 1956), pp. 65–74.

[1] P. B. Shelley, *A Philosophical View of Reform*, ed. T. W. Rolleston (London, 1920), pp. 44–6; also printed in R. J. White, *Political Tracts of Wordsworth, Coleridge, and Shelley* (Cambridge, 1954). Cf. T. J. Hogg, *Shelley at Oxford* (London, 1904), pp. 79–81. Brougham once spoke of attorneys and pettifoggers in terms very similar to those used by Shelley, and added that 'of all the kinds of labour which some writers have denominated unproductive, the labour bestowed on litigation is perhaps the least beneficial to society' (*Edinburgh Review*, January 1804. Referred to by John Clive in *Scotch Reviewers* (London, 1957), p. 141, n. 7).

[2] *O.E.D.* The earliest use noted is 1785; 'respectable' used to describe persons worthy of respect by reason of moral excellence is dated from 1755: used to describe persons 'of good or fair social standing, and having the moral qualities naturally appropriate to this', it is dated from 1758. Neither word appears in Johnson's Dictionary (1755). 'Respectable' (in any sense) appears in only four out of fourteen dictionaries of various dates between 1730 and 1820, in those of 1737, 1791, 1802, and *c*. 1814. 'Respectability' is not included until the dictionary of 1820, which quotes it as in use in 1812. 'Respectable' is often used in Boswell's *Life of Johnson* (1791): 'respectability' rarely.

[3] Quoted from Queen Victoria's Diary for 23 January 1840, by Algernon Cecil in *Queen Victoria and Her Prime Ministers* (London, 1953), p. 77. Melbourne's great-grandfather was a prosperous attorney of Southwell, Notts., and agent to the Coke family. His brother, Peniston, also an attorney, left his fortune to his nephews Robert and Matthew, who also inherited £100,000 from their father.

anachronistic and too general.[1] They ignore, what may be shown from the history of the attorneys, that respectability was a moralising force of immense strength in the civilising of eighteenth-century society, and in the imposing on it of new, necessary, and admirable standards of behaviour—necessary and admirable because they were consonant with the new social structure, as the old were not.

They were ideas which were being canvassed by professional groups other than the attorneys, but in some measure, their activities may be taken as typical of a much wider development. If they were to come to terms with the new structure that was crystallising out of the fluid society of the late eighteenth century, if they were to improve their social status, and avoid all the old abuse which had commonly been their lot, it was clear that they could not secure praise for the deserving without admitting the justice of many of the complaints about the unworthy. This they showed themselves willing to do, and the test they applied was the criterion of the middle classes, that of respectability. A respectable man was one whose affairs would bear looking into, who had nothing to be ashamed of. A respectable attorney was one who could be trusted to put the interests of justice and of his client before those of his own pocket, who would—if only because he could afford to—be fastidious about the sort of work he undertook. He would be concerned for the dignity of his profession, for his own professional character. He would also be jealous of the privileges of the profession, and convinced of the need of professional solidarity. In return for observing high standards of professional conduct, he would expect to obtain the esteem of society. He would certainly have agreed with Adam Smith when he wrote:

We trust our health to the physician; our fortune and sometimes our life and reputation to the lawyer and attorney. Such confidence could

Matthew the younger (later Bart.) attorney and steward to the Coke, Salisbury, and Egremont estates, married the sister and heir of G. C. Coke. It was his son, Peniston, who was (officially at least) the father of the prime minister. Melbourne himself was called to the bar in 1804, but gave up any intention of practising on the death of his elder brother in 1805.

[1] The remarks of Sir Harold Nicolson on this point in *Good Behaviour* (London, 1955), p. 225, seem too sweeping, and to ignore the value of this concept in the process described by G. M. Young as the 'moralizing of society'. Respectability was, moreover, a goal at which all classes could aim, whatever their economic status. On the one hand, the aristocracy itself became respectable; on the other, respectability became the ideal of many sections of the working class. On this last point, see T. R. Tholfsen, 'The Artisan and the Culture of Early Victorian Birmingham', *Birmingham Historical Journal*, IV, 2 (1954), 146–66.

not safely be reposed in people of a very low or mean condition. Their reward must be such, therefore, as may give them that rank in the society which so important a trust requires. The long time and great expense which must be laid out in their education, when combined with this circumstance, necessarily enhance still further the price of their labour.[1]

It was the aim of many men at the end of the century to secure the general recognition of this opinion.

What success the profession achieved in this attempt is partly explained by the fact that social and economic forces were working in its favour. But a great deal was done by the attorneys themselves to take advantage of these conditions, in the ways that have been suggested. Here it may be emphasised how much was done to secure acceptance of the view that this was a respectable calling, of some use to society, and that some at least of its members were respectable men. This was the burden of much of the pamphleteering; even when it was most bitter and unrestrained it was not against the profession as a whole, but only that part of it whose conduct brought all into disrepute.[2] Some, indeed, appealed to the highest motives of social responsibility, such as the author who published in 1811 *An Essay on the Law, being a summary view of the profession of a solicitor in opposition to prejudice and misconception.* The author addressed himself to the public as well as to the profession, and it was his hope that by pointing out the real nature of the profession he would help to remove the prejudice which had long existed against it. He insisted that solicitors were an essential part of the legal system of the country, and, for that reason, that their behaviour was of general importance. 'As constituents of one general system of jurisprudence, even the inferior members of municipal law cannot be without their influence on the welfare of society. However pure the fountain, if the streams are tainted, national health will languish.' He admitted that prejudice still existed against the profession, 'though happily decreasing from its prevalence in former times'. The most alarming consequences would follow if this prejudice were not overcome. The profession would be abandoned by all save those with 'vulgar and degraded minds,

---

[1] Adam Smith, *The Wealth of Nations* (Everyman ed.), 1, 93–4.

[2] The motto of Robert Holloway's *Strictures on the Characters of the most prominent practising Attornies*, was taken from *Timon of Athens*:
'All have not offended,
Like a shepherd, approach the Fold, and cull th'infected forth:
But kill not all together.'

such as are alive only to the base suggestions of gain, and insensible even to merited disgrace when accompanied with the sordid recompence of lucre'.

The author tried to show that the profession could appeal even to the noblest instincts. 'The main design of all human laws, the dispensation of justice, affords the first and brightest ornament to a solicitor's character.... He may rejoice in this animating truth, that fidelity even in his inferior office will not be without its effect in preserving inviolate from the corruptions which too easily infect the purest human laws, the unalterable and eternal nature of justice.' More even than this: 'The dispensation of justice is the most awful attribute of the Deity; and the meanest minister of all human laws, by a fervent zeal to secure the rights of his fellow creatures, imitates, in his humble sphere of action, the eternal purposes of the Supreme Being.'

It was a lamentable truth which he had to admit, that the law could be perverted to serve the ends of the lawyer, rather than those of justice. But the upright solicitor 'must prefer the dignity of his professional character, and the unsullied purity of justice, above any reward attending upon venality, however high, however dazzling'. Wise regulations had been made to discipline the profession, but it was the duty of its present members to observe such standards as would effectively remove such prejudice as remained, and to 'shed lustre on the paths on which darkness has too often brooded'. Solicitors could not hope for the highest rewards of society, nor aspire to its most exalted stations, but they could gain satisfaction from useful work well done, 'from the daily exercise of virtue and disinterestedness, though flowing in a quiet and retired channel'. And if, in spite of all, he fails to obtain a just recompense for his labours, he could take comfort in the knowledge that he had 'learnt to infuse the spirit of justice and benevolence into his whole professional life, from higher motives than the mere love of praise, or a mercenary wish of personal aggrandisement, and when he retires into his own bosom, he will enjoy peace and serenity, which the world can neither give nor take away'.

Such an appeal would hardly have been possible a hundred years earlier. But in its time, there were many attorneys who shared its ideals; and, acting alone or through professional societies, they had already done much to establish the respectability of their calling. Bearing in mind the public reputation of the profession at the beginning of the century, it can be seen that their task was not easy; nor was their success complete. But those who wrote about the profession in the last decades of the eighteenth century no longer indulged in the wholesale abuse which had been the earlier habit. They were reformers, not merely satirists, and they insisted that a clear distinction should be drawn between the respectable attorney and the pettifogger. This was the obvious way to set about reforming the profession and increasing its social status.

Many were ready to admit that this distinction existed. Johnson, declared Boswell, 'seldom encouraged general censure of any profession; but he was willing to allow a due share of merit to the various departments necessary in civilised life. In a splenetick, sarcastical, or jocular frame of mind, however, he would utter a pointed saying of that nature. One instance has been mentioned,[1] where he gave a sudden satirical stroke to the character of an *attorney*. The too indiscriminate admission to that employment, which requires both abilities and integrity, has given rise to injurious reflections, which are totally inapplicable to many very respectable men who exercise it with reputation and honour.'[2] In the same vein, the *Monthly Review* protested against the wholesale abuse of the profession, and pointed out that

an ingenious man, by selecting all the evils attendant on civil society, by displaying them in the most glaring colours, may exhibit such a picture as none but an hypochondriac will for a moment admit to be a faithful representation. In this manner have the law and its professors been treated. Every benefit which is derived from legal institutions has been concealed; while every abuse of them has been magnified with the most malicious industry.[3]

It was significant of this attitude that the respectable members of the profession were beginning to be known as solicitors, a term which, though less well established historically, had not habitually

---

[1] Cf. Boswell, *Life of Johnson* (Everyman ed.), I, 393, 'he did not care to speak ill of any man behind his back, but he believed the gentleman was an *attorney*'. See also Lord MacNair, *Dr Johnson and the Law* (Cambridge, 1948), p. 44.

[2] *Ibid.* II, 536. There are other examples of this attitude in Richard Cumberland's *The Country Attorney* (1787) (noticed in the *General Magazine*, July, 1787); *The Pettifogger Dramatized* (1797); *Observations on the Use and Abuse of the Practice of the Law* (1786); William Smith, *Mild Punishment Sound Policy* (1777); Crabbe, *The Borough* (1810), Letter VI, note at end.

[3] *Monthly Review* (March, 1789), noticing *Speculations upon Law and Lawyers* (1788), written by an irate litigant while immured in the King's Bench Prison.

been coupled with the adjective 'pettifogging' as had the term attorney. The pamphlet of 1811 quoted earlier in this chapter uses this term; it was used by Crabbe in *The Borough*: Shallow was an 'able and upright solicitor'. The habit was noticed by Maria Edgeworth in her novel *Patronage*, published in 1814. 'There are no such things as attorneys now in England', one of her characters remarked, 'they are all turned into solicitors and agents, just as every *shop* is become a *warehouse*, and every *service* a *situation*.'[1]

Linguistic affectations of this sort have their historical origin in the attempt of a rising section of the community to establish itself in society, and the concern with self-justification which it implies signifies, perhaps, a lack of self-confidence in face of the traditional order. But when these sections become sufficiently well-established to have confidence in their own judgments and their own standards, they exert an influence outside their immediate sphere. The respectable attorneys gain control of the profession: the respectable classes come to influence society as a whole.

The attorneys were typical too of those sections of the community which were insisting on higher standards of public and private morality: respectability in its limited aspect in the history of the profession has its counterpart in a wider sphere. These are the years of the evangelical revival and of the awful warning from France, in which men were turning from the assertion of rights to the consideration of duties.[2] But the impact of Wesley[3] and of the French Revolution was not alone responsible for this changing outlook. It reflected important changes in the structure of society itself, demanding a different system of social obligations.

[1] Also quoted in E. Halévy, *England in 1815* (2 ed. London, 1949), p. 21 n. 2. Boswell noted Johnson's amusement at the anxiety of the Society of Procurators in Scotland to be known as solicitors 'from a notion as they supposed, that it was more *genteel*' (*Life of Johnson* (Everyman ed.), II, 404). See also Lord MacNair, *Dr Johnson and the Law*, pp. 57–8. After the Judicature Act of 1873 attorneys were to be known as solicitors.

[2] Cf. such books as Thomas Gisborne's *An Enquiry into the Duties of the Higher Ranks and Middle Classes in Great Britain, resulting from their respective stations, professions and employments* (1794); and *A Defence of Attorneys, with reasons for thinking that no attorney who duly considers the present critical situation of his country, or who has at heart the increasing respectability of the profession, will object to be taxed* (1804).

[3] Methodists were discouraged from going to law with one another, and Wesley himself had a low opinion of lawyers, more than once intervening personally to discourage 'that villainous tautology of lawyers which is the scandal of our nation'. Cf. *Wesley's Journal*, ed. N. Curnock 1910–16), IV, 361–2, and VIII, 70.

It is in this period that the middle classes acquire self-confidence, and arouse the antagonism of men like Shelley and Lord Eldon who deplored their irruption into the old structure. It is in this period also that the professions gain self-confidence and begin to put their houses in order. Both the professions and the middle class became conscious of the role they could play in a society which gave freer scope for the exercise of individual talents than the old, in which influence and patronage had counted for more than individual worth, and Chesterfield could congratulate his fellow peers: 'We, my Lords, may thank Heaven that we have something better than our brains to depend upon.'[1] Now, Maria Edgeworth could write an entire novel with the purpose of showing 'how some lawyers and physicians may be pushed forward for a time, without much knowledge either of law or medicine, (but how)...on the contrary, others may, independently of patronage, advance themselves permanently by their own merit'.

These people, and the attorneys among them, enjoyed in the last years of the century a vastly enhanced position, and provided a strong bulwark to English society in these dangerous years. They had gained much, and stood to gain much more, so that for the moment their influence was exerted to strengthen society, not to weaken it. All over the country men such as Christopher Wallis, James Wheat, Joseph Hodgson, John Ambrose, and many others about whom less is known, like Charles Simeon's father, 'a wealthy and respectable' attorney of Reading,[2] and Mr Messiter of Wincanton,[3] were among the leaders of local society, a society which they were increasingly able to mould to their will. Halévy quotes a single example of an attorney who was secretary of the Corresponding Society, and suggests that the profession as a whole, because of its lack of social standing, 'had every inducement to

[1] Quoted D. Daiches, *Literature and Society* (London, 1938), p. 141.

[2] So described by the Revd. T. Pentycross in a letter to John Thornton, of 28 July 1783, quoted from the *Congregational Magazine* for December 1842, by Charles Smyth in *Simeon and Church Order* (Cambridge, 1940), p. 13.

[3] 'The most eminent attorney in this county and acquainted with all the monied people in it.... The respectability of Messiter is a circumstance on which I build much as well in my expectations that he will be able to do the business if practicable as that justice will be done your Lordship...' (Revd. S. Rogers to Earl Verney, 11 August and 30 November 1780, *Verney Letters of the Eighteenth Century*, ed. M. M. Verney (London, 1930), II, 273). Another example was Caleb Lowdham, a prosperous and well-connected Leicester attorney, and a member of the London and Leicester Pitt Clubs. See W. E. Beasley, *The Early History of an Old Leicester Firm of Attorneys* (Leicester, 1930).

become a discontented class in revolt against a system which condemned them to a position of social inferiority'.[1] But this study leads to a contrary conclusion, and suggests that the attorneys who were acting as officers in the militia, and as secretaries to Church and King Clubs and Associations for the Protection of Liberty and Property, were more typical of their profession than was John Frost.[2] Respectability and Jacobinism rarely went together.

It was in the nineteenth century that the professional classes came into their own, and the standards of professional morality which they set were in some measure those which decided the tone of society as a whole. Certainly the epithet 'respectable' is one which was frequently applied to these people, and it was one which many were proud to deserve. For however justly respectability may sometimes be linked with hypocrisy, at this time it represented a valuable and important attitude, which played its part in the process described by G. M. Young as the 'moralizing of society'.[3] The conditions and complexities of the new age demanded new standards and new organisations for those who had its work to do, and it was of some importance that the attorneys and others entered it with these standards clearly before them, and with suitable organisations either already in existence, or at hand.

[1] Halévy, *England in 1815*, p. 22.

[2] John Frost (1750–1842) was educated at Winchester, and became an attorney. He was struck off the Roll in 1797 as a result of a trial for sedition. He was given a free pardon by the Regent in 1813, but a move to have him reinstated as an attorney in 1815 failed, since the 'court held that his want of practice and experience in the profession made him presumably unfit for the employment' (*State Trials*, xxii; *D.N.B.*). William Hone, who was sent to an attorney's office in London in 1790 at the age of ten, was removed by his father when he came under the influence of the Corresponding Society, and sent to another attorney in Chatham. He left the law in 1800 for bookselling and publishing (*D.N.B.*).

[3] G. M. Young, *Victorian England: Portrait of an Age* (Oxford, 1949), p. 4.

THE APPRENTICESHIPS OF RICHARD CARRE AND SAMUEL BERRIDGE

RICHARD CARRE was articled to Thomas Wright and Francis Sitwell, attorneys at Sheffield in the early part of the eighteenth century. His Day Book, which is preserved at Sheffield,[1] gives a detailed picture of his life as an articled clerk in the period 1724-30. It begins appropriately enough on 2 December 1724, 'Engrossed a deed', for this seems to have been one of his principal occupations, together with that of attending his master on his business journeys, especially to hold manorial courts, and to enter indentures of apprenticeship at the Hall of the Cutlers' Company in Sheffield. At sessions time he went with him to Doncaster, York, Rotherham, and Chesterfield. He was sent to Wakefield to buy stamps, he issued subpoenas, collected rents, and when there was no work of this kind to be done, he occupied his time in copying out precedents, or reading from such current legal manuals as Giles Jacob's *Common Law Common Plac'd*.

Carre's masters seem to have taken the task of training him very seriously. The main purpose of the Day Books seems to have been to act as a sort of check on his activities, and may perhaps have served as documentary evidence of his diligence—or lack of it— during his clerkship, and have been produced for the inspection of the judges when he was seeking admission. This at least seems to be the meaning of the various marginal comments added in a hand different from that of the main body of the text, and which is presumably that of the master.

On 31 January 1726/7, the clerk notes, '12 sheets of Bradesford's answer—Bradesford had not the skin till almost noon'. Beneath this is written in a different hand, 'This is the engrossment of the answer and is 39 lines of the skin and is but 10 sheets of the draft and 2 lines though here it is said 12, these sheets are very wide and there happens to be a sheet or more of the 10 struck out, but however all this should have been done in less than two hours and

T[ibbitts] C[ollection] 384.

better done than it is done'. On 6 April 1727 Carre writes: 'Finished Swynson's writ'; to this is added the comment: 'Although you have writ that Swynson's writ is finished I find it is not, let there be a fourth copy made, and stay in your office from 8 in the morning till noon and from 2 to 7 and see if business cannot be better minded. If it be not I must at last come. . . .' This has been heavily scored through, so that the last words are indecipherable; perhaps the clerk was anxious that those looking over his book should not be able to read his master's strictures on his behaviour.

Between the entries for 11 and 12 July 1727, the master had written: 'Friday 14, 10 in the morning I find nothing entered to be done of Wednesday and Thursday and he lay out of my house last night and not yet come in.' On 8 May the master noted: 'Although I required every night you should enter what you had done that day here is nothing done in my absence since Wednesday the 3rd.' On 17 July Carre claimed to have copied out a conveyance, but his master noted: 'At 10 o'clock of Monday night there was not a sheet of this conveyance copied, and he not in when the doors were locked. . . .' Again the remainder has been scored through too heavily to be legible. Some days afterwards Carre noted that he had nothing before him to do. On such occasions he might be employed in running errands for Mrs Wright.

On 3 February 1727/8, Carre went up to London with Sitwell, and returned to Sheffield on 21 March. The details about this visit are not recorded in the Day Book, but are apparently given in a note book preserved at Renishaw Hall. He travelled, wrote Sir George Sitwell,[1] 'Carrying the portmantle and mail leather bag strapped with rings and staples on the saddle behind him'. Both travellers carried a pair of pistols. Once in London, the clerk was kept busy with the legal business of the visit which was entrusted to him, while his master did the more important work, and paid social calls on his relatives. He was 'kept busy running about between the King's Bench, the Green Seal Office, Register Office, Custos Brevium Office, King's Silver Office in Brick Court, Alienation Office, Cursitor's Office, Chirographer's Office, Return Office, Warrants of Attorney Office, and so forth'.[2]

On his return to Sheffield the Day Book begins again. On 10 July he records that he 'read several trials for High Treason, not

[1] G. R. Sitwell, *The Hurts of Haldworth* (Oxford, 1930), ch. xv, p. 267.
[2] *Ibid.* p. 269.

having any other book to inform myself in', and on 22 July, 'Had
nothing before me and read all day in Bridall's works upon conveyances to the 32nd page'. On 29 August he was 'with Mr Sitwell
at Town taking the Master Cutler's account and afterwards at the
Feast'.[1] On 25 September he spent the morning making a fair copy
of a will, and attended the school burgesses feast in the afternoon.
He kept an account of all the money spent and received by him on
his master's account—payments for letters, stationery, rents and
fines received at manorial courts.[2]

In the same collection at Sheffield is another Day Book which
seems also to have been Carre's. Apart from the single note saying,
'lay out of my house a second time . . .', there are no more strictures
on his behaviour, but he still had to account for himself, and still
noted the books he had been reading. These included the *Compleat
Attorney*, the Statute Laws, Littleton's *Tenures*, Nelson's *Justice
of the Peace*, Brown on Fines, *Common Law Common Plac'd*, and
the *Guide to the Conveyancer*. He read up such subjects as baron
and feme, settlements and removals, and the practice of the ec-
clesiastical court. On one occasion he was able to put his legal
knowledge to his own use. '1 October 1729. Went over to my
mother's to inquire and meet people who were about presenting a
watercourse belonging to her when having produced and examined
our witnesses, convinced them of their error. 8 October, went about
3 miles about a little business of my own with master's leave.'[3]

Samuel Berridge was articled to William Leigh a solicitor of
Bardon, near Taunton, and the correspondence between Leigh,
Samuel's father (a Leicester attorney), and a friend of both parties,
Mr Huxtable, a master at Rugby School, in 1820, illustrates the
conditions under which Leigh's articled clerks lived.[4]

On 19 April Leigh wrote to Huxtable:

. . . I have always been very particular upon such occasions which the
peculiar situation and circumstances of my home and family in which
my clerks are more than ordinarily inmates and part of the society
render more than usually requisite; and as in January last I articled my
own son . . . it is become more essential to my comfort to be very cautious

---

[1] Sitwell was Clerk to the Cutlers' Company.
[2] T.C. 385.   [3] T.C. 386.
[4] These letters are printed in W. E. Beasley, *The Early History of an Old
Leicester Firm of Attorneys, 1767–1865* (privately printed, Leicester, 1930),
pp. 24–7. I am most grateful to the Leicester City Librarian for sending this
book to Cambridge for my use.

in the selection both as my two articled clerks will be so young in the office at the same time, and as I would not for any consideration on earth introduce to the society of my son a young man in the least degree likely to set him a bad example upon any one point, as he is in himself, I am most thankful to say, as well disposed a youth as can possibly be. I will therefore enter at some length into my views. I have been led to think not only that a very good classical education is necessary for the profession.... My clerks work very hard and we do not know the meaning of 'office hours'. All hours within which I want them are office hours.... My articled clerks must look up to and respect my highly respectable managing clerk, Mr Rowcliffe, whom I have brought up and who has been with me upwards of 14 years. My writing clerk is as good a lad as can possibly be; we never hear of a dog or a gun. Business and study fill up the hours here. The situation and peculiar circumstances of my family prevent my taking any young gentleman who is not of the Established Church. My terms are 600 guineas, and my clerks pay for their washing out of the house, and I always stipulate...for obvious reasons that in the case of sickness the clerk should be provided with lodging and attendants as well as medical assistance by his father. You do not mention the age of the young gentleman...and as the distance is too great to propose an interview, which I have always wished, as so much depends upon the manners of the young gentleman and the way in which he has been brought up, and as my clerks are certainly cast with the best society in the neighbourhood, I trust it would not be considered indelicate towards either you or Mr Berridge that I make these general inquiries, that the reasons into which I have thought it best to enter so fully, necessarily will require my having most satis-factorily answered; at the same time I shall be happy to hear from you whether you think your young friend will answer the description I have endeavoured to give of what I wish my clerks to be.

On 27 April Mr Berridge wrote to Huxtable approving these conditions—except the 600 guineas which he wanted reduced to 500—and said, '...he requires no more as to character and conduct than every gentleman similarly circumstanced ought to do'. He added that his son would 'be 16 on 22 May next and from his infancy was taught to revere the King and the Established Church'. These conditions were eventually agreed to. Samuel was told to write to Leigh sending a specimen of his handwriting, and Leigh wrote that he thought it would develop into a good business hand, but that he regretted that the young man was not acquainted with law hands. When the period of articles was over Samuel returned to Leicester and became a partner in his father's firm.

APPENDIX II

THE ADMISSION OF AN ATTORNEY

IN his Memoirs William Hickey describes very vividly the way in which he was examined and admitted as an attorney before leaving London for Jamaica in 1775.[1] Mr Justice Yates, one of the judges of the Court of King's Bench, and an old friend of his father's, had promised to sign the fiat. He invited Hickey to breakfast so that he could be examined as to his being 'equal to the practice of an attorney', and was told to send his articles in advance to Yates's clerk. Hickey goes on:

At the time appointed I attended, and in a terrible fright I was at the ordeal I imagined I had to pass through, and the probable loss I might be at in answering some of the many questions I understood would be put to me upon points of practice. Being conducted into his parlour where the breakfast things were all arranged, in five minutes the Judge entered. We sat down, and he recommended his French rolls and muffins as of the best sort, but so predominant were my fears about the dreaded examination that I had no inclination to eat. Breakfast being over, he asked me how I liked the Law, how long I had been out of my clerkship, and two or three other questions equally unimportant, when a servant entered to announce the carriage being at the door, whereupon he desired his clerk to be called, upon whose appearance he enquired whether Mr Hickey's Certificate was ready. The clerk having it and other papers in his hand, the Judge took it from him, and after perusal subscribed his name, and then said, 'Now, Mr Hickey, if you will be so good as to accompany me to Westminster Hall, I will get you sworn, and the business concluded.' I accordingly stepped into his coach which conveyed us to Westminster, and immediately going into Court, where he had taken his seat upon the Bench, the proper officer was asked whether he had the roll, and answering in the affirmative my Certificate was delivered to him and read as was also an affidavit of my Master Mr Bayley's. This being done the Judge ordered the oaths to be administered to me, after which, and my subscribing my name to each, I was entered upon the Roll as an attorney, and making a respectful bow to the Bench and the Bar, I retired, most agreeably relieved from my apprehensions respecting the various interrogatories I had expected would be put to me on the subject of my qualifications.

[1] *Memoirs of William Hickey* (London, 1913), I, 331–2, also quoted Holdsworth, *History of English Law*, XII, 62.

On 11 November 1759 Robert Nevill went up to London from Tamworth to get himself admitted as an attorney.[1] He seems to have spent a clerkship very like that of Richard Carre—collecting rents, serving notices to quit, mentioning very carefully when he had by chance torn an agreement he was copying. He took with him to London a bill for £10 on Mr William Ayre, Grocer in Newgate Street, and £6. 14s. 6d. in his pocket. In the portmanteau in the coach he took 'A Banyan, waistcoat and Breeches, 4 Ruffle Shirts, 4 plain do., 6 Stocks, 2 Cravatts, 3 pair of black stockings, 4 Night Caps, a Periwig, 4 Pockett Handkerchiefs, and 2d. in my pockett'. He seems to have stayed in London until the following June.

On 21 November 1759 he was admitted an attorney of the Court of Common Pleas, and noted down the expense in detail:

> To a treble 40s. Stamp and Parchment on which Admission
> engrossed: £6. 1s. 0d.
> To a treble 6d. Stamp and Paper for an Affidavit of Service of
> my Articles of Clerkship annexed to one part and filed in
> Court: £0. 1s. 7d.
> For the Oath, (taken before a Judge) 1s., for the Judge's Fiat
> 6/6 and gave the Judge's clerk 3s.   £0. 10s. 6d.
> To the Clerk of the Warrants for searching for the Affidavit
> of the due execution of Articles of Clerkship (which Af-
> fidavit is taken to the Secondary of the Prothonotary in
> whose office you are admitted to be read in open court
> before the oaths are taken):   £0. 3s. 6d.
> To the fees in Court and the Crier   £0. 10s. 6d.
> To the Clerk of the Warrants for the inrollment of
> Admission: £0. 2s. 6d.

On 30 November, Nevill was admitted a solicitor in the High Court of Chancery. This cost him 13s. 1d.

> To a treble 6d. Stamp and paper for Affidavit of seeing the
> Gent. who sign the Cert. or Testimonial of your ability,
> and sign it (annexed to the Cert. and filed): £0. 1s. 7d.
> For the oath taken before a Master Ordinary 1/6 and for
> exhibit 2/6:   £0. 4s. 0d.

[1] These details are derived from his note-book which was lent to me by his great-grandson, Mr R. C. Reginald Nevill, who is also a solicitor. Richard seems to have had an extensive practice, attending the sessions for Warwickshire, Bedfordshire, and Staffordshire, and having frequent business in Birmingham. He put out money on loan, and had election business at Tamworth and Leicester, and acted as estate agent for Lord Donegal at Fisherwick.

To Mr Leach (Public Clerk to the Masters) for ingrossing
   my admission and getting it signed by two Masters: £o. 5s. od.
To Mr Richd. Asheton Senr., Clerk of the Petty Bag for the
   inrollment: £o. 2s. 6d.

There is no note of any examination. Nevill took the opportunity
of buying several law books when he was in Town. These included
Horseman's three volumes on Conveyancing, £2. 4s. od.; Jacob's
Law Dictionary, £1. 1s. od.; the *Attorney's Pocket Book*, 6s.; the
Attorney and Solicitor's Practice, 6s. 6d.; the *Impartial Lawyer*,
6d.; Jacob's *Common Law Common Plac'd*, 6s.; and Manwood's
Forest Law, 6d. Nevill was back in Tamworth in June 1760, in
time to attend the Summer Assizes at Warwick.

CHRISTOPHER WALLIS: NOTES FROM THE JOURNAL

I. ESTIMATED PROFITS FROM BUSINESS

25 December 1793–25 December 1794	£ 560
25 December 1794–25 December 1795	£ 580
1797	£ 722
1798	£ 750
1799	£ 800
1800	£ 823
1801	£1800
1802	£1930
1803	£1970
1804	£2130
1805	£1610

To these sums were to be added his profits from rents and mines. In the six years ending in December 1805 he estimated that he had made a clear saving of £13,763.

More detailed accounts of his professional affairs are given for certain years.

1799

Lord Arundell's business	£ 50
Exor's of Rev S. Sandys	£ 50
Rowe Clerk ats. Price and others in Chancery	£ 40
Exchequer business	£ 40
Six vessels and Cargoes claimed in Exchequer	£120
Conveyancing etc.	£ 60
Law	£ 60
Ecclesiastical Courts	£ 30
Chancery	£ 30
Droits of Admiralty	£ 26
Wrecks, etc.	£ 20
A great variety of attendances	£120
	£646
Profits on bargains in the course of the year	£154
	£800

1804

Lord Arundell's business	£200
Annuities	£200
Conveyancing	£150
Commissions on sales	£100
Mr Rowe's assignments	£300
His business	£400
Ships and Cargoes	£ 50
Exchequer	£ 30
Conveyancing	£ 80
Fines etc.	£ 50
Chancery	£ 30
Law	£300
Ecclesiastical Courts	£100
Attendances	£100
Parish business	£ 40
	£2130

1805

Lord Arundell's business	£100
Annuities	£100
Conveyancing	£100
Commissions on sales	£300
Mr Rowe's business	£ 50
Ships and Cargoes	£250
Exchequer	£100
Conveyancing	£ 50
Fines etc.	£ 20
Chancery	£ 30
Law	£300
Ecclesiastical Courts	£ 50
Attendances	£120
Parish Business	£ 40
	£1610

2. AN ATTORNEY'S WEEK

1796 *Sunday, 27 March*

Easter. Set off this morning in the Royal Caroline Diligence for Exeter and Bodmin. Breakfasted at Oakhampton, dined at Launceston, slept at Bodmin. At Bodmin and there attended Miss Fr. Harme and consulting about the claims made on her estate by the widow of the late Mr Jno. Harme and about the suit between her and Mr Mountsteven, etc. Slept at Bodmin. Bed at 11. Wind N.W. some snow and cold.

Monday, 28 March

Up at ½ past 4. Wind N.W. some snow and cold. At Truro and there attended Mr Warner undersheriff for a warrant on attachment against Robt. Snell in Harris and anor. agst. Basset and ors. for non payment of costs. At Falmouth, and there intended to arrest Robt. Snell, but Mr Pearse attorney requested it might not be done, and he undertook to settle the business in three days.

At Helston and there left Mr Scantlebury, and then to Trevarno. Bed at ½ past 9. Wind W. very gloomy and cold.

Tuesday, 29 March

Up at 6. Wind W. very cold and gloomy, but not so cold as yesterday. Ther. 42.

A great number of attendances, and writing and reading many letters. Attended Miss Huthrance at Gwincar about her sister's mortgage. Viewing several lands at Trevarno for spring tillage.

Entering up several accounts, and making up costs of London journey. Quitted office at ½ past 8. Wind W. rather gloomy and cold.

Wednesday, 30 March

Up at ½ past 6. Wind N.W. some rain and wind. Ther., 43. Writing many letters and entering several accounts.

At Helston and there attended Mr Jno. Polyglass.

Consulting about Mr Scantlebury's patent, and about carrying the same into execution.

Attended Cuthbert Tremayne agst. Treloar and received directions to prosecute.

Attended Rev. Mr Sandys on several mortgages.

Attended Sandys about several parish matters.

Quitted office at ½ past 8. Wind W very gloomy and looks like rain.

Thursday, 31 March

Up at ½ past 6. Wind S.W. gloomy but mild. Ther. 45.

Many attendances and writing several letters.

Making out and stating several accounts and entering them in the cash books.

Making bill of costs in Harris and Harris agst. Basset Bart. and settling with Mr Pearse the costs taxed and demanded by sbpa.

Quitted office at ½ past 9. Wind S very thick rain.

Friday, 1 April

Up at ½ past 6. Wind S very soft thick rain. Ther 48.

A great number of attendances and writing many letters.

Making out and stating several accounts, and making out the accounts of the Bog Mine.

At the Bog and there paying the men and viewing the mines.
Quitted the office at ½ past 8. Wind S soft thick rain.

Saturday, 2 April

Up at ½ past 6. Wind S.W. very fair and mild. Ther. 49.
A great number of attendances and writing several letters.
Attended at Helston Mr Thos. James of Trelandoen, and talking over
the matter between him and Nichs. Andrew a prisoner in Bodmin at
his suit. When Mr James desired he might be discharged from custody
and I wrote to my brother for that purpose.
Attended Mr James relative to his demand of Hearne and Trean Bankrupts and consulting how to proceed therein, taking minutes for that
purpose.
Attended Mr Rowe and Capt. Edward Richards about Wheal Bog and
Wheal Prosper in Polladras Sett.
Attended Mr Grylls and purchased Ruth Dower Stamps and tenements
off him for £400 on the lives of Mrs Grylls 27 and Mrs Short 24 last
lease granted in 1777 Mrs Grylls then 8 Mrs Short 5.
Attended Mr Bull agst. Boulton and Watt, and consulting on further
proceedings therein.
Attended Mr Grylls on the same cause and consulting on further
proceedings.
Quitted office at ½ past 6. Wind N.W. very fair and very mild.

A NOTE ON NUMBERS

IT was a frequent source of complaint that there were too many attorneys, so that pettifogging practice was inevitable. It is obviously impossible to estimate how many attorneys would have been sufficient for any district, but it may be suggested that the figures put forward by the critics of the profession were generally too low, and failed to take into account the growing complexity of English society. The returns made to the House of Commons under the 1729 Act stated that there were 2236 attorneys of the Court of Common Pleas, 893 of the Court of King's Bench, and 1700 solicitors in Chancery. These figures, however, are probably not accurate, and they do not take account of the fact that many men were accredited in all three courts. Some information is available in the various town and county directories, but, again, this is hardly reliable as to numbers. The Law Lists do not begin until 1775, and these too, in the early stages, are obviously incomplete, omitting many attorneys, and containing the names of some who were not on the Roll. Browne's Law List was replaced by Hughes's in 1798. John Hughes was an official of the Stamp Office, and had access to the returns made to that office under the act of 1785 which introduced the annual practising certificate. The volume for 1798 is clearly incomplete, but by 1800 these lists, in so far as they tally with the Stamp Office returns, are the most accurate source available for names and numbers of attorneys. In the lists that follow, the numbers of attorneys in certain towns are given for the years 1790 and 1800. These figures are derived from the Law Lists, and I am grateful to the council of the Law Society for letting me examine these and other volumes in their library in Chancery Lane. The towns selected were not chosen with any special purpose in mind; they are merely the towns for which, for one reason and another, I happened to want this information.

	1790	1800
Bath	24	31
Berwick	9	7
Beverley	10	7

	1790	1800
Birmingham	40	44
Bristol	61	71
Cambridge	15	16
Carlisle	15	11
Chelmsford	5	4
Chester	29	34
Chesterfield	10	9
Cockermouth	7	4
Colchester	10	15
Gisborough	1	4
Helston	9	7
Hexham	10	5
Hull	16	20
Knaresborough	8	5
Leeds	26	23
Lincoln	13	12
Liverpool	68	76
London[1]	c. 1755	
Malton	1	7
Manchester	40	61
Nantwich	11	5
Newcastle under Lyme	12	12
Newcastle upon Tyne	29	25
North Shields	6	7
Northwich	6	3
Norwich	32	33
Pickering	1	2
Prescot	5	3
Salisbury	22	15
Scarborough	9	5
Sheffield	11	19
Stockport	7	11
Sunderland	11	10
Warrington	9	10
Whitby	7	2
Whitehaven	14	5
Wigan	6	6
York	20	38

[1] E. Halévy, *England in 1815*, p. 21 n. 2, quotes Gneist, *Verfassungs- und Verwaltungsrecht*, vol. 1 (Berlin, 1857), p. 509, as giving the number of solicitors in London in 1800 as 1800, and in the provinces as 3500.

APPENDIX V

THE PROFESSIONS IN THE EIGHTEENTH CENTURY: A BIBLIOGRAPHICAL NOTE

SOME support is given to the conclusions reached in this work by other studies of different professions in the eighteenth century. In his unpublished Fellowship dissertation on the *English Parish Clergy, 1660–1800*, in the Library of Trinity College, Mr P. A. Bezodis describes the development from the position in which the country clergyman was a man of no social prestige, when there was a great and almost impassable gulf fixed between him and those who occupied the high places of the Church, to the point at which, although vast economic and social differences persisted, yet all were conscious of belonging to a single professional body, and when they were more liable to be criticised for neglecting the duties of the cloth than for being socially pretentious upstarts. Dr B. M. Hamilton, in her London Ph.D. thesis dealt with the *Medical Professions in the Eighteenth Century*. (The results are summarised in an article in *Economic History Review*, 2nd series, IV.) She discerns two strands in the development among the doctors, a revolution in medical training, and a growth of professional feeling. She writes:

As a result of these two movements and of the great expansion of the middle classes, by 1800 the professional scene of a hundred years before had been completely transformed: the apothecaries, once mere tradesmen and the 'servants of the physician', had become practising doctors; the surgeons had dissociated themselves from the barbers, and the 'pure' or hospital surgeon had become a specialist of high reputation; whilst the physicians, originally few in numbers and of a good social position, had received an influx of hard-working middle-class graduates from Leyden and Edinburgh. All types met in the wards of the London and provincial hospitals. Professional honour, etiquette and status were now matters of the liveliest debate, and by the end of the century a man could achieve social standing as well as reputation through his profession. In 1660 a physician was a gentlemen, while apothecaries and surgeons were mere craftsmen: by 1800 it is possible to see them all as part of the new professional classes.[1]

[1] *Econ. Hist. Rev., loc. cit.* p. 141.

These conclusions were underlined in Dr C. E. Newman's Fitzpatrick Lectures for 1954, which, though mainly devoted to the nineteenth century, described the growth of professional solidarity and professional societies among the physicians and apothecaries, and showed the aims and achievements of the apothecaries to be very similar to those of the attorneys.

There are no comparable studies of the other professions in this period, but there are suggestive comments in such work as has been done. Technical, as opposed to, or in addition to, social qualifications, were beginning to be demanded in the army and the navy. (Cf. Norbert Elias, 'Studies in the Genesis of the Naval Profession', *British Journal of Sociology*, 1 (1950), 291–309; M. A. Lewis, *England's Sea Officers* (London, 1939); H. W. Richmond, 'The Navy', in *Johnson's England*, ed. A. S. Turberville (2nd ed. Oxford, 1952), 1, 39–65; E. Robson, 'Purchase and Promotion in the British Army in the Eighteenth Century', *History*, XXXVI, nos. 126 and 127 (1951), 57–72; Sir John Fortescue, 'The Army', in Turberville, *op. cit.* 1, 66–87.) The Royal Military Academy at Woolwich was founded in 1800, and the Military School at High Wycombe in 1802, under the inspiration of the Duke of York, but these were only first steps, and the name of the Duke of York cannot be called to mind without thinking also of Mary Anne Clarke.

The growth of professional feeling and of professional societies among architects was noticed by H. M. Colvin in his *Biographical Dictionary of English Architects, 1660–1840* (London, 1954). 'Architecture', he wrote, 'had become a reputable and remunerative occupation which the professional man could view with favour for his son—one which no longer depended on the uncertainties of aristocratic patronage or the doubtful devices of speculative building. The architect had at last taken his place alongside the doctor and the lawyer, and it would not be long before he began to formulate his own standards of professional conduct and to create an organisation through which they could be enforced.'[1]

The growth of the banking profession had recently been described by Dr L. S. Pressnell in his *Country Banking in the Industrial Revolution* (Oxford, 1956). The works of A. S. Collins on *Authorship in the Age of Johnson* (London, 1927), and *The Profession of Letters, 1780–1830* (London, 1928), consider the improving status

[1] Colvin, *op. cit.* p. 15; see also p. 25.

of authors. The examples of Garrick and of Reynolds did much to enhance the position of actors and artists.

Many of these conclusions are summarised by Professor Edward Hughes in his article on 'The Professions in the Eighteenth Century', in *Durham University Journal*, new series, XIII, ii (1952), 46–55, and the part played by the professions in one part of England is described in chapter III of his book *North Country Life in the Eighteenth Century* (Oxford, 1952).

These studies suggest certain significant similarities, but there are important differences, due to the differing natures of the various professions. Only in the case of the legal and medical professions did the actual ability to perform certain professional functions have a very significant effect on the rewards which were obtained; only in these cases was there an accepted body of technical knowledge which would make it possible for professional ability to be tested— and even here the opportunity was not fully exploited. The other professions—the army, the navy, the church—were more naturally spheres in which the patronage system worked, and increased. None of those who practised in these fields were under the necessity of the doctors and the lawyers of attracting clients by their individual qualities. In all three cases a certain number of vacancies existed, so that it was natural that in these professions men were appointed to certain places, than that they carved out careers for themselves. But there were signs that even here the position was changing, and that new conceptions of the duties of such men, as well as the new needs of society—such influences as that of Wesley on the idea of a clergyman, and the urgent needs of the Napoleonic wars on the military profession, are of importance—are pointing in the general direction of professional advancement on the basis of proved ability alone. That professional men should also be gentlemen had been clearly enough accepted in the cases of the army and the navy: the story here is of the process by which it ceases to be the only qualification insisted on. In the case of the clergy the process is in some ways reversed—the clergy come to aspire to gentility, and gentility in a clergyman comes to be insisted on by patrons and by society, perhaps to the neglect of professional qualifications and aptitudes.[1]

[1] Theological colleges for the training of clergymen were founded in 1839 at Chichester, in 1840 at Wells, and in 1854 at Cuddesdon, but some concern was felt about the matter before this. See W. O. Chadwick, *The Founding of Cuddesdon* (Oxford, 1954).

Commenting on William Hutton's assertion in 1780 that 'Every man has his future in his own hands', Professor Ashton has said: 'That, it is needless to say, has never been true, or even half true; but anyone who looks closely at English society in the mid- and late eighteenth century will understand how it was possible for it to be said, for at this time vertical mobility had reached a degree higher than that of any earlier, or perhaps of any succeeding age.'[1] The professions were important factors in this 'vertical mobility', and one of the main ways in which the old society with its emphasis on 'status' was broken down. Professor Pares has suggested that 'The enormous growth of the organised professions (is) perhaps the greatest change in the whole of modern history',[2] and Professor Woodward has spoken of the professional classes of mid-Victorian England as 'perhaps the most important new social phenomenon of the age'.[3] The professions are important in two ways, for, apart from serving as a sort of social ladder, they are examples of social organisations in which individual merit must necessarily count for more than inherited status, and their history is, therefore, doubly important for understanding the differences between eighteenth and nineteenth-century England.

[1] T. S. Ashton, *The Industrial Revolution* (Oxford, 1949), p. 17.
[2] R. Pares, *George III and the Politicians* (Oxford, 1953), pp. 16–17.
[3] E. L. Woodward, '1851 and the Visibility of Progress', in *Ideas and Beliefs of the Victorians* (London, 1949), p. 61.

LIST OF PRIMARY SOURCES

(a) MANUSCRIPTS, ETC.

Birmingham Law Society, Minutes, 1818–30.
Bristol Law Society, Minutes, 1774–80.
Bristol Law Library Society, Minutes, 1819–30.
Cumberland Record Office: Joseph Hodgson MSS.
Essex Record Office:
    Day Book, 1798–1806, D/DGg 1
    Bill Book, 1772–1782   5
    Day Book, 1779–1801   6
    Bill Book, 1766–1772, D/DO 14/1
    Solicitors' Letter Books, 1731–1815, D/DO 17/1–4
                                 18/1–2
                                 19/1–30
                                 20/1–5
    Precedent Books, 1760–1795, D/DRc B 11 and 12
    Account Books, 1794–1807, D/DRc B 15
    Account Books and Letters, D/DR B 1, 1 A, 5
                            D/DRc B 1–7
                            C 1
                            F 10 and 17
                            F 73–79
                    D/DEl T 1/1–21
                          T 2/1–48
    Justice's Notebook, D/DVf 8
    Attorney's Letter Book and Diary, 1746–59, D/DEl F 3
    Attorney's Precedent Books, D/DEl B 1–3
    Bills, etc. D/DEl 2, 3, 4, 8; B 19–26
    Bill Book, 1770–1800, D/DHw
    Accounts, 1775–1800, D/DHw
    Bills, receipts, etc. D/DHw A 5–23, 69, 70, 73
    Misc. Letters G 2, H 18, F 10–12, 15, 16
Liverpool Underwriters' Association, Cases and Opinions of a Liverpool
    Attorney, 1732–80.
Munby MSS. in the possession of A. N. L. Munby, Esq., Librarian of
    King's College, Cambridge.
Nevill: Robert Nevill's Diary in the possession of R. C. Reginald Nevill,
    Esq. of Ringwood, Hampshire.
Potts: Account Book of Charles Potts in the possession of Henry Potts,
    Esq. of Chester.

Public Record Office, Stamp Office Registers (Apprentices). I.R. 1/1
    19, 38, 42, 51, 70.
Report of the Select Committee on Legal Education, 1846: Reports,
    Committees (1846), vol. x.
Sheffield City Libraries:
  Athorpe Muniments, AM 692, Lawyer's Account Book
  Beauchief Muniments, section II, Steade Papers, BM 198
                                    Steade Letters, BM 202
                                    Steade Receipts, BM 203
  Tibbitts Collection
    T.C. 379 Thomas Wright's Cash Book, 1701–4
        380 Cash Book, 1703–4
        381 Personal Note Book, 1712–13
        383 Thomas Tofield's Cash Book, 1714–16
        384 Richard Carre's Day Book, 1727–9
        385 Richard Carre's Cash Book, 1727–8
        386 Richard Carre's Day Book, 1729–31
        517 Private Correspondence of Samuel Dawson
        518 Thomas Wright's Letters to Dawson, 1733–73
        519 Misc. Personal Bills
        520 Letters from J. Richardson, Furnival's Inn, 1750–69
        521 Letters from Daniel Fox, Chancery Office, 1753–77
        522 General Correspondence, 1718–76
        523 Correspondence of William Hoyle, 1759–88
        524 Letters to John Hoyland, 1775
        525 General Correspondence of John Hoyland
        526 Letters to John Redfearne, 1750–6
        527 Letters to Thomas Wright
        528 Letters to Francis Sitwell, 1721–2
        530 Letters to John Redfearne, 1742–70
      1050 Samuel Dawson's Statement for legal expenses
Wentworth Woodhouse Muniments:
  Bright Papers, 112–155
  Letters and Papers of 2nd Marquis of Rockingham,
      Richard Fenton's Letters and Accounts, 1765
  Papers and Correspondence of 2nd Earl Fitzwilliam
    F 34–42, 48–50, Letters concerning elections
      67–69, Letters from Charles Bowns, etc.
      70–71 Papers relating to Fitzwilliam Estates
      72–81 Correspondence about Malton Estates, 1787–1830
  Elections
    E 1–36 Yorkshire County Election, 1784
      37–208 Yorkshire County Election, 1807

Wentworth Woodhouse Muniments: Elections (*cont.*):
> 219 Account Book of Richard Fenton with Rockingham on
> election of William Thornton, M.P. for York City, 1758

Wheat Collection:
> W.C. 1258–75 Letters to and from James Wheat
> 1276–86 Bills, Wheat, household and professional
> 1298 Cash Book, 1787–8
> 2237 Wilberforce's Committee Bills, 1807
> 2258 Office Accounts, 1785
> 2259 Wheat's building accounts, 1772–4
> 2260 Bills of James Milne of Newark

Diary and Account Book of William Adam.

Society of Gentlemen Practisers in the Courts of Law and Equity, Records, ed. Edwin Freshfield, London, 1897.

Truro: Royal Institution of Cornwall, Journal of Christopher Wallis, 1790–1815.

Yorkshire Law Society Minutes, 1786–1834.

Library of the Incorporated Law Society:
> Browne's Law List, 1775–1796; New Law List (Hughes') 1798–.

Lawyers' and Magistrates' Magazine, 1790–4.

(b) PAMPHLETS

E. LEACH. *Downfall of the Unjust Lawyers and Rising of the Just* (1652).

THOMAS MANLEY. *The Sollicitor; declaring both as to knowledge and practice how such an undertaker ought to be qualified* (1663).

M. HILDESLEY. *Religio Jurisprudentis: or, a Lawyer's advice to his son* (1685).

ANON. *The Young Lawyer's Recreation: Being a collection of several pleasant passages and customs in the law* (1694).

ANON. *Observations on the Dilatory and Expensive Proceedings in the Court of Chancery in relation to the Bill now depending in the House of Commons, for lessening the Number of Attorneys and Solicitors, and regulating their practice, etc., together with some methods of redressing the same* (1701).

ANON. *True Picture of an ill practiser of the Law. In a dialogue between a sollicitor and his intended client* (1703).

AN ATTORNEY. *Proposals Humbly Offered to the Parliament for remedying the great charge and delay of Suits of Law and in Equity* (1707).

ANON. *An Essay in Praise of Knavery* (1723).

ANON. *The Pettifogger, a satire in hudibrastick verse, displaying the various frauds, deceits and knavish practices of the pettifogging counsellors, attornies, solicitors and clerks, in and about London and Westminster, and all market towns in England, with characters of the chief of them* (1723).

ANON. *A Certamen Epistolare: Letters between an Attorney and a Dead Parson* (1724).

ANON. *An essay on the Amendment and Reduction of the Laws of England, for the ease of the subject, the advancement of justice, and regulating the profession of the law* (1724).

ANON. *Law Quibbles; or, a treatise of the Evasions, Tricks, Turns, and Quibbles commonly used in the profession of the law, etc* (1726).

SASSON (Dim). *Law-Visions, or, Pills for Posterity, (with) Plain Truth by way of a dialogue between Truman and Skinall, two Attorneys, and Season, a Bencher* (1736).

READ HODSHON. *The Honest Man's Companion: or, the Family Safeguard. Illustrated with Copper Plates, and done at the Request of Several Gentlemen and Others, occasion'd by an Attorney's defying any Person to paint him or his Brotherhood in their proper Colours, or to propose any method to regulate them or their Practice. As also Remarks upon Roman-Catholick Lawyers practising as Chamber-Counsel and Conveyancers, etc.* (Newcastle upon Tyne, 1736).

R. CAMPBELL. *The London Tradesmen, being a compendious view of all the trades, professions, arts both liberal and mechanic, now practised in the cities of London and Westminster, calculated for the information of parents, and the instruction of youth in the choice of business* (1747).

ANON. *Animadversions upon the present laws of England; or, an Essay to render them more useful and less expensive to all His Majesty's subjects. To which is added, A Proposal for regulating the Practice and reducing the Number of Attornies, Solicitors, etc., with a supplement humbly submitted to the serious consideration of both Houses of Parliament* (*c.* 1749).

ANON. *An Address to all the Electors of all the Counties, Cities, and Counties of Cities, and Boroughs of England—Earnestly recommending to them to insist upon their respective representatives moving for, and procuring, a bill to restrain the excessive number of attornies, etc., in England and Wales, and shewing that, including the Newgate attornies, Newgate sollicitors, and pettifoggers, and not reckoning the knights of the post, there are ten thousand more than can live by honest gain* (*c.* 1755).

ANON. *Observations in the duty of an Attorney and Solicitor submitted to the public consideration, but addressed more especially to Young Practitioners of the Law* (*c.* 1759).

ANON. *Reflections or Hints founded upon experience and facts touching the law, lawyers, officers, attorneys, and others concerned in the administration of justice, humbly submitted to the consideration of the legislature* (1759).

JOSEPH SIMPSON, ESQ., Barrister at Law. *Reflections on the Natural and Acquired endowments requisite for the Study of the Law, and the means to be used in the pursuit of it* (3rd ed. 1764).

ANON. *The Attorney's and Solicitor's Complete Assistant, compiled by a Gentleman eminent in practice* (1768).

ANON. *A Report on the Proceedings...in the cause between Thomas Harrison, Esq., Chamberlain of the City of London, and John Alexander, attorney of the Court of King's Bench* (1769).

ANON. *Pettifogging Display'd, with a remedy against it. Whereby justice may be distributed in a more equitable, impartial, speedy, and less expensive manner than at present, and above twenty millions yearly saved the public. In a Letter from an English gentleman at Piossi to his correspondent in England* (c. 1769).

ROBERT HOLLOWAY, Gent. of Gray's Inn. *A letter to John Wilkes, Esq., Sheriff of London and Middlesex; in which the extortion and oppression of Sheriffs' officers and many other alarming abuses are exemplified and detected, and a remedy proposed. The infamous practice of attornies clearly pointed out, and many other real grievances which the common people have long groaned under without relief* (c. 1771).

ANON. *Friendly Hints to young gentlemen who are or desire to be bound by Articles to Attornies and Solicitors, MS.* (n.d.).

ROBERT HOLLOWAY. *The Rat Trap* (1773).

ROBERT HOLLOWAY. *The Mirror of Iniquity* (n.d).

ANON. *A Word to the Wise, or, a hint to the minister about taxing attornies, solicitors, proctors, etc., by an untaxed attorney* (1785).

ANON. *A Free Inquiry into the enormous Increase of Attornies, etc.* (1785).

ANON. *Considerations on the Attorney Tax, and proposals for altering and equalising the same, so as to render it easy in operation, and just in practice* (1786).

ANON. *Observations on the Use and Abuse of the Practice of the Law; interspersed with Remarks on the Character and Conduct of Persons of a Description more numerous than respectable, who encourage litigious Disputes to the great Inconvenience of Mankind in general and the Disgrace of the better part of the Profession of the Law, and illustrated with several professional anecdotes. By a Friend to the Profession* (1786).

ANON. *Speculations upon Law and Lawyers, applicable to the manifest hardships, uncertainty, and abusive practice of the common law* (1788).

EDWARD WYNNE. *Strictures on the Lives of Eminent Lawyers* (1790).

ANON. *Advice to a certain Lord High Chancellor, 12 Judges, 600 Barristers, 700 English and 800 Irish Students of the Law, and 30,000 Attornies, etc.* (1792).

ANON. *A Letter to the Right Honourable William Pitt upon the proposed Tax on the Admission of Attorneys* (1794).

ANON. *Remarks on the Education of Attorneys, designed to promote a reform in the inferior order of the Profession of the Law* (1794).

THOMAS GISBORNE. *An Inquiry into the Duties of Men in the Higher Ranks and Middle Classes in Great Britain, resulting from their respective stations, professions, and employments* (1794).

JOSEPH DAY. *Thoughts on the Necessity and Utility of the Examinations directed by the Acts of Parliament previous to the Admission of attorneys at law and solicitors* (1795).

A. GRANT. *The Progress and Practice of a modern Attorney, exhibiting the Conduct of Thousands towards Millions* (1796).

JOSEPH DAY. *An Address to the Attorneys at Law and Solicitors practising in Great Britain upon the proceedings of the London Law Club relative to the Bill . . . for incorporating and better regulating the practitioners, etc* (1796).

T. B. JUNR. *The Pettifogger Dramatized* (1797).

CHARLES MARTYN. *Considerations of the Qualifications, Clerkships, Admission and Practice of Attorneys; with Hints of the Necessity and Means of correcting several prevailing Abuses* (1804).

CHARLES ILSLEY. *A Brief Inquiry concerning the origin, progress, and impolicy of taxing attorneys; including remarks ascribed to a suggestion from the late Right Honourable Lloyd, Lord Kenyon* (1804).

ANON. *A Defence of Attornies, with reasons for thinking that no attorney who duly considers the present critical situation of his country, or who has at heart the increasing respectability of the profession will object to be taxed* (1804).

ROBERT HOLLOWAY. *Strictures on the Characters of the most prominent practising attornies* (1805–11).

ANON. *An Essay on the Law, being a summary view of the Profession of a Solicitor in opposition to Prejudice and Misconception* (1811).

WILLIAM WRIGHT. *Advice on the Study and Practice of the Law to attorneys' clerks* (2nd ed. 1815).

ANON. *The present state of the practice and the practisers of the Law, by an impartial hand; in a familiar dialogue between Philalethes and Philonomous* (n.d., after 1729).

RICHARD EDGEWORTH. *Professional Education* (1808).

179

INDEX